Search models and applied labor economics

Search models and applied labor economics

NICHOLAS M. KIEFER
Cornell University

GEORGE R. NEUMANN
University of Iowa

*The right of the
University of Cambridge
to print and sell
all manner of books
was granted by
Henry VIII in 1534.
The University has printed
and published continuously
since 1584.*

CAMBRIDGE UNIVERSITY PRESS

Cambridge
New York   New Rochelle   Melbourne   Sydney

CAMBRIDGE UNIVERSITY PRESS
Cambridge, New York, Melbourne, Madrid, Cape Town, Singapore, São Paulo

Cambridge University Press
The Edinburgh Building, Cambridge CB2 2RU, UK

Published in the United States of America by Cambridge University Press, New York

www.cambridge.org
Information on this title: www.cambridge.org/9780521360531

First published 1989
This digitally printed first paperback version 2006

A catalogue record for this publication is available from the British Library

Library of Congress Cataloguing in Publication data
Kiefer, Nicholas M.
Search models and applied labor economics/Nicholas M. Kiefer, George R.
Neumann.
p. cm.
ISBN 0 521 36053 6
1. Job hunting. 2. Unemployment. 3. Wages. I. Neumann, George R.
II. Title.
HF5382.7.K43 1989
331.12'5 – dc19   88-15302
                                                                     CIP

ISBN-13 978-0-521-36053-1 hardback
ISBN-10 0-521-36053-6 hardback

ISBN-13 978-0-521-02464-8 paperback
ISBN-10 0-521-02464-1 paperback

To Charlotte and Margaret

Contents

viii   **Contents**

Preface

The search approach to labor economics allows a productive interaction between economic theory and applied work because it incorporates uncertainty about the economic environment from the outset of the analysis. Optimal decisions derived in the search framework take account of market opportunities and market uncertainties, as well as considerations of costs of search or the "value of nonmarket time." In this sense, search models represent a sharp break with conventional practice in empirical modeling of employment and labor force participation. Because these models are explicitly stochastic, the distinction in tone between theoretical arguments and econometric and empirical arguments is much less pronounced than is usually the case. Indeed, theory and econometrics can be made to blend quite smoothly.

The chapters in this volume represent our work in labor economics, in the search framework, over roughly the decade 1977–87. We began our work at the University of Chicago, and the effort continued at the Center for Operations Research and Econometrics (CORE), University of Louvain, and Cornell (NMK), and at Northwestern and Iowa (GRN). Over the years we have received many useful comments and suggestions from teachers, colleagues, and students, including Gary Becker, Ken Burdett, Hyun Joon Chang, Theresa Devine, Ron Ehrenberg, James Heckman, Tony Lancaster, Ed Lazear, Steve Lippman, Bob Lucas, Shelly Lundberg, John McCall, Lars Muus, Melvin Reder, Geert Ridder, Sherwin Rosen, Sunil Sharma, Robert Topel, and Neils Westergaard-Neilsen. We are grateful to all of those named and especially to Dale T. Mortensen, who has, as this volume shows, influenced us as teacher, coauthor, and critic. Many others, including participants at numerous seminars, made additional helpful comments. We are grateful for all of them. This work has been supported over the years by the National Science Foundation and by the Department of Labor. We appreciate their support.

CHAPTER 1

Introduction

The labor market is a fascinating and important market in modern economies. Imperfect and asymmetric information, heterogeneity among workers and firms, labor unions and bargaining, implicit and explicit long-term employment arrangements are all present in the labor market. Thus, this market has a much more complicated and diverse structure than, say, spot markets for homogeneous goods or financial markets. Yet understanding the labor market is crucial for understanding movements in macroeconomic aggregates – business cycles – as well as for evaluating the important welfare questions associated with the presence of unemployment. Payments to labor make up about two-thirds of gross domestic product in the United States, in the United Kingdom, and across the European Economic Community. How well do economists understand this important component of the economy? Perhaps it will suffice to point out that a wage equation, run on a sample of individual workers, is considered to have a "good fit" if it explains about 25 percent of the variance in wages.

The literature on job search represents a breakthrough in modeling the labor market. In the search framework, uncertainty is explicitly handled in the theoretical treatment of the worker's behavior. Employment is determined as workers sample wage offers from a distribution and accept jobs that have acceptable wages. In this model, "lucky" workers may earn more than identical workers who were not so lucky in their draws from the wage distribution. Thus, at least a portion of the unexplained variance in a wage regression is part of the model; there is no presumption that the equation should fit perfectly apart from specification and measurement errors. From a macroeconomic theory point of view, the search framework is attractive because it admits the existence of unemployment. Indeed, it is possible to begin to ask questions about the efficient level of unemployment – the level that allows workers time to find suitable jobs without enduring hardship due to lack of offers.

1

2 Introduction

The search literature began with Stigler's pioneering articles (1961, 1962) on information in the labor market. Stigler formulated the job-shopping problem facing a worker as an optimal sample size problem. The worker chooses a sample of offers from a wage distribution at some cost per offer. The worker then accepts the job at the highest wage sampled. The decision problem for the worker is to choose the sample size so as to maximize the expected net return to search. In this framework, the worker applies for a number of jobs at once.

The next round of theoretical work on job search introduced a sequential approach based on the literature on optimal stopping in statistical decision theory. In this work, the worker samples a wage in one period and decides whether to accept employment at that wage or to wait, sampling another wage in the next period. In most of the models the worker's optimal policy is a "reservation wage" policy – the worker chooses a reservation wage and accepts the first offer above the reservation wage. In this approach the sample size, that is, the number of offers received, is random, rather than determined by the worker in advance of sampling, as in Stigler's model. The sample size has an interpretation in terms of duration of search since each observation corresponds to a period of time. Thus, this framework has implications for lengths of spells of unemployment as well as for reemployment wages. The relevant literature includes Gronau (1971), McCall (1970), and Mortensen (1970). A key insight of this literature is that the reservation wage depends not only on the value of "nonmarket production," but on market opportunities. This insight represented a sharp break with standard approaches to labor force participation and labor supply.

The search paradigm was the basis for many of the contributions in the celebrated "Phelps volume" (Phelps et al. 1970), which announced a new and rigorous approach to macroeconomics. Since then the theoretical development has been continuous and search ideas have continued to be influential in macroeconomics, demography, and other areas as well as in labor economics. Theoretical developments, adding to the applicability of the search framework, include continuous-time models (avoiding the theoretically clean but empirically awkward problem of defining a "period"), utility-maximizing models, models allowing layoffs and on-the-job search, models explicitly treating unemployment insurance variables, models in which the offer distribution must be learned, models with capital or asset constraints, and many others. The literature is carefully unified and reviewed in the insightful survey by Mortensen (1986).

At least one empirical study using search ideas appeared even before the formal sequential search models of the 1970s. Kasper (1967) studied data on a sample of 3,000 unemployed workers in Minnesota. These workers were asked for their reservation wages – "What wage are you seeking?" – as well as for their previous wages and other information. Kasper addressed two questions: (1) Are unemployed workers willing to accept a lower wage than that received in their previous job? and (2) does the reservation wage decline with the duration of a spell of unemployment? Kasper used the term "asking wage" rather than the now conventional "reservation wage." Although he presented no formal model, the reasoning Kasper used in forming these equations was exactly that suggested by the search models developed later.

The 1970s saw an expansion of interest in search models, following the publication of the papers by Gronau (1971), McCall (1970), and Mortensen (1970). This interest was due in part to the fact that an important policy question, namely, the effect of unemployment insurance benefits on unemployment, appeared to be amenable to analysis within the search framework. Unemployment insurance benefits subsidize search costs and therefore allow workers to be more choosy about jobs. This leads to longer unemployment spells and therefore possibly to higher unemployment rates. Of course, workers whose search costs are subsidized can be expected to find better jobs, and this effect must be considered as well in evaluating the welfare effects of an unemployment insurance system. The effects of benefits on the duration of unemployment spells and on reemployment wages were investigated by Ehrenberg and Oaxaca (1976). This study examined the regressions of durations and reemployment wages (both in logarithms) on a variety of demographic variables and the "replacement rate" – the ratio of benefits to previous wages. Coefficients were interpreted within the search framework in terms of costs of search and so on. No formal search model was presented in the published paper, although the appendix, regrettably unpublished, was an advance in linking empirical and theoretical search models.

Estimation of an empirical model closely tied to a theoretical job search model was the aim of the paper "Estimation of Wage Offer Distributions and Reservation Wages," which appears here as Chapter 2. Before turning to a discussion of this and the following chapters, we present a simple, stylized job search model and discuss some issues involved in estimating such models. A full review of the empirical literature on job search models, loosely interpreted, is given by Devine and Kiefer (1987).

1.1   A simple job search model

This section sets out the basic job search model in continuous time. The discrete-time version can be obtained simply from the continuous-time model, as indicated at the end of the section. For simplicity, we focus here on one transition, that from unemployment to employment. This is sufficient to introduce the central ideas of search theory. Assume that (1) workers maximize expected lifetime income, discounted over an infinite horizon at constant rate r; (2) the income flow while an individual is unemployed, net of search costs, is a constant b, fixed over the duration of a given spell (thus, the income received over a short interval of unemployment of length h is bh); (3) the probability that a worker receives an offer during a short interval of length h is δh, where δ is constant over the duration of a spell; (4) a job offer is characterized by a wage rate w, which will be received continuously over time if the job is accepted; and (5) job offers are independent draws from a fixed distribution $F(w)$ known to the worker.

These assumptions are obviously unrealistic. The interesting questions are whether they can form the basis of a model that increases our understanding of the working of the labor market, and whether that model is helpful in organizing and interpreting labor market data. Assumption (1) involves an infinite horizon. This assumption simplifies calculations substantially, and examples seem to show that an infinite horizon is not much different from a "long" horizon as long as there is discounting. Thus, the model may have to be modified for workers nearing retirement, as in Chang (1985). Assumption (1) also restricts attention to income-maximizing workers. Generalizing to utility maximization is straightforward. The assumption of a constant discount rate r does not seem objectionable. Assumption (2) abstracts from the possibilities that workers draw down assets significantly when unemployed or that unemployment insurance benefits vary over the course of a spell. The model has been modified to study the effects of benefit exhaustion (Burdett 1979; this is also an example of a utility-maximization model). Generally, data on workers' financial status through the course of a spell of unemployment are either unavailable or unreliable, with the occasional exception of records of unemployment insurance benefits paid. Assumption (3) implies that offers arrive according to a Poisson process; that is, the probability of receiving an offer in an interval is proportional to the length of the interval. This assumption eliminates the possibility that a worker will vary the effort devoted to search over the course of an unemployment spell or that firms will use elapsed duration as an indicator of a worker's suitability. This assumption is probably too restrictive. More work should be done on the determination of offer arrivals in labor markets. Assumption (4), that a job once accepted is held forever, is obviously unrealistic but is easily modified to allow future layoffs or quits. The basic implications for the unemployment-to-employment transition remain unchanged. Assumption (5), that draws from the offer distribution are independent, means that firms cannot take duration into account when determining the size of an offer, for example. It also requires that the offer distribution remain fixed over the course of an unemployment spell, abstracting from business cycle effects or deterioration of human capital.

We are now in a position to construct the value function for a worker in the labor market. First, consider the maximum expected discounted income for a worker who becomes employed at wage w. Under our assumptions no expectations are involved, and that value is

$$V_e(w) = w/r.$$

This value is a function of the wage w, but not of the offer distribution due to the simplifying assumption that the job is held forever. The value, or discounted expected income, for a worker who is unemployed is a little harder to calculate. It is defined by the equation

$$V_u = \frac{bh}{1 + rh} + \frac{\delta h}{1 + rh} E \max\{V_e(w), V_u\} + \frac{1 - \delta h}{1 + rh} V_u + o(h),$$

where h is a short time interval. The first term on the right side is the discounted present value of net unemployment income over the interval. The second is the probability of receiving an offer in the interval times the discounted expected value of following the optimal policy if an offer is received. The third is the value of continuing search if no offer is received in the interval weighted by the probability of that event. The last term allows for the possibility that more than one offer is received in the interval h. Under our assumptions $o(h)/h$ goes to zero as h goes to zero. Multiplying through by $1 + rh$, rearranging and taking limits as h goes to zero gives an expression for V_u not depending on h,

$$V_u = b/(r + \delta) + \delta/(r + \delta)E \max\{V_u, V_e(w)\},$$

where the expectation is taken using $F(w)$, the distribution of wage offers. The value function for the worker is $V(w) = \max\{V_u, V_e(w)\}$, so the optimal policy is for the worker to accept employment when $V_e(w)$ is greater than V_u and decline employment otherwise. Now, V_u is a constant, depending on the parameters of the model including the distribution F, but not depending on the offered wage. The value of employment $V_e(w)$ is an increasing function of the wage offer. Consequently, the optimal policy is a *reservation wage* policy: Define w^* by $V_e(w^*) = V_u$. Then an offer above w^* will be accepted by a worker following the optimal policy; an offer below w^* will be declined. In order to make the model interesting, we assume that there are potential offers above and below w^*. Otherwise, the worker either is always employed or is out of the labor force.

A simple interpretation of the equation defining the reservation wage can be made in our model. Note that $V_u = w^*/r$ and so we have

$$w^*/r = b(r + \delta) + \delta/(r + \delta)[w^*/rF(w^*) + (1 - F(w^*))/rE(w \mid w > w^*)],$$

where $F(w^*)$ is the probability that a wage draw will be less than w^* and $E(w \mid w > w^*)$ is the conditional expectation of a wage offer, conditional on its being greater than the reservation wage. Upon reexpressing the expectation as the expected increment in wages over the reservation wage and rearranging terms, we obtain

$$(w^* - b)r = \delta(1 - F(w^*))E(w - w^* \mid w > w^*).$$

The left side of this equation is the marginal cost of rejecting an offer equal to w^*. This is the imputed interest income on the difference between w^* and b, unemployment income. The right side is the marginal expected gain from continued search using reservation wage w^*. The reservation wage is thus the wage rate that equates the marginal cost and marginal benefit of search.

In this model the probability of an unemployed worker finding a job in a short time interval h is given by $\lambda h = \delta h \pi$, where $\pi = (1 - F(w^*))$ is the probability that an offer is acceptable. The probability that the worker will become employed is the product of the probability that he or she will receive an offer and the probability that the offer received will be acceptable, that is, greater than the worker's reservation wage. Note that the probability of finding a job in the interval h does not depend on elapsed duration. This implies that the duration of a spell of unemployment, the random variable T, has the exponential density $f(t) = \lambda \exp\{-\lambda t\}$. The reemployment wage is an observation from the wage offer density truncated from below at w^*; $f(w \mid w > w^*) = f(w)/(1 - F(w^*))$ $(w > w^*)$. Since offer arrivals and the values of the offer are independent, the joint density of unemployment duration and reemployment wages is given by

$$f(t, w) = f(t)f(w \mid w > w^*), \qquad 0 < t < \infty, \qquad w^* < w < \infty.$$

Note that the theoretical model has led to a data density that can form the basis for an estimated model without the ad hoc introduction of error terms. In Chapters 2 through 4 we study this joint density (actually, a discrete-time version), attempting to exploit the relationship between $f(t)$ and $f(w \mid w > w^*)$ implied by the theory.

Actually calculating the reservation wage can be quite tricky, though some properties of the reservation wage considered as a function of parameters can be obtained from the implicit equation derived above. As an example, consider the simple case of a standard exponential offer distribution, $f(w) = \exp\{-w\}$. Here we have

$$(w^* - b)r = \delta \int (w - w^*) \exp\{-w\} \, dw$$
$$= \delta \exp\{-w^*\}$$

upon integrating. This implicit equation is easy to solve numerically and obviously has a unique solution (recall that b is greater than zero), although a simple formula for w^* as a function of b, r, and δ is not available. It is straightforward, however, to calculate quantities like

$$\partial w^*/\partial b = r/(r + \delta \exp\{-w^*\})$$
$$= r/(r + \lambda),$$

where $\lambda = \delta\pi$ is the transition rate from unemployment to employment. Thus, an increase in b, income while an individual is unemployed, increases the reservation wage, but by an amount less than the increase in b. The increase in the reservation wage will lead to longer durations and higher reemployment wages. If information on wages, durations, and unemployment income is available, these are testable implications of the model.

The discrete-time version of this model is obtained by dropping the assumption of Poisson arrivals for offers and assuming instead that one offer is received each period. In this framework the random variable "time unemployed" is discrete and the probability of becoming employed in any period, conditional on being unemployed at the beginning of the period, is simply π, the acceptance probability. The distribution of reemployment wages is unchanged, and the joint distribution of duration and reemployment wages is again the product of the marginal distributions. These marginal distributions have structural parameters in common, so it pays to study them together, even though the random variables "duration" and "wages" are independent.

1.2   Wages, reservation wages, and durations

Chapter 2 provides an initial approach to identifying, separately, the policy function, the reservation wage, and the wage offer function. In keeping with the theoretical treatment of McCall and Mortensen, the search model is set up in discrete time, and the arrival rate of offers, λ, is fixed at one per period. The wage distribution is assumed to be lognormal.

The central focus of this chapter is whether data on unemployment duration and accepted wages provide sufficient information to identify w^* and $F(w)$. A condition leading to identification is given in Proposition 1, which states how the reservation wage changes in response to a translation of the wage offer function. This condition, coupled with a known discount factor, makes the identification problem similar to the ordinary identification problem of simultaneous equations, and it is resolved by exclusion restrictions.

Once one has identified w^* and $F(w)$, it is natural to inquire how well the data support the structure that is imposed. Because observations on w^* are not available, we are left to inquire how well a truncated (at w_i^*) log-normal distribution $F(w_i \mid w_i^*, x_i)$ fits the data. The last part of the chapter provides a tentative answer to that question. Our approach uses "generalized residuals" similar to those defined by Cox and Snell (1968) in an article we had not seen when we did our work (but we wish we had . . .). Our test statistic is not quite correct in that the Kolmogorov–Smirnov "goodness of fit" test is used without adjusting for estimation error in the parameters (Durbin 1973). In essence, a degrees of freedom correction is needed, and the test results reported without such adjustment will be too conservative. Practical methods of making the adjustment are still needed.

In Chapter 3, the basic search model is estimated without the assumption of a constant reservation wage. The specification used – the addition of a linear trend term in duration – provides a superior fit to the data. The linear dependence of the reservation wage on duration can be interpreted as a linear approximation to a more complicated dependence, in keeping with our interpretation of the reservation wage function specification as a linear approximation. Of course, the specification could be inappropriately restrictive, so an examination of specification diagnostics is in order.

Misspecification, or heterogeneity, can lead to incorrect inferences about the effect of elapsed duration on the probability of reemployment. Distinguishing between duration dependence, brought about by a changing reservation wage, and heterogeneity is a difficult problem, as Bates and Neyman (1951) and Heckman and Borjas (1980) have noted. Attempts to sort these out are the subject of Chapter 4 and of much current research. Chapter 4 attempts to model heterogeneity with a random-effects specification. The value of this approach has since been questioned (see the references in Kiefer, 1988) and is the topic of debate. The standard errors reported in Chapter 4 are inappropriate, since the constraint that observed wages will be greater than reservation wages leads to a violation of the usual regularity conditions for asymptotic theory. The standard errors are probably overestimated. A recent, insightful discussion of asymptotic theory under nonstandard conditions is Self and Liang (1987).

The models estimated in Chapters 2 through 4 involve rather complicated specifications of the joint density of wages and durations. In Chapter 2 fairly simple estimation techniques, related to those used in an older literature on deterministic models of labor force participation, are used. Chapters 3 and 4 rely on maximum likelihood techniques. These involve complicated numerical issues, especially in Chapter 4. Much simpler estimation strategies can be used if attention is restricted to the distribution of durations alone, especially in the case of continuous-time models.

1.3 Continuous-time models of durations

Duration distributions are conveniently specified using the notion of a hazard function. Suppose the distribution of a duration T is specified as usual in econometrics by its density $f(t)$ or its distribution function $F(t) = \Pr(T < t)$. Two alternative specifications are the survivor function $S(t) = 1 - F(t) = \Pr(T \geq t)$ and the hazard function

$$\lambda(t) = f(t)/S(t) = -d \ln S(t)/dt.$$

The hazard function at the point t gives, roughly, the conditional probability that a spell will end at t given that it lasts until t or longer. That is, the probability that a spell will end in the interval $t + h$, given that it lasts at least until t, is $\lambda(t)h$. In contrast, the density function gives the unconditional probability, so that the probability of ending in the interval $t + h$ is $f(t)h$. Clearly, $\lambda(t) \geq f(t)$. The density and hazard functions provide alternative equivalent methods of specifying a distribution; given a hazard one can calculate the density and vice versa.

Specification of the density of wages and durations seemed to be easier and more natural than direct specification of the hazard in the models used in Chapters 2 through 4. In these models the duration distribution is discrete and the wage distribution is continuous. In succeeding chapters we focus on the marginal distribution of durations and specify a continuous distribution. The choice between continuous and discrete specifications is not trivial. The discrete specification most closely mimics the theoretical models of McCall and Mortensen, in which offers are received once each period. In empirical implementation, the period must be chosen, and in the absence of information on offer arrivals, the choice is somewhat arbitrary. In Chapters 2 through 4 we assume that offers are obtained at the rate of one per week. This assumption clearly affects the interpretation of coefficients. The continuous-time specification enables us to model offers arriving at random intervals. Thus, in principle, durations can end at any moment upon arrival of a suitable offer. This approach seems theoretically superior, but in fact the data are available in weeks, not continuously, so the continuous-time model must be interpreted as an approximation to a discrete-time model. Still, the continuous specification allows us to finesse the problem of the definition of an appropriate period.

The hazard function is useful for characterizing duration dependence. If the hazard function is increasing, $d\lambda(t)/dt > 0$, then the probability that a spell will end is increasing with duration. In the context of a job search model, an increasing hazard for unemployment duration would be implied by a decreasing reservation wage, which could arise, for example, if the unemployed worker was drawing down a stock of assets over the course of a spell of unemployment. This finding appeared in the data studied in Chapter 3. The increasing hazard property is often referred to in the economics literature as positive duration dependence. Similarly, a decreasing hazard, $d\lambda(t)/dt < 0$, exhibits negative duration dependence. This can occur if the worker becomes discouraged and searches less enthusiastically over time, or because employers interpret long spells of unemployment as a negative signal and are less likely to make offers to the long-term unemployed. The constant hazard $\lambda(t) = \lambda$ characterizes the exponential distribution $f(t) = \lambda \exp\{-\lambda t\}$. The exponential specification, typically with λ depending on explanatory variables, is often a natural initial specification in a duration analysis, much as the linear regression model is often used in preliminary analyses in other contexts.

Estimation is straightforward using maximum likelihood methods. For illustration, consider the popular exponential regression specification

$$\lambda(t, \mathbf{x}, \boldsymbol{\beta}) = \exp\{\mathbf{x}'\boldsymbol{\beta}\},$$

where $\mathbf{x}$ is a column vector of explanatory variables and a constant term and $\boldsymbol{\beta}$ is a column vector of coefficients to be estimated. With this specification the duration distribution is exponential with mean $\exp\{-\mathbf{x}'\boldsymbol{\beta}\}$; the hazard function does not depend on duration. The density function for these durations is given by $f(t) = \lambda(t)S(t) = \exp\{\mathbf{x}'\boldsymbol{\beta}\} \exp\{-t \exp\{\mathbf{x}'\boldsymbol{\beta}\}\}$. Given a sample of N independent observations, indexed by i, from this distribution the log-likelihood function for the parameter $\boldsymbol{\beta}$ is

$$L(\boldsymbol{\beta}) = \sum_{i=1}^{N} \ln f(t \mid x_i, \boldsymbol{\beta})$$

$$= \sum_{i=1}^{N} [\ln \lambda(t_i \mid x_i, \boldsymbol{\beta}) + \ln S(t_i \mid x_i, \boldsymbol{\beta})]$$

$$= \sum_{i=1}^{N} [x_i' \boldsymbol{\beta} - t_i \exp\{x_i' \boldsymbol{\beta}\}].$$

This log-likelihood function is concave in $\boldsymbol{\beta}$, and maximum likelihood estimates are not difficult to compute, using, for example, Newton's method. Programs for fitting the exponential regression model are now readily available in common statistical software packages. The discussion so far assumes that a sample of completed spells is available. Of course, the distinguishing feature of duration data is that some of the spells in a sample are incomplete – that is, censored. For example, we might study lengths of employment spells, but see workers only over a four-year period. In this case the longest employment spell possibly observed is four years – but it would still be in progress when our observation ended. Such a spell contributes a probability term to the log-likelihood function rather than a density term. The appropriate probability is, of course, exactly the survivor function evaluated at the duration at which censoring occurred. This point is discussed in Chapter 5. Other issues of sampling affect the formulation of the appropriate likelihood function as well. See the discussions in Cox and Lewis (1966) and in Kiefer (1988), for examples. Hazard functions were fit to unemployment duration data by Lancaster (1979) and Nickell (1979). Identification in hazard function models with heterogeneity is treated by Elbers and Ridder (1982).

Thus, the continuous-time model for durations (not for durations and wages jointly) turns out to be far simpler to estimate than the models treated in Chapters 2 through 4. Chapters 5 through 8 focus on these models. In this framework it is easy to generalize the model to allow for several potential labor market states, here employment, unemployment, and nonparticipation in the labor force. The previous models concentrated on the unemployment-to-employment transition and hence on durations of unemployment spells. Clearly, lengths of employment spells are also of interest in explaining macroeconomic fluctuations and in understanding the operation of the labor market. New entrants to the labor force, for example, might expect to experience a number of short duration spells of employment before settling into a satisfactory job (if only to learn what sorts of jobs are available!), whereas established workers with specific training may expect to stay with the same employer for some time. The hazard function approach is ideal for considering these possibilities. The question of labor force participation is also important: How long do potential workers stay out of the labor force? What variables influence the decision to enter the labor market?

With empirical models of the durations of employment, unemployment, and labor force participation within reach, we need to concentrate on a sensible way to fit the pieces together into a model of turnover in the labor market. Suppose the hazard functions associated with employment, unemployment, and nonparticipation are λ_e, λ_u, and λ_n, constants not depending on duration. Each of these hazard functions can be decomposed into the sum of destination-specific hazards, for example, $\lambda_e = \lambda_{eu} + \lambda_{en}$. To interpret this decomposition we can multiply by h – the length of a short interval of time – and reason in terms of probabilities. Then, the probability of leaving employment in a short interval is equal to the sum of the probabilities of leaving employment for unemployment and of leaving employment for nonparticipation. We can add these probabilities because the events ($e \rightarrow u$ and $e \rightarrow n$) are mutually exclusive (as $h \rightarrow 0$). With this specification the labor market history for an individual follows a *Markov process*. The practical implication of the Markov specification is that the transition rates out of any state and into another depend only on the origin and destination states. Markovian models for labor market transitions have been considered by Marston (1976) and Toikka (1976). The assumptions that have to be made to obtain a Markov model are fairly strong. As discussed in Chapter 5, the arrival rate of offers must be Poisson, although the rate can depend on the state occupied. Further, offers must be drawn from a distribution fixed over time and duration. Finally, the option of declining an offer to keep the last offer must *not* be available. Some early articles on this topic (including one of ours, Burdett, Kiefer, Mortensen, and Neumann 1980) assumed employed workers could keep their current wage and decline a new offer when it arrived. Though arguably more realistic than the specification finally adopted in our work, namely, that an offer to an employed worker consists of a new wage and a new value of leisure time, allowing current wages to be kept as offers arrive leads to a model that is not Markovian in labor market states. Of course, the model can be made Markovian by a suitable redefinition of the state space, but the simple three-state structure is lost.

The destination-specific transition rates (hazards) are given, from a theoretical point of view, by the products of offer arrival rates, which depend only on the state occupied, and acceptance probabilities, which depend on the joint distribution of offers. In Chapter 5 the joint distribution of offers is assumed to vary across individuals only in its mean. The optimal search strategy can be analyzed and used to develop predictions about the effect of differences in mean wage offers across individuals on their labor market histories. In fact, those predictions of the model hold up fairly well when confronted with data.

The Markovian structure allows the calculation of steady-state distributions. In the three-state models the steady-state distribution can be interpreted as giving the fraction of individuals with particular characteristics occupying each state at any time, or as the fraction of time over a long period that an individual with particular characteristics will occupy each labor market state. Thus, the steady-state probability associated with unemployment can be interpreted as a "natural" or "equilibrium" fraction of the population unemployed. A corresponding unemployment rate can be obtained by dividing this probability by the participation rate, namely one minus the steady-state probability of nonparticipation. The steady-state probabilities are calculated in Chapter 5, and their sensitivity to expected wages is examined.

The analysis of Chapter 5 yields estimates of the transition rates λ_{ij}, but not separate estimates of the arrival rates and acceptance probabilities. Chapter 6 reports the results of an attempt to sort the transition rates into the separate arrival rates and acceptance probabilities. Let us abstract for the moment from the inclusion of regressors. Note that there are six origin- and destination-specific transition rates in the three-state model. There are three distinct offer arrival probabilities. Under the assumption that the offer distribution does *not* depend on the state currently occupied, there are two acceptance probabilities, one associated with each state and one eliminated by the constraint that the probabilities sum to 1. Thus, the six transition rates are determined by five underlying parameters. We can obtain estimates of the underlying parameters using the transition rates as data. In fact, this logic shows that the arrival rates and acceptance probabilities can be estimated by maximum likelihood; further, a test of the restriction is available since the underlying parameters are overidentified. This approach is pursued in Chapter 6, where the arrival rates are called "chance" and the acceptance probabilities "choice."

In Chapter 7 the exponential distribution of employment durations is generalized to Weibull. The theoretical model has layoff probabilities depending on experience. The resulting model is no longer Markov, but it is *semi-Markov*, in that a record of the transition alone, that is, the sequence of states occupied, is a Markov chain (the embedded chain). Employment durations are found to be different from exponential. Indeed, the distribution of employment durations exhibits negative duration dependence: The longer a job is held, the less likely it is to be lost.

1.4   Applications

Chapters 8 and 9 consider direct applications of empirical search models. In Chapter 8, the model developed in Chapters 3 and 4 is used to study the potential effects of changes in unemployment insurance (UI) benefit levels and alternative direct wage subsidies. Since the wage subsidy programs were not in place in our sample, their effects cannot be estimated directly by reduced-form methods, but must be inferred from parameters having a behavioral interpretation. The basic finding is that increasing UI benefits leads to slightly longer unemployment spells and slightly higher reemployment earnings. Both of these effects are so small that the practical implication is that income maintenance at the levels considered is unlikely to have much impact on the labor market. A direct wage subsidy program is estimated to have larger effects – including moderate reductions in unemployment durations. In Chapter 9 the model developed and estimated in Chapter 5 is used to provide evidence on the effects of the Baily–Tobin targeted wage subsidy proposal on equilibrium unemployment rates. Our results are not encouraging with regard to the possibility of reducing overall unemployment rates with targeted subsidies, though the employment status of targeted groups can be influenced. (The responses of other groups to the tax necessary to pay the subsidies and the participation response of the targeted groups work against a reduction in the overall unemployment rate.)

Chapter 10 considers a problem with data and the measurement of lengths of spells of unemployment. This is the least theoretical chapter in this book. Here, we use hazard function methods, without stressing a tight link to a search model, to examine an important data issue. Most data used to study durations of unemployment spells come from the Current Population Survey (CPS). The CPS is a point-in-time survey and can give an incomplete view of the underlying duration distribution. Potential problems with CPS methods of measuring durations have been widely discussed. In an effort to assess the empirical importance of these problems we apply CPS sampling methods to panel data for which we know unemployment durations. We find that predicted duration distributions derived from our CPS-like data can be quite different from the actual distributions.

1.5 Mobility and contracting

Sources of "stickiness" or slow adjustment to shocks in the labor market are of interest to macroeconomists trying to explain the persistence of business cycles. The search models we have discussed permit a break in the link between the marginal value of leisure and the wage rate; breaking this link is crucial for the Keynesian view of the macroeconomy. However, our models do not focus on the dynamics of adjustment in labor markets. Models of contracting in labor markets, developed by Azariadis (1975) and Baily (1977), specify a mechanism, an implicit or explicit contract, with which workers and firms can avoid the continuous adjustment of wages and hours implied by the spot market view of the labor market. The incorporation of aspects of contracting ideas into search models is considered in Chapters 11 and 12. In Chapter 11 workers are assumed to be immobile across markets, and, within markets, firms' demands are correlated. A contract consists of a wage rate (payment while an indi-

vidual is employed), a layoff benefit (payment while an individual is unemployed), and a layoff probability. This model is used to explain state-
to-state variation in unemployment rates. The main finding is that employment risk has been declining over time, which supports the need to
consider models in which workers have long-term attachments to firms.
In Chapter 12 the worker's optimal behavior when faced with a particular
form of contract is analyzed. Specifically, the worker is assumed to sample job offers, where the offer consists of a wage rate and a number of
hours per week worked. Thus, the worker is not free to adjust hours on
a job – so the link between the marginal value of leisure and the wage
is broken. The worker can adjust hours only on the extensive margin, by
changing jobs. The main result is that the theorems obtained in the simpler models on the effects of translations in the wage offer distribution
cannot be expected to hold when the offer is a contract. A generalization
of a theorem (proved in Chapter 2) on the effect of a wage translation
on acceptance probabilities to the utility maximization framework is obtained (in the case when wages alone vary across offers).

In Chapter 13, job-to-job transitions are considered explicitly. The idea
is to sort out three different explanations of the positive relationship between experience and earnings. In the first, the "pure search" explanation, the positive relation is due to selectivity. Workers with high wages
are unlikely to search actively for alternatives and therefore accumulate
experience. In the second, the "pure experience" or "matching" explanation, workers slowly accumulate information about the quality of the
match with their job. Productivity depends on the quality of the match,
and wages evolve according to expected productivity. Wages and tenure
will be positively correlated because only "good" matches last. Finally,
there is the "on-the-job-training" explanation, in which wages are deterministic functions of training. Reduced-form results indicate that no one
of the "pure" explanations alone is satisfactory. This topic remains an
active area of research.

It has often been observed that hourly wages depend on hours worked,
so that the observed wage is not the marginal price of leisure. Estimation
for models of this type is the topic of Chapter 14.

1.6   Open areas

The major area for future research using search ideas or the search framework is the incorporation of the demand side of the labor market in a

sensible way into empirical work. With the exception of the last three chapters, we have focused on the "supply side," that is, on a worker's reservation wage behavior given the configuration of arrival rates and offers he or she faces. The work in Chapter 6, as well as recent work by Devine (1988), suggests that variation in arrival rates across workers may be at least as important in understanding labor turnover as variation in reservation wages due to interindividual differences in offer distributions or search costs. Although arrival rates can be modeled from the supply side as dependent on the time or effort allocated to job search, we suspect that this approach is unlikely to be empirically fruitful. In the absence of data on offer arrivals (except when a transition occurs) we are unlikely to be able to make firm inferences about the relative effects of variables on arrivals and on acceptance probabilities, although we can obtain suggestive results by relying heavily on theoretical models. Jensen and Westergaard-Neilsen (1987) studied one of the rare data sets with observations on offer arrivals, a sample of newly graduated lawyers in Denmark, and found that arrival rates significantly affect reservation wages. What is really needed is a satisfactory model of the firm's decision to make an offer and the data to fit and evaluate the model, much as models of the worker's behavior have been fit and evaluated.

Other areas for research in the job search framework include the following:

1. Techniques for choosing among competing models, frequently nonnested and invariably nonlinear. This is an area in which much has been accomplished recently (see the survey by MacKinnon 1983). Residual analysis is an important and largely neglected tool for specification analysis in models of this type. Generalized residuals can always be defined, calculated, and plotted. Test statistics based on generalized residuals, though less useful perhaps than the plots themselves, can typically be obtained in a straightforward manner. Residual analysis is discussed in Chapters 3 and 5.

2. Incorporation of the results from microeconometric studies of the labor market into models of the macroeconomy. Explaining movements in economic aggregates, particularly unemployment, was one of the original goals of search theory – indeed some of the major early articles had a strong macroeconomic flavor (see Phelps et al. 1970). We now know a great deal about the mi-

croeconomic relevance of search models. What about the macroeconomic relevance?

Finally, although our work has concentrated exclusively on search ideas applied to the labor market, it is clear that the ideas and empirical methods of the search approach can be applied in many other settings. Methods developed for job search models can be applied, perhaps with some modification, in any setting in which we are interested in studying the optimal behavior of an individual who is making sequential decisions under uncertainty. We anticipate seeing fruitful applications in finance, marketing, resource economics, and other areas.

References

Azariadis, C. (1975). "Implicit Contracts and Unemployment Equilibria," *Journal of Political Economy, 83*, 1183–1202.

Baily, M. N. (1977). "Wages and Employment Under Uncertain Demand," *Review of Economic Studies, 41*, 47–50.

Bates, G., and Neyman, J. (1951). "Contributions to the Theory of Accident Proneness. II: True or False Contagion," *University of California Publications in Statistics, 1*, 215–53.

Burdett, K. (1979). "Search, Leisure, and Individual Labor Supply," in S. A. Lippman and J. J. McCall (eds.), *Studies in the Economics of Search*, North-Holland, Amsterdam, 157–70.

Burdett, K., Kiefer, N. M., Mortensen, D. T., and Neumann, G. R. (1980). "A Dynamic Model of Employment, Unemployment and Labor Force Participation: Estimates From the DIME Data," University of Chicago Working Paper.

Chang, H. (1985). "Age and the Length of Unemployment Spells: A Structural Hazard Analysis," Ph.D. dissertation, Cornell University, Ithaca, N.Y.

Cox, D. R., and Lewis, P. A. W. (1966). *The Statistical Analysis of Series of Events*, Methuen, London.

Cox, D. R., and Snell, E. J. (1968). "A General Definition of Residuals (with discussion)," *Journal of the Royal Statistical Society B, 30*, 248–75.

Devine, T. J. (1988). "Search Models and Employment," Ph.D. dissertation, Cornell University, Ithaca, N.Y.

Devine, T. J., and Kiefer, N. M. (1987). "Empirical Labor Economics in the Search Framework," Cornell University working paper, Ithaca, N.Y.

Durbin, J. (1973). *Distribution Theory for Tests Based on the Sample Distribution Function*, SIAM, Philadelphia.

Ehrenberg, R. G., and Oaxaca, R. L. (1976). "Unemployment Insurance, Duration of Unemployment, and Subsequent Wage Gain," *American Economic Review, 66*, 754–66.

Elbers, C., and Ridder, G. (1982). "True and Spurious Duration Dependence: The Identifiability of the Proportional Hazard Model," *Review of Economic Studies, 49*, 403–11.

Gronau, R. (1971). "Information and Frictional Unemployment," *American Economic Review, 61*, 290–301.

Heckman, J. J., and Borjas, G. (1980). "Does Unemployment Cause Future Unemployment? Definitions, Questions and Answers from a Continuous Time Model of Heterogeneity and State Dependence," *Economica, 47,* 247–83.

Jensen, P., and Westergaard-Neilsen, N. (1987). "A Search Model Applied to the Transition from Education to Work," *Review of Economic Studies, 54,* 461–72.

Kasper, H. (1967). "The Asking Price of Labor and the Duration of Unemployment," *Review of Economics and Statistics, 49,* 165–72.

Kiefer, N. M. (1988). "Economic Duration Data and Hazard Functions," *Journal of Economic Literature, 26,* 646–79.

Lancaster, T. (1979). "Econometric Methods for the Duration of Unemployment," *Econometrica, 47,* 939–56.

MacKinnon, J. (1983). "Model Specification Tests Against Non-Nested Alternatives," *Econometric Reviews, 2*(1), 85–110.

Marston, S. T. (1976). "Employment Instability and High Unemployment Rates," *Brookings Papers on Economic Activity, 1,* 169–210.

McCall, J. J. (1970). "Economics of Information and Job Search," *Quarterly Journal of Economics, 84,* 113–26.

Mortensen, D. T. (1970). "Job Search, the Duration of Unemployment, and the Phillips' Curve," *American Economic Review, 60,* 505–17.

(1986). "Job Search and Labor Market Analysis," in O. Ashenfelter and R. Layard (eds.), *Handbook of Labor Economics,* Elsevier, New York, Vol. 2, 849–919.

Nickell, S. (1979). "Estimating the Probability of Leaving Unemployment," *Econometrica, 91,* 39–57.

Parsons, D. O. (1977). "Models of Labor Turnover: A Theoretical and Empirical Survey," in R. Ehrenberg (ed.), *Research in Labor Economics,* Greenwich, Conn., JAI Press, Vol. 1, 185–225.

Phelps, E. S., et al. (1970). *Microeconomic Foundations of Employment and Inflation Theory,* Norton, New York.

Self, S. G., and Liang, K.-Y. (1987). "Asymptotic Properties of Maximum Likelihood Estimators and Likelihood Ratio Tests Under Nonstandard Conditions," *Journal of the American Statistical Association, 82,* 605–10.

Stigler, G. J. (1961). "The Economics of Information," *Journal of Political Economy, 69,* 213–25.

(1962), "Information in the Labor Market," *Journal of Political Economy, 70,* 94–104.

Toikka, R. (1976). "A Markovian Model of Labor Market Decisions by Workers," *American Economic Review, 66,* 821–34.

PART I

Wages, reservation wages, and duration

CHAPTER 2

Estimation of wage offer distributions and reservation wages

2.1   Introduction

Though theoretical work on job search and the theory of reservation wages has attracted considerable attention, very little empirical work along the lines suggested by theory has been done. Empirical work in this context is potentially useful not only for better understanding of unemployment but for measuring the effects of diverse labor-market programs. For example, the provision of contingency payments such as unemployment insurance may have effects on observed market phenomena such as earnings or unemployment, but these effects are transmitted indirectly through the effect of unemployment insurance (UI) on reservation wages. To evaluate the effects of UI on market phenomena it is necessary to examine the transmission mechanism directly. Similarly, if one wishes to measure the displacement effect of a minimum wage, it is necessary to estimate the number of individuals who have reservation wages less than the minimum wage.

In this chapter we begin the econometric analysis of job search models. We specify an appropriate econometric model and discuss several issues which arise in its estimation and interpretation. We then apply the model to a sample of workers who were permanently separated from previous employment. Throughout the chapter we discuss the model in the context of a labor market, though the empirical model is more general.

The lack of empirical work along the lines suggested by theory is largely due to the identification problems which cloud the issues. Central to all sequential search models is the choice of a reservation wage – and the implications of search theory for empirical phenomena follow from the effects of reservation wages on such phenomena.

In using the term reservation wage we note that the concept is intrinsi-

This chapter is reprinted from *Studies in the Economics of Search*, edited by J. J. McCall and S. A. Lippman (1979), by permission of Elsevier Science Publishers.

cally different from the normal meaning of the term in labor economics. In the theory of labor supply the term reservation wage has come to mean the critical value of the wage rate which will make an individual indifferent between participating in market activities or engaging in nonmarket work. In this framework the reservation wage is determined solely by "tastes," or in the spirit of the new economics of consumption, by productivity in nonmarket alternatives. It is not affected by market wages, at least not directly. By contrast, the term reservation wage as we use it and as is generally used in the search literature denotes the critical value which equates the marginal gain from an additional search with the marginal cost of one more search. Since the marginal gain from search depends upon the distribution of wages, it is clear that the reservation wage must also depend upon the wage distribution. It is this dependence, reflecting the investment nature of search activity, that differentiates the two concepts of reservation wages.

Reservation wages are not, however, directly observable; this makes it difficult to test the implications of search theory directly. Consequently, one must rely heavily on restrictions implied by the theory. In this chapter we describe a method for estimating the wage offer distribution facing individuals from incomplete data – that is, from information on accepted wage offers. We then examine the conditions under which this information enables one to identify reservation wages. We present one method of identification based on an implication of the underlying theoretical model. The plan of the chapter is as follows.

In Section 2.2 we set out the model to be estimated and discuss its implications. Section 2.3 introduces the data source we use and presents the estimation technique and the estimates of the wage offer distribution (which do not depend on the crucial identification assumption). Section 2.4 discusses the identification and estimation of reservation wage functions and presents a discussion of the results and potential applications. Section 2.5 is the conclusion.

2.2   The model

In the simplest form of job search model studied by McCall [6] and Mortensen [8], the decision problem which the individual faces is that of wealth maximization with uncertain wage offers generated by a known wage offer distribution. Denoting wage offers by w^0 and reservation wages by ξ, the reservation wage which maximizes wealth is found as the solution to the following necessary condition:

$$(1 - F(\xi))\{h(\xi) - \xi\} = (m + \xi)\theta, \tag{1}$$

where $F(\xi) = \int_{-\infty}^{\xi} f(w^0)\, dw^0$ is the distribution function of wage offers,

$$h(\xi) = \frac{\int_{\xi}^{\infty} w^0 f(w^0)\, dw^0}{\int_{\xi}^{\infty} f(w^0)\, dw^0}$$

is the mean of w^0, given that $w^0 \geq \xi$, θ is the rate of discount, and m is the direct costs of search per period.

Under the assumptions of the models in [6] and [8] – risk neutrality, no capital constraints and agelessness – the value of ξ which solves (1) is constant across time but varies with θ and m across individuals. Although (1) can in principle be solved, empirical testing is made difficult since ξ is unobservable; thus one cannot proceed directly to estimating the determinants of ξ. An alternative is to use the implications of (1) for analyzing observed employment and earnings patterns across individuals. If two otherwise identical individuals differ in their costs of search, then their expected probability of finding a job in any number of periods will differ as will their expected earnings upon reemployment, and these will both differ in a systematic way. Hence, one can in principle use these implications to test the theory. To use these implications requires not only that the sources of differences in cost of search be specified, but also that the manner in which these differences affect observed phenomena be specified as well. This necessarily involves some assumptions about the distribution $F(w^0)$, but, as we indicate below, these assumptions can themselves be tested.

Let the wage offer distribution facing the ith individual be:

$$\ln w_i^0 = x_i'\beta + \varepsilon_i^0 \tag{2}$$

with

$$\varepsilon_i^0 \sim N(0, \sigma_0^2).$$

The vector $x_i' = (x_{1i}, \ldots, x_{ki})$ contains all characteristics of the worker and the labor market which affect the job search process. The reservation wage of the ith individual is generated by:

$$\ln \xi_i = Z_i'\gamma + \varepsilon_i^r \tag{3}$$

with

$$\varepsilon_i^r \sim N(0, \sigma_r^2).$$

The independent variables Z_i are again worker and labor market characteristics. We further assume that the error terms are jointly distributed as bivariate normal with covariance $\sigma_{0,r}$.

This characterization of the reservation wage function merits comment. If (3) is viewed as the exact solution of (1), then no error should be contained in it. An alternative interpretation is that ε_i^r represents interindividual variation in ξ_i which is not captured by Z_i. We will maintain this latter interpretation throughout.

An individual accepts a job if and only if $S_i \equiv \ln w_i^0 - \ln \xi_i$ is greater than zero, which from (2) and (3) is:

$$\begin{aligned} S_i &= x_i'\beta - Z_i'\gamma + \varepsilon_i^0 - \varepsilon_i^r > 0 \\ &= x_i'\beta - Z_i'\gamma + \varepsilon_i > 0 \end{aligned} \tag{4}$$

with

$$\varepsilon_i \sim N(0, \sigma_0^2 - 2\sigma_{0,r} + \sigma_r^2).$$

Since the condition for observing an individual's wage is that (4) hold, it is clear that the distribution of observed wages is truncated – offers below ξ_i are not accepted and therefore not observed. The observation on the wage offer distribution comes from a conditional distribution where the condition is that (4) holds. If w_i^0* is the logarithm of a drawing from the observed wage offers, then it is distributed with:

$$E(w_i^0*) = x_i'\beta + \rho\sigma_0\lambda_i, \tag{5}$$

$$\text{var}(w_i^0*) = \sigma_0^2(1 + \rho^2 r_i\lambda_i - \rho^2\lambda_i^2), \tag{6}$$

where:

(a) $\lambda_i = \dfrac{\phi(-r_i)}{1 - \Phi(-r_i)}$,

(b) $r_i = \dfrac{x_i'\beta - Z_i'\gamma}{\sigma}$, $\tag{7}$

(c) $\rho = \dfrac{\sigma_0^2 - \sigma_{0,r}}{\sigma_0\sigma}$,

(d) $\sigma = (\sigma_0^2 + \sigma_r^2 - 2\sigma_{0,r})^{1/2}$.

Here ϕ and Φ are the standard normal density and distribution function respectively. If λ_i were known, the regression:

$$w_i^0* = x'\beta + \rho\sigma_0\lambda_i + \varepsilon_i \tag{8}$$

could be run and β and $\rho\sigma_0$ estimated. Heckman [3] shows that probit estimates of the normalized version of (4), that is

$$S_i^* = \frac{S_i}{\sigma} = \frac{x_1'\beta - Z_i'\gamma}{\sigma} + \frac{\varepsilon_i}{\sigma}$$
$$= x_i'\beta* - Z_i'\gamma* + \varepsilon_i^*, \tag{4'}$$

can be used to estimate λ_i consistently, which in turn provides consistent estimates of β and $\rho\sigma_0$. Generalized least squares can be used to improve efficiency.

This framework is useful for interpreting two issues which arise in previous work on wage offer distributions, [1], [2]. Suppose λ is omitted from (6), but instead some elements of Z' are included. To the extent that truncation is important, these variables will serve as an approximation to λ and thus may become significant for that reason alone.[1] Thus variables which affect an individual's reservation wage but not his wage offer in the market, such as variables representing the level of UI payments, may appear significant in a wage equation. The significance of UI variables in a wage equation is correctly interpreted as evidence of misspecification. The second issue concerns the requirements for an observation to be included in a sample. Most studies use observations only for completed spells of job search, which elminates any information from (4) because (4') is always greater than zero. Since individuals with long spells of job search are likely to have the highest reservation wages, relative to potential earnings, selection by employment status results in a truncation of the reservation wage distributions.

Collecting equations with observable or partially observable dependent variables, we have:

$$w_i^0* = x_i'\beta + \varepsilon_i^0 \qquad \text{(wage offer function)} \tag{2'}$$

and

$$S_i^* = x_i'\beta* - Z_i'\gamma* + \varepsilon_i^* \qquad \text{(employment function)}, \tag{4'}$$

---

[1] For example, some elements of x_i may also be elements of Z_i; in this case their coefficients in a regression which does not include λ will confound market wage effects with reservation wage effects.

Table 2.1. *Sample characteristics of male workers*

	Mean	Maximum	Minimum
Education/years	10.2	21.0	0.0
Number of dependents	1.7	9.0	0.0
Per cent married	83.6	—	—
Per cent union members	70.4	—	—
Local unemployment rate (per cent) at layoff	5.30	9.00	2.20
Age	47.8	75.0	19.0
Unemployment benefits per week ($1967)	62.7	117.11	0.0
Maximum benefit period, weeks	41.5	65.6	0.0
Previous weekly earnings ($1967)	149.0	457.0	19.20

where the sign of S_i^* is observed and w_i^{0*} is observed if S_i^* is positive. In the following sections we provide estimates of the parameters of these equations.

2.3 The data and the wage offer distribution

The data are from a survey of workers in 14 states conducted by the Institute for Research on Human Resources of the Pennsylvania State University. The data were collected under contract to the Department of Labor for a study of the effects of the Trade Adjustment Assistance program (TAA); full details of the survey are reported in [8]. The individuals sampled had all become unemployed within the four year period 1969–1973. The survey took place in October of 1975. In this chapter we restrict attention to male workers. Summary statistics for this subsample are reported in Table 2.1.

The sample consists of workers who were permanently displaced from their jobs during the period 1969–1973. Over half of the sample (54 per cent) were recipients of unemployment benefits under TAA, which was considerably more liberal in terms of benefits than existing state programs. The remaining individuals were permanently separated from jobs in the same labor market but were not recipients of TAA. Because individuals were separated in different years, earnings are expressed in 1967 dollars. As a glance at Table 2.1 indicates, this sample of workers is not typical; in general, they are older, less educated and more heavily unionized than the entire male population. Since our interest is primarily methodological, this lack of representativeness is not a serious drawback. The

Table 2.2. *Employment equations*

	1	2
Constant	0.781	−2.18
	(0.494)	(1.02)
Education	−0.112	−0.222
	(1.08)	(1.82)
Dependents	−0.058	−0.049
	(1.08)	(0.917)
Married	0.248	0.227
	(1.44)	(1.32)
Unemployment rate	−0.166	−0.200
	(3.80)	(4.09)
Age	0.115	0.064
	(2.44)	(1.25)
Age × Ed	0.0019	0.0035
	(0.962)	(1.63)
Age^2	−0.002	−0.0017
	(4.85)	(4.07)
Unemployment benefit	−0.0052	−0.0062
	(1.27)	(1.47)
Maximum duration of benefits	0.0059	0.0056
	(0.977)	(0.923)
Tenure on previous jobs	−0.014	—
	(2.32)	—
Wage at previous job	0.0018	—
	(1.32)	—
Expected W^0	—	1.15
		2.04
χ^2	114	111
ln L	−281.45	−282.59

Note: Probit estimates of (4′) and (12′) in the text. The χ^2 test is a test against a binomial specification, $df = 11$ in 1, 10 in 2. Numbers in parentheses are asymptotic t-statistics. There are 517 observations.

value of this particular sample for our purpose is that it excludes all individuals on temporary layoff.

In order to estimate the parameters of the wage offer distribution, we first estimate (4′) by probit, then use the estimated probit coefficients to calculate a series on λ, the adjustment for the truncation in the observed wage offers. Then, conditioning on our series for λ, we estimate (8) by GLS. Estimates of the employment equation are presented in column 1 of Table 2.2. The dependent variable is a 0–1 variable which takes the value 1 if the originally unemployed individual has become employed within 65 weeks and zero otherwise. Note that the choice of 65 weeks is arbitrary under this specification of the job search model. Since reservation wages for each individual are assumed constant across time, as is the wage offer function, it makes no difference (asymptotically) what cut-off point is chosen. The equation is significant as measured by a chi-squared test against the binomial model (analogous to the F-statistic in an ordinary regression model).

The coefficient estimates obtained are "reduced form" coefficients; that is, they represent the net effect of the wage offer distribution and the reservation wage. Thus, being married increases the probability of employment, age has a positive but decreasing effect on employment, and the size of unemployment benefit payments reduces the probability of employment. Surprisingly, the effect of education is estimated to be negative and the maximum potential duration of unemployment benefits has a positive effect. Neither of these effects is significant, however. The local unemployment rate has a strongly negative effect on the probability of employment – a finding which is intuitively reasonable (the "discouraged worker" hypothesis) but which has implications about the appositeness of the simple job search model. These implications and a detailed interpretation of these coefficients are discussed in Section 2.4. For now we turn to the wage offer distribution.

Table 2.3 reports the estimates of the parameters of the wage equation estimated by ordinary least squares and generalized least squares. The equation is estimated over the sample of individuals who were employed and the series on λ constructed from the employment probit was entered as a regressor. The dependent variable was the logarithm of weekly wages. The strongest effect seems to be that of previous wages – the coefficient of the logarithm of lagged weekly wages is 0.32. The local unemployment rate has a positive (though insignificant) effect on the mean of the wage offer distributions facing individuals in the local labor market. This is somewhat difficult to interpret; in part the high unemployment rate could reflect queuing for the higher paying jobs, but then supply pressures could be expected to reduce the market wage. In the job search context there is no reason to believe that higher mean wage offer distributions will lead to higher unemployment – this depends on the response of reservation wage functions to changes in the wage offer distribution. Below we present evidence that this response is not complete (i.e., that reservation wages do not fully adjust to changes in the wage offer distribution). Tenure on an individual's previous job has a negative effect on the

Table 2.3. *Wage equation*

	OLS	GLS
Constant	1.42	1.54
	(2.25)	(2.55)
Education	0.106	0.097
	(2.96)	(2.80)
Age	0.036	0.034
	(1.59)	(1.57)
Age^2	−0.00016	−0.00016
	(0.594)	(0.659)
Age × Ed	−0.0016	−0.0014
	(2.21)	(2.02)
Unemployment	0.027	0.023
rate	(1.32)	(1.22)
Tenure on	−0.0068	−0.006
previous job	(2.60)	(2.55)
(Log of)	0.319	0.316
previous wage	(4.46)	(4.51)
λ	−0.056	−0.050
	(0.679)	(0.793)
R^2	0.199	0.438
N	327	327

Note: The dependent variable is the log of weekly wages.

wage the individual subsequently faces in the market. This can be interpreted as, holding previous earnings constant, an individual with greater job tenure has more firm-specific capital and less general capital. Consequently, the wage offer function facing such individuals is lower because the firm-specific capital is now worthless. Age, age squared and education have the usual effects.

The coefficient on λ is small, negative and insignificant. Recall from (5) and (7c) that this coefficient is

$$\frac{\sigma_0^2 - \sigma_{0,r}}{(\sigma_0^2 - 2\sigma_{0,r} + \sigma_r^2)^{1/2}};$$

therefore $\sigma_{0,r}$ is greater than σ_0^2. Thus, the error terms in the wage equation and in the employment equation are slightly negatively correlated, although the correlation between the "errors" in the wage offer equation and the reservation wage equation are positively (and substantially) correlated.

Although a high positive correlation between reservation wages and market productivity seems intuitively reasonable, there is no *a priori* reason why this should be so. One plausible explanation runs along the following lines. Suppose that there is an omitted variable $\bar{x}$, call it ability, uncorrelated with all other exogenous variables, which affects both market wages and reservation wages. Then if the true $\sigma_{0,r}$ were zero, the estimated $\sigma_{0,r}$ would be positive. It is straightforward to show under this specification that our estimate of the coefficient on λ is biased upwards if ability affects market wages more than or the same as reservation wages, and biased downwards if ability has a greater effect on reservation wages.

2.4   Reservation wages

An individual's reservation wage is assumed to be a function of the wage offer distribution faced and the costs of searching. In our model

$$E(\ln \xi_i) = f(x_i'\beta, \text{costs}_i) = Z_i'\gamma \tag{9}$$

since the higher moments of the wage offer distribution are assumed to be the same for everybody.

This formulation requires then that all elements of X be contained in Z, necessarily because they affect w^0 (i.e., through $x_i'\beta$), and possibly because they affect the costs of search as well – e.g., more educated individuals may need less time to read the help wanted section of the newspaper. Define x_i^j as the set of variables which affect wage offers and costs of search, x_i^k as the set of variables which affect wage offers but not costs of search, and Q_i as the set of variables which affect costs of search but not wage offers. Thus

$$Z_i' = [x_i'^j, x_i'^k, Q_i']. \tag{10}$$

By employing a Taylor series expansion on the middle expression in (9), the parameter vector γ can be decomposed as

$$\gamma = (f_1 B_j + \gamma_j, f_1 B_k, \gamma_Q), \tag{11}$$

where

$$f_1 = \frac{\partial \xi_i}{\partial x_i'\beta}.$$

Using (10) and (11) the employment equation (4) can be rewritten in normalized form as:

$$S_i^* = \frac{\ln(w_i^0) - \ln(\xi_i)}{\sigma} = x_i^{ij}\left(\frac{(1 - f_1)B_j - \gamma_j}{\sigma}\right)$$

$$+ x_i^{\prime k}\frac{(1 - f_1)B_j}{\sigma} - Q_i'\frac{\gamma_Q}{\sigma} + \frac{\xi_i}{\sigma} \qquad (12)$$

or, equivalently,

$$S_i^* = \frac{\ln(w_i^0) - \ln(\xi_i)}{\sigma} = (x_i'\beta)\frac{1 - f_1}{\sigma} - x_i^{ij}\frac{\gamma_j}{\sigma} - Q_i'\frac{\gamma_Q}{\sigma} + \frac{\varepsilon_i}{\sigma}. \qquad (12')$$

The question is, can we identify separately, σ, $1 - f_1$, and γ? The estimates in (12), which we shall call the reduced form estimates, are obviously of no help. The structural estimates of (12') provide some possibility, however. Since consistent estimates of $x_i'\beta$, the mean of each individual's wage offer function, can be obtained, it is possible to enter it separately into a probit model. This raises the central identification problem referred to in Section 2.1. If all variables which affect earnings also affect the costs of search, then (12') will be perfectly collinear. In order to identify the parameters of the reservation wage function it is necessary that some elements of x_i' affect reservation wages solely through their effect on wage offers. A priori restrictions are thus required on x_j'. These restrictions permit identification of $(1 - f_1)/\sigma$, (γ_j/σ), and γ_Q/σ, but except in the degenerate case of $f_1 = 0$, they are not sufficient to separately identify the remaining parameters. However, information on f_1 is available from at least two other sources; one is the requirement that the estimated error covariance matrix be positive semidefinite (this restricts f_1 because it restricts σ and we can estimate $(1 - f_1)/\sigma$). From the coefficient on λ in (5) and the definition (7c) and the interpretation of the coefficient on expected wages in (12') (denote this k) we find that feasible $(f_1, \sigma_{0,r})$ pairs lie along the line

$$f_1 = -kw^{-1}\sigma_0^2 + kw^{-1}\sigma_{0,r}$$

where w is the coefficient on λ in (5). Only points with $f_1 < 1$ satisfy the requirement that the estimated standard deviation σ is positive (for positive k; $f_1 > 1$ for negative k). The only other constraint arising from the consideration of definiteness which will ever be binding is the requirement that $\hat{\sigma}_r > 0$. The set of points $(f_1, \sigma_{0,r})$ for which $\sigma_r = 0$ is given by:

$$\left(\frac{1 - f_1}{k}\right)^2 - \sigma_0^2 + 2\sigma_{0,r} = 0;\tag{13}$$

feasible $(f_1, \sigma_{0,r})$ pairs lie to the right of this curve.

The second source of additional information is given in the following proposition.

Proposition 1. Let g, the wage offer density, be differentiable, with finite mean, and let u be a translation of the wage offer density. Then, $0 \le \partial \xi / \partial u \le 1$.

Proof.[2] Define the necessary condition (1) as:

$$H(\xi, u) = \int_\xi^\infty (w^0 - \varepsilon)g(w^0 + u)\, dw^0 - \theta[\xi + m] = 0$$

and note that

$$\frac{d\xi}{du} = -\frac{\partial H/\partial u}{\partial H/\partial \xi}.$$

We have

$$\frac{\partial H}{\partial u} = \int_\xi^\infty (w^0 - \varepsilon)g'(w^0 + u)\, dw^0.$$

Integrating by parts yields

$$\frac{\partial H}{\partial u} = (w^0 - \varepsilon)g(w^0 + u)|_\xi^\infty - \int_\xi^\infty g(w^0 + u)\, dw^0$$
$$= -[1 - G(\xi + u)],$$

where the first term on the right hand side vanishes if (1) has a solution. Also

$$\frac{\partial H}{\partial \varepsilon} = -\int_\xi^\infty g(w^0 + u)\, dw^0 - \theta$$
$$= -[1 - G(\varepsilon + u) + \theta].$$

---

[2] We are indebted to Roger Kormendi for correcting and generalizing an earlier version of this point.

Therefore

$$\frac{\partial \xi}{\partial u} = \frac{1 - G(\varepsilon + u)}{(1 - G(\xi + u)) + \theta} = \frac{\alpha}{\alpha + \theta} \leq 1. \qquad \text{QED}$$

This result bounds $f_1(=\partial \xi/\partial u)$ to the $[0, 1)$ interval, since α is necessarily contained in the interval $[0, 1]$, and θ is assumed to be positive; this implies that our estimate of k must be greater than zero. It can be shown that α is equal to the inverse of expected duration; consequently, data on duration can be combined with *a priori* values of θ to yield estimates of f_1. This allows estimation of the entire reservation wage function.

Proceeding to its application, we assume that two variables which enter the wage offer function do not affect the cost of search: an individual's tenure on his previous job and his previous wage. Both of these variables significantly affect the mean of the wage offer distribution. The advantage of imposing more than one restriction is that a test of the (overidentifying) restrictions can be made.

The second row of Table 2.2 reports probit estimates of (3) with the zero restrictions imposed. The variables in Q, which are assumed to affect costs of search but not the wage offers, are: the number of dependents, marital status, potential unemployment benefits and the maximum potential duration of benefit payments. The coefficient of the mean of the wage offer distribution, which up to a positive constant is $1 - f_1$, is of particular interest. *A priori* we expected f_1 to be nearly one; however, the estimates show that f_1 is significantly less than one. Thus, when the wage offer distribution shifts, reservation wages do not shift by as much.

This is consistent with observed patterns of unemployment over the business cycle, which are usually "explained" by sticky wages. However, an alternative interpretation, consistent with our evidence, is that wages are not sticky but that reservation wages are. In this view, changes in average observed wages will not fully reflect changes in market wage offers.

A check on the appropriateness of the identifying restrictions can be made on the basis of a likelihood ratio test between (1) and (2) of Table 2.2. The resulting χ^2 (1) statistic is 1.14; thus, the restrictions cannot be rejected under usual standards of significance. This is a test of whether the two variables, tenure on previous job and previous wage, enter the reservation wage function in the same relative amounts (i.e., the same linear combination up to a constant) that they enter the wage offer function. To the extent that these variables do affect costs of search in the same relative proportion that they affect the offer distribution, our test would be misleading. The procedure tests only the overidentifying restriction. Note that this likelihood ratio test is conservative; if the test were done without conditioning on the estimated β vector (i.e., if the wage offer equation and the employment equation were estimated simultaneously), the resulting test statistic would take a lower value.

A further check on the appropriateness of our division of variables into those affecting costs only and those affecting the costs of search and the wage offer distribution is available. The coefficients γ, those variables which affect only cost, should be the same under both versions of the employment equation (with and without the predicted wage). From Table 2.2 we see that the coefficients on dependents, marital status, unemployment benefits and maximum duration of benefits are practically the same for the two versions of the equation. Consequently we are reasonably confident about our classification of variables.

In order to estimate f_1 and, therefore, interpret our model in more detail we must obtain estimates of α and θ.[3] A natural estimate of α is the inverse of mean duration of unemployment in our sample. The mean duration in our sample is 34 weeks. We present estimates of the reservation wage function based on an annual value of θ of 0.1, a traditional value for discount rates. The implied value of f_1 is 0.94. The estimated parameters of the structural and reduced forms of the reservation wage equations corresponding to this value of f_1 is given in Table 2.4. Comparing the structural and reduced form estimates is of interest and shows, for example, that age and education affect reservation wages primarily through their effect on the wage offer distribution facing an individual.

To estimate the variance structure note that the coefficient on expected wage, $X\hat{\beta}$, in the structural employment probit is equal to $\sigma^{-1}(1 - f_1)$. Consequently, for $\theta = 0.25$

$$\sigma^2 = \sigma_0^2 - 2\sigma_{0,r} + \sigma_r^2 = 0.148 \tag{14}$$

and since the coefficient on λ in the GLS regression in Table 2.3 has interpretation

$$\frac{\sigma_0^2 - \sigma_{0,r}}{\sigma} \tag{15}$$

---

[3] The variance restriction noted in the text above was not binding for these data (i.e., the only f_1 violating the $\hat{\sigma}_r > 0$ constraint were greater than one).

Table 2.4. *Reservation wage function,[a]* $\theta = 0.1$

	Structural equation	Reduced form equation
Constant	0.113	1.56
Education	0.0115	0.103
Dependents	0.0025	0.0025
Marital status	−0.012	−0.012
Unemployment rate	0.0104	0.032
Age	−0.0033	0.0286
Age × Ed	−0.00018	−0.0015
Age^2	0.0000088	−0.00006
Unemployment benefits	0.00032	0.00032
Maximum duration	−0.00029	−0.00029
Expected wage[b]	0.94	
Tenure previous job		−0.0056
Wage previous job		0.297

[a] Derived using $f = 0.94$, corresponding to a discount of 0.10.
[b] The mean of the wage offer distribution.

we have

$$\sigma_0^2 - \sigma_{0,r} = 0.006. \tag{16}$$

An estimate of σ_0^2 is available (and was used in constructing the GLS estimators, following Heckman [3]) from the squared residuals from (1). The estimate is $\sigma_0^2 = 0.1866$. Consequently, $\sigma_{0,r} = 0.193$ and σ_r^2 can be obtained from (14). The resulting variance–covariance matrix for the joint distribution of ε^0 and ε^r is

$$V = \begin{bmatrix} 0.187 & 0.193 \\ 0.193 & 0.214 \end{bmatrix}, \tag{17}$$

which implies a correlation of 0.97 between the errors in the wage offer distribution and those in the reservation wage function.[4]

The high correlation between errors in the wage offer function and those in the reservation wage function indicates that the amount of "pure" wage

---

[4] The corresponding variance–covariance matrix for the errors in the offer and employment equations are

$$\begin{bmatrix} 0.187 & -0.006 \\ -0.006 & 0.015 \end{bmatrix},$$

which implies a correlation between the errors in the offer equation and the employment equation of −0.116.

variation is not as large as one would have expected merely from looking at the unexplained variation in the wage offer function. Taken literally the amount of unexplained variation would be 56.2 per cent of the total – a degree of randomness that is difficult to accept. If 97 per cent of this is accounted for by unmeasured factors – that is, if the correlation between reservation wages and market offers is due solely to omitted productivity factors – then obviously the amount of pure wage variation is considerably less. An interesting research question is how to appropriately decompose the observed variance into unmeasured individual specific components and pure wage variation. We defer this topic to Chapter 4.

A central assumption used in estimating this model of search activity is that the distribution of wage offers is distributed log-normally. This assumption greatly facilitates the computation of the estimates, since the conditional mean of a normal variable can be easily estimated. Alternative distributions could be considered, but their use would require full maximum likelihood estimation. It is beyond the scope of the present chapter to pursue this approach; instead we employ a direct test of the distributional assumption. Distributional tests are not usually performed on cross-section data, in part because the large number of observations available usually means that some peculiar outlier will occur. In the present context, however, the nature of the distribution, in particular the appropriate truncation point, suggests that such a test be applied. Although the failure to pass such a test will not indicate the appropriate area in which further work needs to be done, the passing of such a test would be fairly persuasive evidence in favor of the model.

We note here that the distribution of the errors in the equation for observed wages does not have a simple form. Although these errors are independently distributed, conditional on the parameters being known, they are not identically distributed. The density of the errors can be derived as follows. Let $p(\varepsilon^0, \varepsilon)$ be the joint density of the errors in the earnings and employment equations. This is assumed to be bivariate normal with zero means, variances σ_0^2 and σ^2 and covariance $\rho\sigma_0\sigma$. If the distribution is truncated so that only points for which $\varepsilon > -s$ are observed the joint density becomes (Johnson and Kotz [4])

$$\left[1 - \Phi\left(-\frac{s}{\sigma}\right)\right]^{-1} p(\varepsilon^0, \varepsilon) \qquad \begin{cases} -\infty < \varepsilon^0 < \infty, \\ -s < \varepsilon < \infty. \end{cases}$$

To find the marginal density of ε^0 we integrate ε out of this density. Write the joint density as the product of the conditional and the marginal

$$p(\varepsilon^0, \varepsilon) = p(\varepsilon|\varepsilon^0)p(\varepsilon^0).$$

Using properties of the normal distribution it is clear that

$$p(\varepsilon|\varepsilon^0) = \phi\left(\frac{\varepsilon/\sigma - \rho(\varepsilon^0/\sigma^0)}{\sqrt{(1-\rho^2)}}\right)(\sigma\sqrt{(1-\rho^2)})^{-1}$$

and

$$p(\varepsilon^0) = \phi(\varepsilon^0/\sigma^0)\sigma_0^{-1}.$$

Therefore,

$$f(\varepsilon^{0*}) = \int_{-s/\sigma}^{\infty} \left[1 - \Phi\left(-\frac{s}{\sigma}\right)\right]^{-1} p(\varepsilon^0, t)\, dt$$

$$\Rightarrow f_i(\varepsilon^{0*}) = \frac{\sigma_0^{-1}\phi\left(\dfrac{\varepsilon_i^{0*}}{\sigma^0}\right)\left[1 - \Phi\left(\dfrac{(-s_i/\sigma) - (\rho\varepsilon_i^{0*}/\sigma^0)}{\sqrt{(1-\rho^2)}}\right)\right]}{1 - \Phi\left(\dfrac{-s_i}{\sigma}\right)}, \qquad (18)$$

where ϕ is the standard normal density function and Φ is the corresponding cumulative distribution function. It is clear that the density of ε_i^{0*} depends on s_i unless ρ is zero. The first two moments of this density were given above. The implication of having nonidentically distributed errors is that the residuals cannot be used directly to form a simple test of the distributional hypothesis such as the Kolmogorov–Smirnov test. However, a transformation which makes the errors identically distributed is available. Let $F_i(x)$ be the distribution function corresponding to the density $f_i(x)$, that is

$$F_i(x) = \int_{-\infty}^{x} f_i(t)\, dt.$$

Then the random variables

$$y_i = F_i(x) \qquad (19)$$

are distributed according to the uniform distribution on $[0, 1]$. To show this let $g(y)$ denote the density of y and standard formulae give:

$$g(y) = f_i(F_i^{-1}(y))\frac{dF_i^{-1}(y)}{dy},$$

but from (19),

$$dy = dF_i(F_i^{-1}(y)) \, dF_i^{-1}(y)$$
$$= f_i(F_i^{-1}(y)) \, dF_i^{-1}(y),$$

so

$$g(y) = 1, \qquad 0 \le y \le 1.$$

This property of probability distributions is discussed in, for example, Kendall and Stuart [5]. In order to test our distributional hypothesis we transform the residuals to independently identically distributed uniform random variables using the above transformations.[5] Under the null hypothesis that the underlying error distribution is bivariate normal these transformed residuals will have the uniform distribution. A Kolmorogov–Smirnov test can be performed to test whether the observed distribution is significantly different from the uniform.

To perform this test we need the integral of $f_i(\varepsilon)$ from minus infinity to ε. Since a closed form solution to the integral of (18) does not exist, numerical methods were required. We evaluated the integral over the range -11 to ε by a 24-point Gaussian quadrature.[6] The Kolmorogov–Smirnov test is based on the statistic $\sqrt{N} \cdot D$ where D is defined as

$$D = \max \left| \frac{i}{N} - S_N(y_i) \right|$$

and S_N is the empirical CDF. The value of the K–S statistic obtained was 1.86, which exceeds the 90 per cent critical value of 1.32. Thus the data in this sample do not completely support this specification of the model. The source of this discrepancy is not clear; the K–S statistic tests the full specification of the model – both distributional assumptions and the functional form of the equations. Thus, although the model yields results which are plausible and intuitively appealing, the rejection by the K–S test indicates that further investigation is necessary.

2.5   Conclusion

In this chapter we have examined the econometric issues involved in estimating a simple job search model, and presented some preliminary econometric work on the topic. Subject to the identification problems

[5] This method of constructing identically distributed random variables is quite general and can be used to test distributional assumptions other than that used in this chapter.
[6] In practice this procedure was fast and efficient.

discussed – that some variables must affect wages but not costs of search, and conditional on the value of θ, the average rate of time preference – it is possible to estimate the determinants of reservation wages. The advantage which this approach possesses is that a broader set of questions about labor market behavior can be asked, and more accurate estimates of the quantitative effects of various policy measures can be obtained. For example, it is possible in this framework to analyze exactly how unemployment insurance payments affect wages or duration of unemployment. Although this chapter represents a start, there is clearly much more that needs to be done. Our investigation was in the context of a simple job search model, and the empirical results obtained, while generally consistent, indicate that more complex models may be required.

Acknowledgments

We thank James Heckman, Roger Kormendi, Robert E. Lucas, Jr., Tom MaCurdy, Melvin Reder and Sherwin Rosen and two anonymous referees for helpful comments on earlier versions.

References

[1] Classen, K., "The effects of unemployment insurance: evidence from Pennsylvania," CNA mimeo, April 1975.

[2] Ehrenberg, R., and Oaxaca, R., "Unemployment insurance, duration of unemployment, and subsequent wage gain," *American Economic Review*, 66 (1976), 754–766.

[3] Heckman, J., "Sample selection bias as a specification error," *Econometrica*, 47 (1979), 153–162.

[4] Johnson, N., and Kotz, S., *Distributions in Statistics: Volume Four, Continuous Multivariate Distributions*, John Wiley, New York, 1972.

[5] Kendall, M., and Stuart, A., *The Advanced Theory of Statistics*, Vol. II, 2nd edition, Hafner Publishing Company, New York, 1967.

[6] McCall, J. J., "Economics of information and job search," *Quarterly Journal of Economics*, 84 (1970), 113–126.

[7] Mohabbat, K. A., and Simos, E. O., "Consumer horizon: further evidence," *Journal of Political Economy*, 85 (1977), 851–858.

[8] Mortensen, D. T., "Job search, the duration of unemployment and the Phillips curve," *American Economic Review*, 60 (1970), 847–862.

[9] Neumann, G., "The direct labor market effects of the trade adjustment assistance program," in (ed. Dewald, W. G.), *The Impact of International Trade and Investment on Employment*, GPO, Washington, DC, 1978, pp. 100–122.

CHAPTER 3

An empirical job-search model, with a test of the constant reservation-wage hypothesis

In the 17 years after Stigler's work on search theory, economists have relied increasingly on the notion of search activity to explain diverse economic phenomena. The explanation of one type of unemployment – search, or frictional unemployment – is sometimes considered to be the essential contribution of search theory, but this is a narrow view.[1] The concept of productive investment in search has been used to explain such diverse phenomena as price rigidity (Gordon and Hynes 1970), advertising expenditure (Gould 1970; Butters 1974), duration of unemployment spells (Ehrenberg and Oaxaca 1976; Classen 1977), retention of military personnel (Gotz 1975), the effects of minimum wages (Mincer 1976), quits and layoffs (Mortensen 1977; Parsons 1973), and marriage and divorce rates (Becker, Landes, and Michael 1977). Despite the wide and growing list of empirical phenomena which have been "explained" by search theory, it seems a fair assessment of the subject would have to state that, apart from tightening some theoretical arguments on several topics, the concept has had little effect on the way economists interpret data and almost no effect on matters of public policy.[2]

A major reason for this current situation is the lack of empirical work on search theory. Moreover, what empirical research has been done generally has been only minimally related to the underlying theory. In consequence, it has been difficult to interpret the empirical results, and, more important, it has been impossible to infer whether a given set of results is or is not consistent with a search-theoretic interpretation.

This chapter is reprinted from *Journal of Political Economy*, vol. 87, no. 11 (1979). © 1979 by the University of Chicago.
[1] For a skeptical view of the empirical relevance of a search interpretation of unemployment, see Tobin (1972).
[2] A partial exception is the recent debate over unemployment insurance (UI). However, as Feldstein (1976) has demonstrated, much of the issue has to do with the appropriate means of financing UI payments, and not with search theory per se.

The lack of empirical work reflects the fact that estimating models of individual behavior based upon a sequential decision process involves a higher order of difficulty than normally encountered in static models. Subtle issues of model specification and identification arise which render customary empirical techniques (i.e., least-squares regression) inappropriate. The source of these problems lies in the structure of search problems. Central to all search problems is the adoption of a search strategy – in the simplest case, a reservation price – which is intrinsically unobservable. As a consequence, the observed outcomes of any search process are "contaminated" by the individual selection process, and it becomes difficult to distinguish variations in outcomes due to the environment – taxes, policy parameters – from variations due to search strategies.

In this chapter we examine the empirical implications of one job-search model and we develop the appropriate means of estimating such a model. We abstract from general equilibrium considerations and deal only with a partial equilibrium framework.[3] Although the model we examine is fairly simple, it appears to characterize unemployment behavior adequately. Moreover, this particular model illustrates many of the difficulties which will be encountered in estimating more refined search models and, thus, is of interest apart from the particular application to labor markets. Our techniques permit a test of the hypothesis that reservation wages are constant with duration of unemployment; this hypothesis is soundly rejected. Finally, we provide a tentative estimate of the fraction of wage heterogeneity which is due to search and information considerations.

The chapter is organized as follows. In Section 3.1 we present the essentials of the search model and develop an appropriate empirical model for estimation. Two variants of the simple model are examined: version I, which assumes a constant reservation wage, and version II, which allows the reservation wage to vary over time. The central question of identifying the structure of the reservation wage is discussed and methods of solution are proposed. Section 3.2 contains estimates of the search model and a discussion of their implications. Because both models are developed on an assumption about the wage-offer distribution, diagnostic checks not commonly used in cross-section studies are reported in this section also. The implications of our results for interpreting other labor market phenomena are discussed in Section 3.3 and a summary is given in the final section.

---

[3] Telser (1978) provides a treatment of search strategies and equilibrium price distributions.

3.1   Job-search models: specification and interpretation

In the simplest form of job-search model studied by McCall (1970) and Mortensen (1970), an individual attempts to maximize expected wealth by accepting an employment offer only if it exceeds his reservation wage, w^r. Facing a known stationary distribution of wages, the sequence of reservation wages, $\{w_t^r\}$, which maximizes expected wealth, must satisfy[4]:

$$[1 - F(w_t^r)][h(w_t^r) - w_t^r] = (w_t^r + m)\theta, \qquad t = 1, \ldots, T, \qquad (1)$$

where:

$F(w_t^r) =$ the distribution function of wage offers, w^o;

$$h(w_t^r) = \int_{w_t^r}^{\infty} w^o f(w^o) \ dw^o / [1 - F(w_t^r)]$$

$\qquad\qquad =$ the conditional mean of w^o, given that $w^o \geq w^r$;   (2)

$\qquad \theta =$ discount factor;[5]

$\qquad m =$ direct costs of search.

Equation (1) states a familiar marginal relationship: The reservation wage should be set in each period such that the expected gain – the wage differential – from an additional search equals the cost of that search – the amortized value of the forgone earnings and the direct cost of search. If the horizon of the individual is taken as infinite, the distribution of offers is known, and the costs of sampling are constant, then the reservation wage is constant, $w_t^r \equiv w^r$, $t = 1, \ldots, \infty$.

In general, reservation wages could change over time for a number of other reasons, including wealth effects or learning about the offer distribution. In the latter case, a reservation-wage solution need not even exist.[6]

---

[4] Let the per period gain from an additional search be ξ. Then an offer, w^o, is accepted if $w^o > \xi$. The gain from searching, according to the optimal policy, is

$$\frac{\xi}{\theta} = \frac{1}{1 + \theta} E\left[\frac{1}{\theta} \max(\xi, w^o)\right] - m.$$

Multiplying through by θ and collecting terms gives the equation in the text.

[5] In the infinite horizon case, θ, equals the discount rate i. In the finite horizon case, θ, is the present value at time 0 of a dollar of income received in period t; i.e., $\theta_t = 1/(1 + i)^T \{[(1 + i)^{T-t+1} - 1]/i\}$.

[6] Danforth (1978) obtains a declining reservation wage because of asset decumulation, while Mortensen (1977) produces a similar result due to changes in the direct cost of search, m_t, occasioned by a termination of UI payments. Rothschild (1974) treats the case of an unknown offer distribution.

In any case, assume the reservation wage can be solved from (1) as

$$w_t^r = g[F(w^o), \theta_t, m].^7 \tag{3}$$

If w_t^r were observable, one could estimate (3) directly, and it would be straightforward to test hypotheses about search behavior.[8] Such information is typically not available, however, and one must rely heavily on the underlying theory. In particular, an assumption about the form of the wage-offer function must be made. Below we show how this assumption can be tested.

Assume that the wage-offer distribution facing the ith individual is

$$w_i^o(t) = x_i'\beta + \varepsilon_{it}^o, \tag{4}$$

with $\varepsilon_{it}^0 \sim$ i.i.d. $N(0, \sigma_0^2)$.

The vector $x_i' = (x_{i1}, \ldots, x_{in})$ contains all characteristics of the worker and the labor market which affect earnings.

The assumption that the errors in the wage offer equation are independently distributed over time embodies the assumption of random search made in simple models of job-search activity. In other words, the individual does not persistently search the same employment opportunity.

Let the reservation wage function be given as

$$w_i^r(t) = Z_i'(t)\gamma + e_{it}^r, \tag{5}$$

with $e_i^r \sim$ i.i.d. $N(0, \sigma_r^2)$ and $E(\varepsilon_i^r \cdot \varepsilon_{it}^0) = \sigma_{or}$. The independent variables $Z_i(t)$ are again worker and labor market characteristics.

The specification of the error term in the reservation-wage equation is similar to that of the wage-offer equation, that is, independent over time. We shall argue below that this assumption follows logically from the specification of the wage-offer equation.

Individuals accept employment if and only if $w_i^o - w_i^r(t) = S_i(t)$ is greater than zero,[9] which from (4) and (5) and the temporal independence of the error term is:

---

[7] As an example, suppose that the wage offers are distributed uniformly in the interval $(0, 1)$. Then the solution to (1) is given by the positive root of $(w_t^r)^2 - 2\{1 - 2[\theta/(1 - \theta)]m + 1\theta_t\}w_t^r - 2(m - 1) = 0$.

[8] "Straightforward" is somewhat of an exaggeration since the parameters and form of $F(\cdot)$ would have to be determined exactly if the interrelationships between reservation wages and unemployment were to be examined.

[9] Eq. (5) is the solution to (1) implied by (3), where the error term represents the determinants of reservation wages which are not available to the researcher.

$$S_i(t) = x_i'\beta - Z_i'\gamma + \varepsilon_i^o - \varepsilon_i^r > 0$$
$$= x_i'\beta - Z_i'\gamma + \varepsilon_i > 0, \tag{6}$$

with $\varepsilon_i \sim N(0, \sigma^2)$ and $\sigma^2 = \sigma_o^2 + \sigma_r^2 - 2\sigma_{or}$.

Since the condition for observing the wage outcome of the job-search process is that (6) hold, it is clear that the distribution of observed wages is truncated – offers below $w_i^r(t)$ are not accepted and therefore not observed. Furthermore, if the reservation wage is time dependent, then the point of truncation varies over time and depends upon the actual realization of the job-search process. Note that the point of truncation is stochastic.[10]

Although simplifications are available to bypass these problems when the reservation wage is constant over time (see Kiefer and Neumann 1979), admitting the possibility of a changing reservation wage requires that all information on the search process be utilized. One must resort then to maximum-likelihood methods for this problem. The probability that an individual searches exactly D periods is

$$\Pr(D_i = D) = \prod_{t=1}^{D-1} [1 - \alpha(t)]\alpha(D), \tag{7}$$

where $\alpha(t)$ is the probability of receiving an acceptable offer in period t. From (6) and our distributional assumption

$$\alpha(t) = \Phi\left(\frac{x_i'\beta - Z_i'\gamma}{\sigma}\right), \tag{8}$$

where Φ is the standard normal cumulative distribution. We could estimate each of these probabilities by probit, but additional information is gained by working with the joint distribution of duration and the reemployment wage of those workers who become reemployed. This distribution is, using results from conditional normal distribution theory,[11]

---

[10] The model specified here provides a rigorous interpretation of the employment probits used in Kiefer (1978), with only a reference to the existence of a search-model interpretation.

[11] The "trick" is to note that the joint distribution is the product of a marginal distribution (denoted here by ϕ) and a conditional, and that the conditional normal distribution has a simple form (see Johnson and Kotz 1972).

$$\Pr(D_i, w) = \prod_{t=1}^{D-1} [1 - \alpha(t)]\sigma_o^{-1}\phi\left(\frac{w - X\beta}{\sigma_o}\right)$$
$$\cdot \left(1 - \Phi\left\{\frac{(Z'\gamma - x'\beta)/\sigma - \rho(w - X\beta)/\sigma_o}{(1 - \rho^2)^{1/2}}\right\}\right), \qquad (9)$$

where

$$\rho = \frac{\sigma_o^2 - \sigma_{or}}{\sigma\sigma_o}, \qquad (10)$$

the correlation between the errors in the offer and the employment equations and ϕ is the standard normal density. The likelihood function for this problem consists of products of probabilities for those who do not become reemployed and products of probabilities and densities for those who do. Thus observations on both completed and uncompleted spells of unemployment can be used.

The question which arises naturally is whether one can identify the basic parameters of interest: β, γ, σ_o, σ_r, σ_{or}. Clearly, β and σ_o can be identified from the wage offer function (see Heckman, 1979). The correlation parameter between wage offers and the employment decision can also be identified. Problems arise in attempting to identify the remaining parameters since w_i^r and, hence, σ_r are not observed. However, observations on reemployment wages, and suitable restrictions, will provide identification. Consider equation (3) for the case of constant reservation wages under the distributional assumptions we have made. We have

$$E(w_i^r) = f(x_i'\beta, \theta_i, m_i) = Z_i'\gamma.^{12} \qquad (11)$$

This formulation requires, then, that all elements of x be contained in Z, necessarily because they affect w^o (i.e., through $x_i'\beta$), and possibly because they affect the costs of search, m_i, as well – for example, more educated individuals may need less time to read the want ads in the newspaper. Define x_i^j as the set of variables which affect wages offers and costs of search, x_i^k as the set of variables which affect wage offers but not costs of search, and Q_i as the set of variables which affect costs of search but not wage offers. Thus,

$$Z_i' = (x_i'^j, x_i'^k, Q_i'). \qquad (12)$$

---

[12] We explicitly assume that the variance in wage offers is constant across all individuals and, thus, will be absorbed into the constant term of the reservation-wage function.

Interpreting the parameter vector γ as a Taylor series expansion of the middle term in (11), we have

$$\gamma = (f_1\beta_j + \gamma_j, f_1\beta_k, \gamma_Q), \tag{13}$$

where $f_1 = \partial w^r / \partial x_i'\beta$.

Combining this with the definition of S_i above yields

$$S_i = -\left\{ x_i^{ij} \frac{[(1 - f_1)\beta_j - \gamma_j]}{\sigma} + x_i^{\prime k} \frac{(1 - f_1)\beta_k}{\sigma} - Q_i' \frac{\gamma_Q}{\sigma} \right\} + \varepsilon_i \tag{14}$$

or, equivalently,

$$S_i = \left[-(x_i'\beta) \frac{1 - f_1}{\sigma} + x_i^{ij} \frac{\gamma_j}{\sigma} - Q_i' \frac{\gamma_Q}{\sigma} \right] + \varepsilon_i. \tag{14'}$$

If x_i^k is null, that is, if all factors which affect an individual's market productivity also affect his costs of search, then it is impossible to obtain estimates of γ_j/σ. This is the central identification issue to which we referred in the introduction. Thus a necessary condition for estimating the parameters of the reservation-wage function is that some elements of x_i' affect reservation wages solely through their effect on wage offers.[13]

Assuming that this identification condition holds, we can estimate from (9) and (14') β, σ_o, γ_i/σ, γ_Q/σ, $\rho = (\sigma_o - \sigma_{or})/(\sigma \cdot \sigma_o)$, and $(1 - f_1)/\sigma$. Except in the degenerate case of $f_1 = 0$, these estimates provide insufficient information to identify the basic parameters of the reservation-wage function. This is of no consequence for some purposes – for example, estimating, correctly, the impact of UI payments on duration of unemployment – but for other problems it may be of critical importance. In order to determine the basic parameters, additional information is needed.

Kiefer and Neumann (1979) have shown that

$$0 \leq \frac{dw^r(t)}{dx'\beta} = f_1 = \frac{\alpha(t)}{\alpha(t) + \theta_t} \leq 1. \tag{15}$$

Since $\alpha(t)$ can be estimated from the reduced-form parameters alone and θ_t determined by knowledge of an individual's length of time until retirement and the appropriate discount rate i, it is possible to obtain an estimate of the mean value of f_1. Combining this with the estimate of

---

[13] That an identification issue arises is not surprising since the model is essentially a special case of an ordinary simultaneous equation problem.

$(1 - f_1)/\sigma$ provides an estimate of σ which serves to identify both σ_{or} and σ_r.[14]

3.2 Empirical results

In this section we apply the model discussed above to a sample of unemployed male workers. This particular sample of workers consists solely of individuals who were permanently separated from employment and thus were not eligible for recall. The survey was conducted by the Institute for Research on Human Resources of the Pennsylvania State University to study the effects of the Trade Adjustment Assistance Program. A full description of the data is found in Neumann (1978). The use of this data set has advantages and disadvantages. Its major disadvantage is that the workers included are not representative of the entire U.S. population or even of the unemployed population. Thus the specific results we obtain may not be generalizable to the total population. Since we are concerned primarily with the appropriate methods for estimating search models, we do not view this as a major problem. The advantage of using this source is that, by construction, all individuals were not able to return to their previous employer and, hence, had to engage in search behavior.[15] Additionally, this data set has information on completed spells of unemployment and on reemployment earnings, both of which are required in estimating the model. Summary statistics for this sample are given in Table 3.1.

One problem which arises in examining the search behavior of indi-

---

[14] Two further sources of information about f_1 can be used to place bounds upon the value of σ. By definition, the covariance matrix

$$V = \begin{bmatrix} \sigma_o^2 & \sigma_o^2 - \sigma_{or} \\ & \sigma^2 \end{bmatrix}$$

must be positive definite. The singular curve determined by $|V| = 0$ is defined in the (f_1, σ_{or}) space by $f_1 = -\hat{k}\hat{\rho}^{-1}\hat{\sigma}_o[1 + (\sigma_o/\hat{\sigma}_o^2)]$, where $\hat{k}$ is the estimated coefficient of $(1 - f_1)/\sigma$ obtained from (14'). A further restriction, $\sigma_r^2 > 0$, is available. The singular curve determined by $\sigma_r^2 = 0$ is defined in (f_1, σ_{or}) space by $[(1 - f_1)/\hat{k}]^2 - \sigma_o^2 + 2\sigma_{or} = 0$. These two restrictions provide bounds upon the admissible values of f_1 and σ_{or} which may be used to check the "reasonableness" of the estimates. In the event that $f_1 = 1$ obtains, they provide the only means of identifying the reservation wage parameters.

[15] Including the possibility of recall into the model could be achieved with little increase in complexity, except that search intensity, i.e., a labor-supply function, would have to be estimated also.

Table 3.1. *Sample characteristics of male workers*

	Mean	Maximum	Minimum
Education (Yr.)	10.2	21.0	0
Dependents (N)	1.7	9.0	0
Married (%)	83.6	—	—
Union members (%)	70.4	—	—
Local unemployment rate (%)			
at layoff	5.3	9.0	2.2
Age	47.8	75.0	19.0
Unemployment benefits per week ($1967)	62.7	117.11	0
Maximum benefit period (Wk.)	41.5	65.6	0
Previous weekly earnings ($1967)	149.0	457.0	19.2

viduals is that of uncompleted searches. If a group of workers starts searching for jobs at one time and a survey of these workers is taken x periods later, some will have found employment and thus will have complete information, but others will not. This problem arises in most studies of unemployment (Ehrenberg and Oaxaca 1976; Classen 1977; and Hoelen 1977) and is usually solved by discarding the observations on incomplete spells, a practice which creates censoring problems in addition to those already present.[16] In our approach, the problem of incomplete spells poses no problem and, indeed, provides information – namely, that an individual had x wage offers which fell short of the reservation wage. For these observations, the likelihood contribution will be in the form of a product of probabilities without a density.[17]

The estimates of model I, the constant reservation-wage model, are contained in Table 3.2, and the results for model II, the variable reservation-wage model, are presented in Table 3.3. In both specifications we use the (over-) identifying restrictions that years of experience with the previous employer, tenure, and weekly earnings prior to separation, ln w_{t-1} , affect reservation wages solely through their effect on the mean of the wage-offer distribution, $\hat{w}$. The dependent variable for the wage-offer function is the natural logarithm of the reemployment weekly earnings.

---

[16] One paper which attempts to deal with this issue is Neumann (1978). However, the solution proposed there is correct only in the case of a constant reservation-wage model and is less efficient than the approach of this paper.

[17] We classify a spell as incomplete if the worker is still unemployed after 76 weeks. Any other number would do as well provided that it is large enough to adequately capture systematic changes in reservation wages.

Table 3.2. *Constant reservation-wage model maximum-likelihood estimates*

	Wage-offer function (1)	Normalized reservation-wage function (2)
Constant	2.9452	4.6802
	(7.36)	(3.59)
Education	.0560	.0674
	(2.73)	(2.46)
Dependents	—	.0079
		(.44)
Tenure	−.0070	—
	(3.11)	
Marital status	—	−.1618
		(2.12)
Unemployment rate	.0296	.0900
	(1.50)	(4.06)
Age	.0110	−.0466
	(2.00)	(3.47)
Age (squared)	0	.0009
	(.33)	(5.50)
Education × age	−.0005	−.0008
	(1.35)	(1.56)
Unemployment benefits	—	.0038
		(2.79)
Maximum duration	—	−.0021
		(1.02)
ln W_{t-1}	.2425	—
	(4.67)	
$\hat{w}$	—	.6346
		(2.27)
σ_{w^o}	.4430	
	(6.60)	
ρ	−.4263	
	(1.18)	
ln(ll)	−1,782.96	

Note: Numbers in parentheses are asymptotic *t*-statistics.

Constant reservation wage model

Table 3.2 contains the maximum-likelihood estimates of the simple job-search model when the reservation wage is constrained to be constant. The wage-offer function contained in column 1 of Table 3.2 is similar to the earnings function used in most studies. The only notable exception

Table 3.3. *Changing reservation-wage model maximum-likelihood estimates*

	Earnings function (1)	Normalized reservation-wage function (2)
Constant	2.8043	3.4692
	(18.10)	(3.31)
Education	.0810	.0314
	(3.15)	(1.13)
Dependents	—	−.0120
		(.67)
Tenure	−.0072	—
	(3.03)	
Marital status	—	−.2462
		(3.63)
Unemployment rate	.0309	.0713
	(1.76)	(3.66)
Age	.0248	−.0360
	(1.90)	(3.15)
Age (squared)	−.0001	.0006
	(.41)	(4.47)
Education × age	−.0010	−.0004
	(1.96)	(.65)
Unemployment benefits	—	.0033
		(2.67)
Maximum duration	—	.0013
		(.63)
$\ln W_{t-1}$	.2542	—
	(4.89)	
$\hat{w}$	—	.2728
		(1.31)
g	—	−.01736
		(12.59)
σ_{w^0}	.5239	
	(12.02)	
ρ	−.7160	
	(8.87)	
$\ln(ll)$	−1,685.35	

Note: Numbers in parentheses are asymptotic *t*-statistics.

is that we have available a direct measure of job tenure with previous employer, which is used instead of the conventional age-minus-education-minus-five as a measure of experience. This provides the only unusual empirical finding with regard to the wage-offer function: When tenure is held constant, initial earnings do not exhibit any nonlinearity in age. The significant negative effect of previous job tenure suggests a very strong role for job-specific human capital.[18] Holding previous earnings, education, and age constant, an additional year of employment with a firm results in a reemployment wage 0.7 percent lower. For those workers who become reemployed, the average decline in weekly earnings was 26.7 percent. Since the average job tenure was 16.4 years, job tenure accounted for an 11.5 percent decline, or 43.7 percent of the total loss.

The normalized reservation-wage function estimates in column 2 of each table generally agree with our a priori notions. Higher unemployment benefits significantly increase reservation wages, as do higher market earnings potential, $\hat{w}$, and education. Being married leads to lower reservation wages, as one would expect if the spouse was not working, although having more dependents does not seem to have any effect. In contrast to the earnings function, reservation wages have a pronounced nonlinearity in age, being high in the early work years, reaching a minimum at about 26 years $[.0466/2(.0009)]$, and rising thereafter. One curious effect is the large and significant coefficient on the local unemployment rate. If the local unemployment rate is interpreted as indicating structural difference across labor markets, this finding is consistent, but it raises the question of causality. That is, are local unemployment rates high because reservation wages in that area are high, or is it the case that persistently high unemployment areas develop infrastructures which in some way lower the costs of search to individuals? We shed no light on this issue, but the pronounced effect of unemployment on reservation wages coupled with the absence of any appreciable effect on wage offers merits further study.

Finally, the estimated correlation between errors in the wage-offer equation and errors in the employment decision is negative, although not significant. Since the correlation is equal to $(\sigma_o^2 - \sigma_{or}) \cdot (\sigma \cdot \sigma_0)^{-1}$ from (10), this implies that σ_{or} is positive and of larger magnitude than σ_o^2, which implies that σ_r^2 is also larger than σ_o^2. In other words, the variability in reservation wages is larger than that in market opportunities, a result which appeals to our intuition. An estimate of σ^2 is obtained using (15), the mean value of α, 0.0245, and a weekly discount rate of $.1/52 = .0019$. From (15) this yields a value of f_1 of .9272, which implies $\sigma = (1 - .9272)/ .6346 = 0.1147$.

[18] Specific and general human capital and their effects on life-cycle mobility are discussed in Jovanovic and Mincer (1978). See also Lazear (1976).

The definition of ρ (the correlation coefficient between errors in earnings and employment) in turn allows σ_r to be identified as .5027. Thus the covariance matrix of wage offers and (unobserved) reservation wages is:

$$V = \begin{bmatrix} .1962 & .2179 \\ .2179 & .2527 \end{bmatrix}. \tag{16}$$

The implied correlation between reservation wages and market opportunities is .979, indicating a substantial interrelationship. A stronger interpretation of the model can be made if additional structure is placed on the error terms. Consider ε_r, the residual in the reservation-wage equation (5). Since (5) is considered as the exact solution to (3), the residual ε_i^r represents those factors which are known to the individual but which cannot be controlled for in the empirical analyses. Part of the residual is presumably due to uncontrolled population differences which are likely to affect market productivity, and part is also due to uncontrolled-for differences in the cost of search which do not affect productivity in the market. To the extent that these uncontrolled factors affect productivity, estimates of the variances in wage offers will overstate the true variance since they will include the effects of (unmeasured) population heterogeneity. A method for isolating the effects of pure wage-offer variation from population heterogeneity is given by a one-factor representation of the disturbances. Let the residual in the wage-offer equations be given as

$$\varepsilon_i^0 = k\varepsilon_i^r + \varepsilon_i^*, \tag{4'}$$

with

$$E(\varepsilon_i^r) = \sigma_r^2$$
$$E(\varepsilon_i^0) = \sigma_o^2 = k^2\sigma_r^2 + \sigma_*^2 \tag{5'}$$
$$E(\varepsilon_i^0 \cdot \varepsilon_i^r) = k\sigma_r^2.$$

In this representation, k is a scale factor relating individual-specific disturbances in the reservation-wages equation to market earnings and, by construction, ε_i^* and ε_i^r are uncorrelated. This orthogonalization is always possible in a two-equation model. Moreover, it is suggested by a rational expectations approach: All (unsystematic) variations in wage offers received by an individual should be uncorrelated with the determinants of market productivity.

Using this orthogonal decomposition, the covariance term σ_{or} can be interpreted as $k\sigma_r^2$, and k is solved by dividing by .2527 $(=\sigma_r^2)$. Thus $k = .8623$ and σ_*^2, the variance corrected for population heterogeneity, is .00836 or 4.3 percent of the total unexplained variation in wage offers. While we regard this ratio as a lower bound, its relatively small size raises the possibility that purely random wage variation may be more apparent than real.[19]

Variable reservation wages

The preceding discussion focused upon the simple search model where reservation wages are constant over the search period. Although the conditions under which such a result holds are strong – infinite life, knowledge of the wage-offer distribution, and lack of capital constraints – it is an empirical issue whether this simple model provides an adequate explanation of observed behavior. To examine this question, the search model was evaluated allowing for nonstationarity in the reservation wage. Specifically, the reservation wage is characterized as

$$w_i^r(t) = Z_i'\gamma + g \cdot t, \tag{17}$$

where t is the number of weeks of unemployment experienced to date.[20] The estimates of this version of the job-search model are presented in Table 3.3.

Comparison of the wage-offer function estimates in column 1 of Table 3.3 with those of Table 3.2 reveals only small differences in the coefficients – the effect of education has increased and the nonlinearities due to age are somewhat more pronounced. The reservation-wage function also exhibits little change, except for the effect of duration of unemployment. The statistical superiority of the declining reservation model is indicated both by the very large t-statistic (12.59) and by the likelihood ratio test: $-2\Delta[\ln(\text{ll})] \sim X^2 = 2[-1685.35 - (-1782.96)] = 195.22$. Both tests (they are asymptotically equivalent) provide statistical evidence that

[19] Note that this is an ex post interpretation of our estimates. A more general analysis along these lines would require explicit treatment of the individual effects.

[20] This particular representation of the effect of time unemployed on reservation wages is consistent with, and does not permit identification of, several explanations of why reservation wages decline. If data were available on consumption flows, it would be possible to identify some factors separately, but in their absence a general "drift" term must suffice.

reservation wages decline over time. The parameters of the underlying distributions can be recovered in a manner similar to that previously used.[21] The covariance matrix of market and reservation wages is

$$V = \begin{bmatrix} .2745 & .3996 \\ .3996 & .6362 \end{bmatrix}.$$

We again find that variation in reservation wages is greater than variation in offers. Employing the orthogonalization of (4') and (5'), the variances can be decomposed into:

$$\sigma_r^2 = .6362, \tag{18a}$$
$$k = .6283, \tag{18b}$$
$$\sigma_*^2 = .0234. \tag{18c}$$

Thus, in this interpretation, the variance of wage offers corrected for population heterogeneity accounts for 8.5 percent ($=.0234/.2745$) of the unexplained variation in wage offers.

Before turning to a discussion of these results, it is useful to examine how well the model "fits" the data. By comparison with other studies, the estimates of the wage equation are reasonable and the results for the reservation-wage equation conform to one's a priori notions, but these are rather subjective "tests." The critical issue in terms of fit is whether the distributional assumption of lognormality can be maintained. A casual glance at a histogram of wages would not indicate a tendency towards lognormality, but since the observed wage offers are assumed to be drawn from a truncated lognormal distribution, "eyeballing" the data is not a very powerful technique. To test the assumption of lognormality, we use

---

[21] The primary difference lies in the estimate of σ^2. Under the constant reservation-wage interpretation, this was estimated by: $\hat{\sigma}^2 = [(1 - \hat{f_1})/\hat{k}]^2$, where $\hat{k}$ was the coefficient on expected earnings in the normalized reservation-wage function and $\hat{f_1} = \hat{\alpha}/(\hat{\alpha} + \theta)$. In the previous calculations, θ was taken as .1, and the mean value of α, the probability of an acceptable job match in a week, was 0.0245. In the present context, neither α nor θ is constant, and the question is what values should be used to identify σ^2. We computed the average value of $\hat{f_1}$ as:

$$\sum_{i=1}^{N} \frac{1}{N} \frac{1}{76} \sum_{j=1}^{76} \frac{\alpha_i(j)}{\alpha_i(j) + \theta_i(j)},$$

using a market interest rate of 0.1, the individual's age, and an assumed retirement age of 65. The resulting estimate if 0.909. Therefore, σ^2 is estimated as $[(1 - .909)/.2728]^2 = 0.1113$.

the Kolmogorov–Smirnov (K–S) distributional test.[22] The K–S test is based on the statistic $\sqrt{N} \cdot D$, where

$$D = \max \left| \frac{i}{N} - S_N(y_i) \right| \tag{19}$$

and S_N is the empirical cumulative distribution function. The critical value for the 90 percent confidence interval is 1.32. The actual values obtained were 1.57 for the maximum-likelihood estimates of the constant reservation-wage model and 1.28 for the maximum-likelihood estimates of the changing reservation-wage model. Thus, for the changing reservation-wage model, the assumption of lognormality is supported by the data, a result which reinforces confidence in the structure and specification of the model.

3.3 Implications of search

We return now to the question posed in the introduction: How well does search theory explain unemployment behavior? To avoid repetition we note at the outset that the empirical results obtained in the preceding section are based upon a sample of workers who are not representative of the work force or of the unemployed. Despite this limitation, the results are of sufficient interest that we discuss them as though they were generally applicable; where possible, we note what differences could be expected in a more representative sample.

The most natural starting point is how well does a search model explain the observed unemployment behavior of the sample. Since actual duration

---

[22] See Kendall and Stuart (1973) for a description of the K–S test. In the present case, the distribution of the errors in the wage offer function is given by:

$$f_i(\varepsilon^o) = \frac{\sigma_o^{-1} \phi\left(\dfrac{\varepsilon_i^0}{\sigma_o}\right)(1 - \Phi\{[s_i(t)/\sigma - (\rho\varepsilon_i^0/\sigma_o)]/[(1 - \rho^2)^{1/2}]\})}{1 - \Phi[s_i(t)/\sigma]}, \tag{a}$$

where ϕ is the standard normal density and Φ is the corresponding cumulative distribution function. (See Kiefer and Neumann [1979] for the derivation of this density.) So long as $\rho \neq 0$, the residuals in the wage equation are distributed independently, but not identically. However, using a well-known result (see, e.g., Kendall and Stuart 1973), the random variables $\gamma_i = F_i(\varepsilon^o)$, where F_i is the cumulative distribution function of (a), are distributed according to the uniform distribution on (0, 1). A 24-point Gaussian quadrature was used to integrate (a) over the range -8 to ε^o.

of unemployment enters into the estimation only indirectly – that is, as the number of unsuccessful job searches – it is not guaranteed that there will be any relation between predicted and actual unemployment. For the constant reservation-wage model, the expected duration of unemployment, $E(D_i)$, is defined as: $E(D_i) = 1/[1 - F(w_i^r)]$.

For those who had completed spells of unemployment, the mean of D_i is 38.4, the mean of $E(D_i)$ is 52.7, and the correlation is only .110. The low correlation and the high mean of $E(D)$ are partially due to the presence of several outliers for whom

$$\int_{w^r}^{\infty} f(w) \, dw \approx 0.$$

(One outlier was the oldest individual in the sample, who became reemployed at age 75.) When the two outliers are removed, the results are slightly improved – $\overline{E}(D) = 48.1$, $\overline{D} = 39.4$, and $\rho = .390$ – but the relation is not overwhelmingly strong.

For the changing reservation-wage model, expected duration of unemployment is defined as:

$$E(D_i) = \sum_{j=1}^{\infty} j \left\{ \prod_{k=1}^{j-1} [1 - \alpha_i(k)] \right\} \alpha_i(j), \tag{20}$$

with $\alpha(j) = 1 - F[w_i^r(j)]$.

A closed-form solution to (20) does not exist, and thus it was evaluated numerically. The results, with outliers removed, are: $\overline{E}(D) = 40.2$, $\overline{D} = 39.4$, and $\rho = .583$. This correlation compares favorably with the multiple correlation coefficients obtained in regressions of duration of unemployment upon sets of variables similar to those used in the specification of the reservation-wage function. Comparison of R^2 is not an entirely adequate method for judging the "explanatory" ability of a model, but in the present context it is reasonable to conclude that the restrictions we have imposed from the theory result in an empirical model which is superior to alternative approaches. However, these results imply that search theory, as applied in this approach and as limited by the availability of data, accounts for about one-third $[(.583)^2 = .34]$ of the variability in unemployment duration. It is unclear whether this fraction would be higher or lower in a more representative sample.

Accepting, then, that job-search behavior accounts for a significant fraction of unemployment, it is of some interest what this implies about the structure of unemployment. A major result of the previous section was the finding that reservation wages decline over time. The normalized coefficient in the reservation wage function, g/σ, was estimated as $-.01736$; multiplying this by the estimated value of σ, $.3336$, yields a value of g of $-.0058$. Thus these estimates imply a decline in reservation wages of 0.6 percent per week, or about 2.5 percent per month. This estimate is considerably higher than Kasper's estimate of 0.4 percent and Stephensen's estimate of 0.06 percent for young males. The findings of these two studies are not strictly comparable to ours. Kasper's (1967) study measures the relative decline in asking wages from answers to a survey of the unemployed in Minnesota. Apart from the general problem of what type of response is generated to the question "What wage are you [currently] seeking?" the data actually obtained are "contaminated" due to sample selection – those who have the largest relative decline are least likely to be observed. Stephensen's (1976) study is subject to the same problems. There are reasons for believing that this estimate is larger than the average value in the entire population: These workers are older than the average worker, and thus the effect of finite life should be more pronounced in this sample.

An implication of declining reservation wages is that the escape rate – the fraction of workers who find employment in a given week – should rise over time. Evidence reported by Kaitz (1970) and Marston (1975) indicates that escape rates fall with time in the aggregate, a result which is in contrast with ours. We suspect that the difference is due to the obvious selectivity biases in the aggregate data. We note in passing that it would be possible to check whether the change in the escape rate over time was solely due to a change in the reservation wage. This would be, we suggest, a promising area for future empirical work.

A related point is the cyclical behavior of unemployment duration. By the term cyclical, we refer to fluctuations in the mean of the wage-offer distributions confronting individuals. The results of the previous section imply that the distribution of this unemployment duration is independent of the business cycle. That is, our estimate of f_1 – the effect of the mean wage offer on reservation wages – is insignificantly different from unity. Consequently, temporal fluctuations in real earnings, to the extent that they are foreseen at the commencement of the search process, should have little or no effect on the length of a spell of unemployment. Unanticipated changes in the wage-offer distribution will, of course, lead to changes in observed outcomes, but if this is corrected for, the implication is that the distribution of observed unemployment durations should be constant. We are unaware of any evidence which bears directly on this issue, but the view seems widespread that long-term unemployment becomes proportionately greater in a recession.

One final topic which merits comment is the amount of wage variability which actually exists in a labor market. If wages truly were nonrandom to individuals, then search-theoretic interpretations of unemployment would be vacuous. It is important here to distinguish between variability as observed in a given data set and that which confronts an individual with full knowledge of his ability. Thus, in the wage-offer equation we are able to account for about 30 percent of the variance in wage offers, leaving 70 percent to unobserved personal characteristics and to pure "chance." The importance of search-theoretic interpretations clearly depends upon how much is actually due to chance. Using one tentative specification, we estimate that 8.5 percent of the total unexplained variance can be attributed to pure randomness. This would seem a small amount to account for observed unemployment. It is unclear whether this estimate is related to this particular sample of workers, or whether it reflects a more general phenomenon.

We thank George Borjas, James Heckman, R. E. Lucas, and Tom MaCurdy for useful discussions and comments on an earlier version of this chapter. Daniel Hamermesh and Hirschel Kasper sent us useful comments on a later draft. Financial support was provided by the U.S. Department of Labor. The views expressed here are, of course, not necessarily those of the Department of Labor, its agencies, or its staff.

References

Becker, Gary S., Landes, Elisabeth M., and Michael, Robert T. "An Economic Analysis of Marital Instability." *J.P.E.* 85, no. 6 (December 1977): 1141–87.
Butters, Gerard. "Equilibrium Distribution of Prices and Advertising." Mimeographed. Chicago: Univ. Chicago Press, 1974.
Classen, Kathy. "The Effect of Unemployment Insurance on the Duration of Unemployment and Subsequent Earnings." *Indus. and Labor Relations Rev.* 30, no. 4 (July 1977): 438–44.
Danforth, John. "On the Role of Consumption and Decreasing Absolute Risk Aversion in the Theory of Job Search." In *Studies in the Economics of Search*, edited by S. Lippman and J. McCall. Amsterdam: North-Holland, 1979.

Ehrenberg, Ronald G., and Oaxaca, Ronald L. "Unemployment Insurance, Duration of Unemployment, and Subsequent Wage Gain." *A.E.R.* 66 (December 1976): 754–66.

Feldstein, Martin. "Temporary Layoffs in the Theory of Unemployment." *J.P.E.* 84, no. 5 (October 1976): 937–57.

Gordon, Donald, and Hynes, Allen. "On a Theory of Price Dynamics." In *Microeconomic Foundations of Employment and Inflation Theory*, edited by Edmund S. Phelps et al. New York: Norton, 1970.

Gotz, Glen. "An Analysis of the Retention of Air Force Officers: Theory and Preliminary Results." Mimeographed. Santa Monica, Calif.: RAND Corp., June 1975.

Gould, John P. "Diffusion Processes and Optimal Advertising Policy." In *Microeconomic Foundations of Employment and Inflation Theory*, edited by Edmund S. Phelps et al. New York: Norton, 1970.

Heckman, James. "Sample Selection Bias as a Specification Error." *Econometrica* 47 (1979): 153–62.

Hoelen, Arlene, "Effects of Unemployment Insurance Entitlement on Duration and Job Search Outcome." *Indus. and Labor Relations Rev.* 30, no. 4 (July 1977): 445–50.

Johnson, Norman and Kotz, S. *Distributions in Statistics: Continuous Multivariate Distributions*. New York: Wiley, 1972.

Jovanovic, Boyan, and Mincer, Jacob. "Labor Mobility and Wages: On the Job and over the Life Cycle." Paper presented at NBER conference on Low Income Labor Markets, Chicago, 1978.

Kaitz, Hyman B. "Analyzing the Length of Spells of Unemployment." *Monthly Labor Rev.* 93 (November 1970): 11–20.

Kasper, Hirschel. "The Asking Price of Labor and the Duration of Unemployment [in Minnesota]." *Rev. Econ. and Statis.* 49 (May 1967): 165–72.

Kendall, Maurice G., and Stuart, Alan. *The Advanced Theory of Statistics.* 3d ed., vol. 1. London: Griffin, 1973.

Kiefer, Nicholas M. "Federally Subsidized Occupational Training and the Employment and Earnings of Male Trainees." *J. Econometrics* 8 (1978): 111–25.

Kiefer, Nicholas M., and Neumann, George. "Estimation of Wage Offer Distributions and Reservation Wages." In *Studies in the Economics of Search*, edited by S. Lippman and J. McCall. Amsterdam: North-Holland, 1979. Chapter 2 in this volume.

Lazear, Edward. "Age, Experience, and Wage Growth." *A.E.R.* 66, no. 4 (September 1976): 548–80.

McCall, John J. "Economics of Information and Job Search." *Q.J.E.* 84 (February 1970): 113–26.

Marston, Stephen T. "The Impact of Unemployment Insurance on Job Research." *Brookings Papers Econ. Activity,* no. 1 (1975), 13–48.

Mincer, Jacob. "Unemployment Effects of Minimum Wages." *J.P.E.* 84, no. 4, pt. 2 (August 1976): S87–S104.

Mortensen, Dale T. "Job Search, the Duration of Unemployment, and the Phillips Curve." *A.E.R.* 60 (December 1970): 847–62.

"Unemployment Insurance and Job Search Decisions." *Indus. and Labor Relations Rev.* 30, no. 4 (July 1977): 505–17.

Neumann, George. "The Direct Labor Market Effects of the Trade Adjustment Assistance Program." In *Domestic Employment, Foreign Trade, and Investment*, edited by W. Dewald Washington D.C.: U.S. Gov. Office, 1978.

Parsons, Donald O. "Quit Rates over Time: A Search and Information Approach." *A.E.R.* 63 (June 1973): 390–401.

Wages, reservation wages, and duration

Rothschild, Michael. "Searching for the Lowest Price When the Distribution of Prices Is
    Unknown." *J.P.E.* 82, no. 4 (July/August 1974): 689–711.
Stephenson, Stanley P., Jr. "The Economics of Youth Job Search Behavior." *Rev. Econ.
    and Statis.* 58, no. 1 (February 1976): 104–11.
Telser, Lester. *Economic Theory and the Core.* Chicago: Univ. Chicago Press, 1978.
Tobin, James. "Inflation and Unemployment." *A.E.R.* 62, no. 1 (March 1972): 1–18.

CHAPTER 4

Individual effects in a nonlinear model: explicit treatment of heterogeneity in the empirical job-search model

4.1 Introduction

The theory of job search is a theory which concerns optimal behavior for an individual. In a simple model the ith worker faces a distribution of wage offers with mean μ_i and samples offers with constant sampling costs c_i. A reservation wage policy is optimal (maximizes income) and the reservation wage is determined by μ_i and c_i:

$$w_i^r = g(u_i, c_i).$$

Section 4.2 below examines some properties of the function g. In empirical work the μ_i and c_i are unknown, although of course they are known to the ith worker. We wish to learn about the systematic structure of μ_i and c_i, offer distributions and search costs, as well as about the function g.

In previous work[1] we have supplied and estimated an empirically tractable model of job search. In that work we specified

$$\mu_i = X_i\beta,$$

that the mean of the offer distribution facing the ith individual is an exact linear function of observable characteristics X_i. This procedure gave sensible results, but it is open to the criticism that the results are questionable due to left out variables ("ability") in the wage equation. Indeed, in interpreting our results we conjectured that the influence of left out variables was indicated by the substantial positive correlation between errors in the wage equation and in the reservation wage equation. In the present chapter we incorporate individual means μ_i not necessarily exactly equal

---

This chapter is reprinted from *Econometrica*, vol. 49, no. 4 (July 1981), by permission of the Econometric Society.
[1] Kiefer and Neumann [15, 16].

to $X_i\beta$ explicitly by specifying

$$\mu_i = X_i\beta + f_i.$$

The individual effect f_i enters the model nonlinearly through the function g. In Section 4.2 the discussion is in terms of known μ_i; in Sections 4.3 and 4.4 the empirical problem is considered. Section 4.5 presents the final set of estimating equations and the estimates. As an example of the kind of results obtainable with the individual effect approach, we find that individual effects, fixed for an individual for the duration of a spell of unemployment, accounts for substantially more of the variation in wages (after extracting the variation due to X) than does the variance of the offer distribution for each person.

4.2   The search-theoretic background

In the simplest job-search models (McCall [18], Mortensen [19]) a wealth-maximizing worker calculates a reservation wage policy. The worker samples wage offers w_t from a known (to the worker) distribution F, at a constant cost per sample c. A reservation wage policy is optimal. With such a policy the worker chooses a reservation wage w^r, a function of the distribution F and costs c, such that he will accept the first offer w greater than his reservation wage w^r. It is clear that the reservation wage is the per-period gain from an additional search. An implicit equation in w^r which necessarily holds at the optimal value of w^r is easily obtained and provides a restriction which is empirically useful.

The reservation wage w^r must satisfy the relation

$$\frac{w^r}{\theta} = \frac{1}{1+\theta} E\left\{\frac{1}{\theta}\max\{w^r, w\} - c\right\} \tag{1}$$

with θ a discount rate. To see this, note that the left-hand side is simply the present value of the reservation wage (the optimal strategy) and the right-hand side is the discounted (one period) value of the expected present value of another sample less the cost of taking the sample. Clearly the optimal reservation wage w^r should satisfy this equality. A rigorous derivation, as well as discussion of a number of extensions and of general robustness of the model to changes in the assumptions, is given by Lippman and McCall [17]. Equation (1) can be rearranged to

$$(w^r + c)\theta - [1 - F(w^r)][E(w|w > w^r) - w^r] = 0,$$

where F is the distribution function for wage offers and $E(w|w > w^r)$ is the expected value of a wage offer given that the offer is greater than the reservation wage, i.e., given that the offer is accepted. This equation states that the gain from the marginal search, that is the expected wage advantage resulting from that search, must equal its marginal cost – both the direct cost and the amortized value of earnings foregone.

The following theorem gives a parametric restriction useful in the emprical work below:

Theorem. Let μ be the mean of the wage offer distribution. Then

$$\frac{\partial w^r}{\partial \mu} = \frac{\alpha}{\alpha + \theta}, \tag{2}$$

where $\alpha = 1 - F(w^r)$.

The theorem can be proved by differentiating the necessary condition (2.1) first with respect to μ and then with respect to w^r. Taking the negative of the ratio of these derivatives gives the formula appearing in the theorem. Details are given in Kiefer and Neumann [15]. The quantity α is the probability of receiving an offer greater than the reservation wage, i.e., the probability of becoming employed in a given single draw from the offer distribution. The probability of becoming employed in exactly t periods is

$$(1 - \alpha)^{t-1}\alpha \tag{3}$$

and the expected future duration of a spell of unemployment does not depend on when during the spell the expectation is taken.

Extension of the model to allow for wealth maximization with a finite horizon or for wealth-constrained searching raises the possibility that reservation wages decline with duration of a spell of unemployment. In this case α should be subscripted by t, and the sequence α_t is increasing. The theorem continues to hold, although the derivative $\partial w^r/\partial \mu$ must of course be subscripted by t. The probability of becoming employed in exactly t periods is

$$\prod_{j=1}^{t-1} (1 - \alpha_j)\alpha_t \tag{4}$$

and the expected future duration of a spell of unemployment is a decreasing function of current duration. If the form of the offer distribution is not known to the worker a reservation wage strategy may not be optimal, and if such a strategy is optimal the reservation wage may decline or increase with duration. Rothschild [24] considers this case. In previous work we have concluded that reservation wages decline significantly with duration.

4.3 The empirical model

To begin the simplifications required for empirical work we assume that workers face wage offer distributions identical except for first moments. The tth draw from the offer distribution for the ith individual can be written

$$w_{i_t}^0 = X_i\beta + f_i + \varepsilon_{i_t}. \tag{5}$$

The mean of this offer distribution for the ith person is $X_i\beta + f_i$ and is not indexed by t. While the empirical model could handle offer distributions whose means are not fixed for the length of a spell of unemployment, this seems an unnecessary generalization. The variance of wage offers facing any individual is σ^2; however the variance in wage offers across individuals, controlling for the effects of X, is $\sigma^2 + \sigma_f^2$, where σ_f^2 is the variance of f looking across individuals.[2] Thus variation in offers consists of interindividual variation due to the effects f as well as variation arising from the offer distribution. Of course offers are typically not observed unless they are accepted so the above decomposition does not directly apply to variation in observed wages. The variables in X are variables which determine, or indicate, the productivity of the ith worker, and possibly some structural characteristics of the labor market.

The reservation wage for the ith worker is given by

$$w_i^r = g(X_i\beta + f_i, c_i), \tag{6}$$

where the function g is defined implicitly by equation (1). Only the mean of the offer distribution enters the function g since all other characteristics

[2] The assumption that ε and f are orthogonal is innocuous, i.e., f and ε can always be defined so that this is true. Those who dislike the idea of individual effects having a statistical distribution can, for the time being, simply read (with N the number of individuals in the sample)

$$\frac{1}{N}\sum_i f_i^2 \quad \text{for} \quad \sigma_f^2.$$

of the offer distributions are identical across individuals. We now take an approximation to the function g:

$$w_i^r = \delta + g_{1i}X_i\beta + g_{2i}c_i + g_{1i}f_i$$
$$= g_{1i}X_i\beta + Z_i\gamma + g_{1i}f_i, \tag{7}$$

defining Z_i to include a constant term and variables which affect costs of search (Z_i can include variables in X_i). Thus there is a proportionality restriction between coefficients in the reservation wage equation and in the offer equation. Indeed, given θ and α_i we could calculate the coefficient of proportionality. Note that this coefficient is indexed by i, i.e., the proportionality restriction holds for each individual, but with different coefficients of proportionality.[3] A similar restriction could be imposed on g_{2i}, the coefficient of c_i, if we had direct measures of the costs of search. For our present purposes we approximate $g_{2i}c_i$ by $Z_i\gamma + f_i\eta$. Inclusion of the term $f_i\eta$ allows for inter-individual variation in costs above that accounted for by variation in measurable characteristics. An alternative approach would be to specify $c_i = Z_i\gamma$ and enter $g_{2i}Z_i\gamma$ into the reservation wage equation. There seems to be no advantage to this more complicated approach.

Reservation wages are generally not observed, and wage offers are observed only if they are accepted. Offers are observed, that is employment occurs, at the first t such that

$$w_{i_t}^0 - w_i^r > 0$$

or

$$X_i\beta + f_i + \varepsilon_{i_t} - g_{1i}X_i\beta - Z_i\gamma - g_{1i}f_i > 0. \tag{8}$$

Under the assumption that ε_{i_t} is normally distributed this equation, conditional on f_i, is simply a probit employment equation. A mishmash of reduced form parameters could be estimated by probit if the f_i were known. The expected wage offer for the ith worker is

$$E(w^0) = X_i\beta + f_i$$

but the expected accepted wage is

$$E(w^0|w^0 > w^r) = X_i\beta + f_i + \sigma\lambda_i \tag{9}$$

---

[3] In previous work using a slightly different formulation we have approximated the coefficients g_{1i} by a number k, the same for all i. The actual variation in g_{1i}, and therefore the error in our previous approximation, is calculated below.

and the corresponding variance is (see, e.g., [11])

$$V(w^0|w^0 > w^r) = \sigma^2(1 + r_i\lambda_i - \lambda_i^2), \tag{10}$$

where $\lambda_i = \phi(r_i)/\Phi(r_i)$ and $r_i = [(1 - g_{1_i})(X_i\beta + f_i) - Z_i\gamma]\sigma^{-1}$. ϕ and Φ are the density and distribution function respectively of the standard normal distribution. This is simply the expression for the mean of a truncated normal distribution, where the normal has mean $X_i\beta + f_i$ and the point of truncation is w_i^r. If all the f_i were zero the model could be estimated by a simple modification of Tobit. Amemiya's [1] initial consistent estimator could be applied without difficulty. Kiefer [14] estimates Tobit models for reemployment wages, but does not identify γ. Heckman's [9] reinterpretation of Tobit as a missing data model applies here; cost variables Z certainly affect the mean of the distribution of accepted wages, but they do not affect offers. For example, unemployment insurance payments might influence reemployment wages through their effect on search costs, and therefore may be significant in a reemployment wage equation (see [5, 10, 20]).

Thus, the model under consideration consists of two equations. The first,

$$w_{i_t}^0 = X_i\beta + f_i + \varepsilon_{i_t},$$

is the offer equation. The dependent variable in this equation is observed only if the ith individual is employed. Wages are observed for at most one t for each i. The second equation is the employment equation,

$$w_{i_t}^0 - w_i^r = (1 - g_{1i})X_i\beta - Z_i\gamma + \varepsilon_{i_t} + (1 - g_{1i})f_i. \tag{11}$$

For each i, we observe the sign of the dependent variable, i.e., whether the ith person was employed, for each of the $t = 1, \ldots, T$ periods since the beginning of a spell of unemployment. An individual in our sample is either unemployed for all T periods, or becomes reemployed at some $t < T$. We are now in a position to calculate the contribution of the ith observation to the likelihood. As before, we are dealing conditionally on the individual effects f_i. For those who are unemployed at time T the likelihood contribution is

$$(1 - \alpha_i)^T$$

in the case of the constant reservation wage model and

$$\prod_{j=1}^{T} (1 - \alpha_{ij})$$

in the case in which reservation wages vary with duration of unemployment. The probability α_i is given by

$$\alpha_i = \Phi\left[\frac{(1 - g_{1i})(X_i\beta + f_i) - Z_i\gamma}{\sigma}\right] \tag{12}$$

in the case of the constant reservation wage model. In our specification of the changing reservation wage model a linear trend in t is added into the numerator of the argument of the normal distribution in the above equation. Thus we allow only monotonic changes in reservation wages as a function of duration. The probabilities α_i therefore, in both the constant and the changing reservation wage specifications, depend crucially on the individual effects f_i. A worker who becomes reemployed in period t contributes a density term

$$(1 - \alpha_i)^{t-1}\sigma^{-1}\phi\left[\frac{w_{i_t} - X_i\beta - f_i}{\sigma}\right] \tag{13}$$

to the likelihood, where w_i is the accepted wage. This likelihood term is plainly the product of the probability of becoming employed in period t,

$$(1 - \alpha_i)^{t-1}\alpha_i,$$

and the density of a wage, conditional on its being accepted,

$$\alpha_i^{-1}\sigma^{-1}\phi\left[\frac{w_{i_t} - X_i\beta - f_i}{\sigma}\right].$$

Conditional on the individual effects f_i, therefore, the likelihood can be derived in a straightforward manner following the derivation of the Tobit model. The required modification of the formulas when reservation wages are permitted to vary with duration of unemployment is obvious.

4.4 The unconditional empirical model

After forming the likelihood function conditionally on the f_i, one simple way to move to unconditional inference is to treat the f_i as unknown parameters to be estimated. In the case of fixed effects in the linear regression model with panel data this poses no great difficulty; the fixed effects can simply be differenced away. This is discussed in the huge literature on the ANOVA models and by Mundlak [21] in a useful unifying framework for linear models for panel data. In general nonlinear models the situation is much more difficult. Incidental parameters have been widely discussed; classical references are Neyman and Scott [23], who introduced the conventional terminology of "incidental" vs. "structural" parameters, and Kiefer and Wolfowitz [13]. The latter reference showed that the situation is not hopeless. If one is willing to assume that the f_i follow some sort of distribution through the population, and if some regularity conditions are satisfied, then the model can often be estimated without necessarily specifying the form of the distribution of the effects. In this chapter we adopt the strategy of assuming that the individual effects f_i follow a parametric distribution, namely the normal distribution. The problem is thereby converted into a straightforward regular maximum likelihood problem. Alternately, as described below, a Bayesian interpretation can be given to our estimation strategy. Before moving to our specification, we note that the method of conditional inference, which works for the problem of logit estimation (see E. B. Andersen [2] for the theory and R. Freeman [7] for an empirical application) could in principle be applied to our problem if we could find suitable sufficient statistics for the f_i.[4] We chose not to pursue this strategy for two reasons: (i) The choice (even existence) of suitable sufficient statistics is not obvious, and (ii) we are more interested in σ_f^2 than in the individual f_i.

To move from the conditional (on f_i) densities given above to unconditional densities we assume that the f_i are independently normally distributed among the population with mean zero (this is not a restriction since a constant term is included in the wage offer equation) and variance σ_f^2. We then integrate the individual effect out of each term in the likelihood. This procedure can be given two interpretations: (i) The economic model specifies a normal distribution of the individual effects, or (ii) the economic model says nothing about the individual effects but we have an independent identical normal prior for each of these effects. In fact we estimate σ_f^2, so under (ii) the posterior density for the parameters studied is conditional on a modal value for σ_f^2 under diffuse priors, i.e., priors proportional to a constant. In discussing the results below we essentially follow interpretation (i) since we wish to interpret σ_f^2 as a parameter of the model. However the analysis is the same, and the reader can choose the interpretation he wishes to maintain.[5]

---

[4] See also Chamberlain [4]. Heckman [8] gives Monte Carlo results for a particular nonlinear model with individual effects.

[5] The normality assumption is convenient here because the only new parameter introduced is σ_f^2, a parameter we are particularly interested in. Future research could experiment with other specifications.

Integrating out the individual effects f_i does not lead to a simple set of estimating equations. For those who remain unemployed for the T periods that they are followed the unconditional likelihood takes the form

$$(2\pi)^{-1/2}\sigma_f^{-1} \int_{-\infty}^{\infty} (1 - \alpha_i(f))^T \exp\left\{ - \frac{1}{2} \frac{f^2}{\sigma_f^2} \right\} df, \tag{14}$$

where the function $\alpha_i(f)$ is given implicitly by the formula for α_i, equation (12). For those who become reemployed at period t, the appropriate unconditional contribution to likelihood is

$$(2\pi)^{-1/2}\sigma_f^{-1} \int_{-\infty}^{\infty} (1 - \alpha_i)^{t-1}\sigma^{-1}\phi\left(\frac{w_i - X_i\beta - f}{\sigma}\right) \exp\left\{ - \frac{1}{2} \frac{f^2}{\sigma_f^2} \right\} df. \tag{15}$$

This has the form of a complicated mixture of truncated normal densities, conditional on employment having occurred in period t. In the next section we give the equations in the form in which they will be estimated, derive their implications for the observed dispersion of accepted wages, then describe the data and present the estimates.

4.5   Estimation

The wage offer equation which will form the basis for estimation is

$$w_{i_t}^0 = X_i\beta + f_i + \varepsilon_{i_t}$$

with parameters to be estimated β, σ_f^2, and σ^2. The reservation wage function is given above, but we allow one extension which arises from consideration of the meaning of the individual effects f_i. These effects are interpreted as a left out variable indicating productivity – perhaps an "ability" variable. Such a variable is likely to affect costs of search as well as the location of the offer distribution. For example, a more able worker might search more efficiently. We allow for this possibility with the parameter η. The form of the reservation wage function which is estimated is

$$w_i^r = g_{1i}X_i\beta + Z_i\gamma + (g_{1i} + \eta)f_i, \tag{16}$$

where η is a parameter reflecting the influence of the individual effect on costs of search. The α_i formed as indicated above (taking account of the new cost parameter) and the likelihood contribution for each observation (indexed by i) is in principle easily found by integrating the effect out of the conditional density for each observation. The full set of parameters is β, γ, η, σ_f^2, and σ^2.

Table 4.1. *Sample characteristics of male workers*

	Mean	Maximum	Minimum
Education/years	10.2	21.0	0.0
Number of dependents	1.7	9.0	0.0
Per cent married	83.6	—	—
Per cent union members	70.4	—	—
Local unemployment rate (per cent) at layoff	5.30	9.00	2.20
Age	47.8	75.0	19.0
Unemployment benefits per week ($ 1967)	62.7	117.11	0.0
Maximum benefit period/weeks	41.5	65.6	0.0
Previous weekly earnings ($ 1967)	149.0	457.0	19.20

The theorem given in Section 4.2 gives a cross-equation restriction in the form of an implicit equation

$$g_{1i} = \frac{\alpha_i}{\alpha_i + \theta}.$$

The probability α_i of course depends on g_{1i} (as well as f_i). In previous work we have simply assumed that g_{1i} was constant across i, and we estimated a parameter g_1, but a strict interpretation of the theoretical model requires that the implicit restriction be imposed. Given values for the parameters being estimated we impose the restriction by solving the implicit equation numerically for each i.[6]

The data are from a survey of workers in 14 states who had been permanently separated from their jobs. The data were collected under contract to the U.S. Department of Labor for a study of the effects of the Trade Adjustment Assistance Program. Full details of the survey are reported in Neumann [22]. Summary statistics are presented in Table 4.1. The sample of workers is not completely typical of the pool of unemployed workers; in general they are older and more unionized. The primary advantage of this data set is that it does not include workers on temporary layoff.[7] There are 517 observations. Data on the length of com-

[6] A simple golden-section search method was used. Clearly $g_{1i} \in (0, 1)$ for all i. A discount rate of .1/year was used.

[7] Feldstein [6] discusses the effects of temporary layoffs on the theory of unemployment. Clearly a worker on temporary layoff is likely to have a somewhat different attitude toward job search than an unemployed worker who is not on temporary layoff. The workers in our sample became unemployed when the plants at which they were employed closed.

pleted spells of unemployment and on reemployment earnings are available for those workers who became reemployed. As a dependent variable we use the log of weekly earnings. Variables included in X, i.e., variables which affect the location of the wage offer distribution, are education (years of schooling), tenure on the previous job – a measure of specific human capital – age, its square, and age multiplied by education as variables which indicate general human capital stocks and allow for vintage effects in schooling, the local unemployment rate, reflecting variation in structural characteristics (e.g., information flows) in labor markets, and previous wages (in logs) as another indicator of the total stock of human capital, general and specific.[8] Variables included in Z, i.e., variables affecting costs of search, are: education, which presumably effectively lowers search costs by increasing search efficiency, marital status and number of dependents, the local unemployment rate, age, its square and age times education since the stock of general human capital is likely to affect search efficiency, and two unemployment insurance variables: the benefit amount and the maximum duration of payments. This specification of included variables is consistent with that in our earlier work which did not model the individual effects explicitly. Consequently the resulting coefficients will be directly comparable and we can examine, in a particular applied problem, the effect on coefficient estimates of not allowing explicitly for the individual effects.[9]

Maximum likelihood estimates of the parameters of the constant reservation wage model are given in Table 4.2. The likelihood was maximized using a modified scoring method.[10] The parameters of the offer

[8] A subtle point arises in using lagged wages to determine the location of the offer distribution. In a world of rapid job turnover, the wage on previous jobs would be on average the conditional mean of the wage offer distribution; thus it would be an indicator of costs of search as well as productivity variables. For workers with long job tenure the effects of search costs in the past are likely to be dominated by the effects of information on the workers' productivity. It is this information on productivity that we attempt to capture with our wage variable. In the sample used the average tenure on the previous job was over 16 years.

[9] The previous model (Kiefer and Neumann [16]) did specify correlation between offers and reservation wages for each individual, but did not explicitly allow correlation of offers over time for an individual. In a loose sense, then, we are examining the effect of ignoring dependence in maximum likelihood estimates of parameters.

[10] The method approximates the second derivative matrix of the log-likelihood function by the negative of the mean of the outer products of the gradients of the densities. Using this approximation a Newton step was taken and a linear search was made at each iteration. The method was introduced into economics by Berndt, Hall, Hall, and Hausman [3].

Table 4.2. *Constant reservation wage model*

	Wage-offer equation	Reservation wage equation
Constant	2.8140	2.3711
	(0.456)	(0.775)
Education	0.0214	0.0388
	(0.0146)	(0.018)
Dependents	—	0.0039
		(0.0076)
Tenure	−0.0083	—
	(0.0022)	
Marital status	—	−0.0841
		(0.0393)
Unemployment rate	0.0168	0.0451
	(0.0114)	(0.0121)
Age	0.0132	−0.0236
	(0.0061)	(0.0069)
Age^2 ($\times 10^{-3}$)	0.0416	0.5439
	(0.1014)	(0.1314)
Ed $\times$ Age	−0.0006	0.0004
	(0.0005)	(0.0002)
UI Benefit	—	0.0021
		(0.0009)
MDuR	—	−0.0006
		(0.0009)
ln w_{t-1}	0.2569	—
	(0.0572)	
f_i	—	−0.0017
		(0.0017)
σ^2	0.0198	
	(0.0092)	
σ_f^2	0.1834	
	(0.0175)	
ln(L)	−1,843.62	

Note: Numbers in parentheses are standard errors. The reservation wage parameters are cost parameters (γ and η) in the text.

equation appear sensible; the only unusual finding is the lack of nonlinearity in age. The tenure variable takes a significant negative coefficient. Since the age and previous wage variables are included in the equation this indicates a strong role for specific human capital. This reinforces our previous findings, indeed the tenure coefficient here is greater in magnitude than our previous estimate (by .001). The estimates of the coefficients in the reservation wage function also appear reasonable. The estimate of η, the effect of the individual effect on costs, is .0017, indicating that the effect does indeed lower search costs, though not significantly. Our variance estimates, a main point of this study, indicate that individual effects, i.e., effects of omitted variables, account for almost ten times more of the interindividual variance in wage offers than the pure search variance in the offer distributions facing each individual.[11] Estimates of the parameters of the changing reservation wage model are presented in Table 4.3. The coefficient δ of the trend interpreted as a weekly rate of change in reservation wages, is $-.0023$, and is significant both on the basis of an asymptotic t test and on the basis of the (asymptotically equivalent) likelihood ratio statistic.

The magnitude of this coefficient warrants some comment. In previous work (Kiefer and Neumann [16]) in which we did not allow for heterogeneity explicitly, our estimate of δ was $-.0058$, approximately double the estimate in Table 4.3. If everyone had a constant probability of leaving unemployment (with respect to duration), then heterogeneity in the probability of leaving unemployment, if ignored, would lead to the inference that these probabilities decline with duration. This spurious form of duration dependence would arise because people with high probabilities of exiting will leave the sample earlier, and we would therefore observe a declining rate of employment. In general, ignoring heterogeneity in exit rates produces down biased estimates of the true amount of duration dependence (see Jovanovic and Mincer [12]). If we carried this reasoning over into the present context we might expect our estimate of δ to be smaller than the value previously obtained. However, in our model this corresponds to reasoning in terms of reduced form, and the effects of heterogeneity in the true structural relationship could be quite different. For example, consider the case of the constant reservation wage model. By definition each individual has a constant probability of exiting in any period. Suppose that there is heterogeneity in the location of the wage offer distribution. We know from the theorem given above that this heterogeneity will affect the reservation wage by less than the change in the wage offer distribution and therefore it will alter the probability of exiting. In particular, individuals with high values of the unmeasured component will have higher probabilities of exiting. If there are two types of workers, high and low ability say, the observed data will show high abil-

---

[11] In previous work we have assumed and estimated a constant g_1. As a check on this procedure we calculated the sample variance of our g_{1i}. It is .0016 in the constant reservation wage specification.

Table 4.3. *Changing reservation wage model*

	Wage-offer equation	Reservation wage equation
Constant	2.8263	1.9713
	(0.453)	(0.568)
Education	0.0361	0.0101
	(0.0193)	(0.0080)
Dependents	—	−0.0068
		(0.0145)
Tenure	−0.0078	—
	(0.0021)	
Marital status	—	−0.0824
		(0.0224)
Unemployment	0.0197	0.0161
rate	(0.0117)	(0.0056)
Age	0.0194	−0.0127
	(0.0064)	(0.0037)
Age^2 ($\times 10^{-3}$)	−0.1387	0.1712
	(0.2273)	(0.2038)
Ed $\times$ Age	−0.0008	−0.0003
	(0.0004)	(0.0002)
UI Benefit	—	0.0016
		(0.0007)
MDuR	—	0.0004
		(0.0007)
ln w_{t-1}	0.2574	—
	(0.0563)	
f_i	—	−0.0014
		(0.0015)
δ	—	−0.0023
		(0.0011)
σ^2	0.0283	
	(0.0108)	
σ_f^2	0.2493	
	(0.0201)	
ln(L)	−1,794.83	

Note: See note to Table 4.2.

ity workers having higher wages and shorter durations of unemployment. But if the two groups are observationally identical, the only way to "explain" the data is by a declining reservation wage. Note that this implies that an upward bias will be imparted to the hazard function, exactly the opposite of what would be expected from reduced form considerations. Indeed, it is quite possible for heterogeneity to be very important in a structural equation, e.g., in the wage offer function, and to be unimportant, or even totally absent, in the reduced form; e.g., in our model, if $1 - g_{1i} - \eta \cong 0$, there will be no heterogeneity in the exit function. Thus in general we cannot sign the bias that arises from ignoring heterogeneity from knowledge of the reduced form equations.

The relation between the variances due to individual effects and those due to search remain the same when duration dependence is permitted; individual effects account for about ten times as much interindividual variance as the variance in offer distributions. Both variances are considerably higher in the changing reservation wage model. The coefficient of the number of dependents is negative in this specification (in the reservation wage equation) which is a priori plausible. The age-squared variable became insignificant in the reservation wage equation, and the effect of the maximum possible duration of unemployment insurance benefits became positive.

The major advantage of our present specification is that the variance in wage offers across individuals is explicitly decomposed into a variance in the location of offer distributions across individuals and the common variance of each offer distribution. We find that the population variance (after controlling for the effects of observable characteristics) is due mostly to interindividual variation in the location of the offer distributions, rather than to pure (search-theoretic) variance in offer distributions for each person.

4.6   Implications

The dispersion in wage offers has been separated into that due to individual differences and that arising from wage distributions facing each individual. It remains to translate this distinction into a decomposition of the dispersion of observed wages. Taking expectations over ϵ and f, so that we consider the unconditional distribution of wages, we note that

$$E(w_i \mid w_i > w_i^r) = X_i\beta + \rho\sigma\lambda_i,$$

where

$$\lambda_i = \phi(r_i)/\Phi(r_i)$$

with

$$r_i = [(1 - g_{1i})X_i\beta - Z_i\gamma][\sigma^2 + \sigma_f^2(1 - g_{1i} - \eta)^2]^{-1/2}$$

and with

$$\rho = \pm\sigma_f^2(\sigma_f^2 + \sigma^2)^{-1/2}.$$

Note that we have considerably simplified the problem of taking this expectation by treating g_{1i} as a fixed constant. Under this simplification, ρ is the correlation between the error $f + \varepsilon$ in the offer equation and the "error" $(1 - g_{1i} - \eta)f$ in the employment equation. The sign of ρ is determined by the sign of $(1 - g_{1i} - \eta)$. The variance in accepted wages is approximately

$$\text{var}(w_i \mid w_i > w_i^r) = \sigma^2(1 + \rho^2 r_i \lambda_i - \rho^2 \lambda_i^2). \tag{17}$$

Comparing this expression with (1), the expression for the variance in expected wages facing a particular individual, we can decompose (approximately) total wage variance into that variance due to search – approximated by the mean over i of (1) – and that variance due to individual unobservables, constant over duration of spells of unemployment, approximated by the mean over i of (16) minus (1). We calculate these variances to be .0039 and .040, indicating that 8.66 per cent of unexplained wage variation (after deleting the effects of X) is attributable to search considerations. It is important to note, in closing, that the finding that search considerations do not play a large part in explaining wage variations does not imply that search does not play a large part in explaining the distributions of durations of spells of unemployment. This will be the topic of another paper.

Acknowledgments

We would like to thank J. Heckman, whose comments on our previous work led to the current specification. Financial support was provided by NSF and DOL. Gary Chamberlain and Dale Mortensen and two anonymous referees made useful comments, as did participants in seminars at Bell Laboratories, Harvard, University of Illinois, Michigan State, Northwestern, University of California at San Diego, and the University of Michigan.

References

[1] Amemiya, T.: "Regression Analysis When the Dependent Variable Is Truncated Normal," *Econometrica*, 41(1973), 997–1016.
[2] Andersen, E.: *Conditional Inference and Models for Measuring*. Copenhagen: Mentalhygiejnisk Forsknings Institut, 1973.
[3] Berndt, E., B. Hall, R. Hall, and J. Hausman: "Estimation and Inference in Nonlinear Structural Models," *Annals of Economic and Social Measurement*, 3(1974), 653–666.

[4] Chamberlain, G.: "Analysis of Covariance With Qualitative Data," Harvard University, 1978.

[5] Ehrenberg, R., and R. Oaxaca: "Unemployment Insurance, Duration of Unemployment, and Subsequent Wage Gain," *American Economic Review*, 66(1976), 754–766.

[6] Feldstein, M.: "Temporary Layoffs in the Theory of Unemployment," *Journal of Political Economy*, 84(1976), 937–957.

[7] Freeman, R.: "A Fixed Effect Logit Model of the Impact of Unionism on Quits," Harvard University, September, 1978.

[8] Heckman, J.: "The Incidental Parameters Problem and the Problem of Initial Conditions in Estimating a Discrete Time – Discrete Data Stochastic Process and Some Monte-Carlo Evidence," University of Chicago, 1978.

[9] Heckman, J.: "Sample Selection Bias as a Specification Error," *Econometrica*, 47(1979), 153–162.

[10] Hoelen, A.: "Effects of Unemployment Insurance Entitlement on Duration and Job Search Outcome," *Industrial and Labor Relations Review*, 30(1977), 445–450.

[11] Johnson, N., and S. Kotz: *Distributions in Statistics: Volume 4, Continuous Multivariate Distributions*. New York: John Wiley and Sons, 1972.

[12] Jovanovic, B., and J. Mincer: "Labor Mobility and Wages," in *Studies in Labor Markets*, ed. by S. Rosen. New York: National Bureau of Economic Research, forthcoming.

[13] Kiefer, J., and J. Wolfowitz: "Consistency of the Maximum Likelihood Estimator in the Presence of Infinitely Many Incidental Parameters," *Annals of Mathematical Statistics*, 27(1956), 887–906.

[14] Kiefer, N.: "The Economic Benefits from Four Government Training Programs," *Research in Labor Economics*, Supplement 1(1979), 159–186.

[15] Kiefer, N., and G. Neumann: "Estimation of Wage Offer Distributions and Reservation Wages," in *Studies in the Economics of Search*, ed. by S. Lippmann and J. McCall. Amsterdam: North-Holland, 1979. Chapter 2 in this volume.

[16] Kiefer, N., and G. Neumann: "An Empirical Job-Search Model, with a Test of the Constant Reservation Wage Hypothesis," *Journal of Political Economy*, 87(1979), 89–107. Chapter 3 in this volume.

[17] Lippmann, S., and J. McCall: "The Economics of Job Search: A Survey," *Economic Inquiry*, 14(1976), 155–189 and 347–368.

[18] McCall, J.: "Economics of Information and Job Search," *Quarterly Journal of Economics*, 84(1970), 113–126.

[19] Mortenson, D. T.: "Job Search, the Duration of Unemployment, and the Phillips Curve," *American Economic Review*, 60(1970), 847–862.

[20] Mortenson, D. T.: "Unemployment Insurance and Job-Search Decisions," *Industrial and Labor Relations Review*, 30(1977), 505–517.

[21] Mundlak, Y.: "On the Pooling of Time Series and Cross Section Data," *Econometrica*, 46(1978), 69–86.

[22] Neumann, G.: "The Direct Labor Market Effects of the Trade Adjustment Assistance Program," in *Domestic Employment, Foreign Trade, and Investment*, ed. by W. Dewald. Washington, D.C.: G.P.O., 1978.

[23] Neyman, J., and E. Scott: "Consistent Estimates Based on Partially Consistent Observations," *Econometrica*, 16(1948), 1–32.

[24] Rothschild, M.: "Searching for the Lowest Price When the Distribution of Prices Is Unknown," *Journal of Political Economy*, 82(1974), 689–711.

PART II

Continuous-time models of duration

CHAPTER 5

Earnings, unemployment, and the allocation of time over time

5.1 Introduction

In this study we consider a dynamic model of an individual's allocation of time among the three labour market states employment, unemployment, and nonparticipation. In this model individuals respond in a rational manner to shocks that occur to them from time to time. The optimal strategy of an individual in the assumed environment will imply that his movement among the labour market states can be represented by a Markov chain. The Markovian implications of the theory are studied and the crucial assumptions are identified. The effects of different expected wages on the transition rates are studied in some detail.

Since an individual's labour market history can be described by a Markov chain in state space, it is possible to calculate the steady states. It is natural to interpret the steady state proportion in unemployment for a group of identical workers as the natural rate of unemployment for this group, i.e. it is the expected proportion that would be employed if the environment were to remain constant. It is shown how the natural rate of unemployment is different for different groups. The model is estimated using data from a large U.S. income maintenance experiment. The predictions of the model, with some exceptions, bear up well to confrontation by data.

The empirical findings also accord well with existing evidence on cross section studies of labour supply. We find that labour force participation rates implied by the estimated models are positively related to earnings for all age, sex and race groups, as expected. We demonstrate that the elasticities of the unemployment rates for all groups with respect to expected wage rates are negative, and large in absolute value in the case of adults. While the role of the wage in allocation of time is not novel,

This chapter was written by Kenneth Burdett, Nicholas M. Kiefer, Dale T. Mortensen, and George R. Neumann. It is reprinted from the *Review of Economic Studies*, vol. 51 (1984); © 1984 by the Society for Economic Analysis Limited.

the existing neoclassical labour literature uses static labour supply models to interpret participation rate studies and search and related models of labour supply dynamics to explain unemployment patterns. Showing that these two approaches can be successfully married both theoretically and empirically is the contribution of this chapter.[1]

5.2   The model

At each moment an individual must choose to occupy one of three possible states; employment (1), unemployment (2), or nonparticipation (3). Anyone in the nonparticipation state is neither working nor looking for a job (but may accept an offer if received), whereas an unemployed worker actively looks for job offers.

Let u_i denote the utility flow obtained if state i is currently occupied, $i = 1, 2, 3$. At random intervals of time, events occur which lead to changes in these utility flows. Many of these events will be labour market phenomena, e.g. the worker may receive a job offer, or be fired from a job. Other events, which at first blush appear to have little to do with the labour market, may also influence choice of state, e.g. the individual may break a leg, or win a lottery. The precise time at which these events will occur is not known in advance. Nevertheless, the arrival rate of such events is known. In what follows the following important restriction will be used.

> *Assumption 1.* The arrival rate of events can be described by a Poisson process with parameter μ_i when state i is occupied, $i = 1, 2, 3$.

Thus, when an individual occupies state i, he obtains a utility flow, u_i, and an arrival rate of events, μ_i. In what follows it will be assumed that the arrival rate of events is greatest when the worker is unemployed, i.e.

$$\mu_2 = \max(\mu_1, \mu_2, \mu_3). \tag{1}$$

This restriction does not appear too unrealistic.

Before specifying how events change the utility flows faced by an individual, restrictions are placed on these flows. Since only relative flows

---

[1] Related literature includes Hall (1970), Marston (1976), Clark and Summers (1979), Mincer and Jovanovic (1981), Bartel (1975), and Kiefer and Neumann (1979, 1981).

will be important in choice of state, without loss of generality assume the utility flow for a nonparticipant equals zero at all times, i.e. $u_3 = 0$. Further, it is assumed that the utility flow when employed for a particular individual can be written as $u_1 = z + e$, where e is a realization of a random variable. The number z can be usefully thought of as the human capital wage of the individual which will depend on his fixed characteristics. Thus, an event is a new realization of the random term, e, and of the utility flow when unemployed. Let $F(\bar{e}, \bar{u}_2)$ denote the probability that the utility flow when employed and unemployed are no greater than $z + \bar{e}$ and $\bar{u}_2$ respectively. Hence, $F(\cdot)$ is a distribution function. The following assumption will be used in obtaining our results:

Assumption 2. Events are independent random draws from the distribution $F(\cdot)$.

The environment specified above is simple. At random intervals of time there is a change in the state dependent utility flows faced by the individual. The worker decides which state to occupy, taking into account that the arrival rate of events will depend on the state selected. Let $V_i(z + e, u_2)$ indicate an individual's expected discounted lifetime utility when (a) state i is currently occupied, (b) the utility flows in state 1, 2, and 3 are $z + e$, u_2, and 0 respectively, and (c) optimal choices will be made in the future. If ρ denotes the time rate of discount, then the state dependent value function, $V_i(z + e, u_2)$, can be written as

$$V_i(z + e, u_2) = \frac{1}{1 + \rho h} \{ u_i h + \mu_i h E \max_{k=1,2,3} V_k(z + \bar{e}, \bar{u}_2)$$

$$+ (1 - \mu_i h) V_i(z + e, u_2) \} + o(h) \qquad (2)$$

where h is a small unit of time and, as usual, $o(h)$ denotes the probability that more than one event will occur in interval h multiplied by the expected return given more than one event occurs (note that $o(h)/h \to 0$ as $h \to 0$). Rearranging terms in (2) and then letting $h \to 0$ yields

$$V_i(z + e, u_2) = \frac{u_i + \mu_i T(z)}{\mu_i + \rho}, \qquad (3)$$

$i = 1, 2, 3$, where

$$T(z) = E \max_{k=1,2,3} V_k(z + \bar{e}, \bar{u}_2). \qquad (4)$$

It is straightforward to establish that a unique vector of value functions solving (3) exists (see Blackwell (1965)). The equations of (3) and (4) imply

$$\frac{\partial V_i(z + e, u_2)}{\partial e} = \begin{cases} 0, & \text{if } i \neq 1 \\ \dfrac{1}{\rho + \mu_i}, & \text{if } i = 1 \end{cases} \tag{5a}$$

$$\frac{\partial V_i(z + e, u_2)}{\partial u_2} = \begin{cases} 0, & \text{if } i \neq 2 \\ \dfrac{1}{\rho + \mu_i}, & \text{if } i = 2. \end{cases} \tag{5b}$$

We are now in a position to characterize completely the lifetime utility maximizing strategy of an individual with human capital wage z. Let $A_i(z)$ denote the set of doubletons, (e, u_2), which imply state i is preferred, i.e.

$$A_i(z) = \{(e, u_2) \mid V_i(z + e, u_2) = \max_{k=1,2,3} V_k(z + e, u_2)\}, \tag{6}$$

$i = 1, 2, 3$. The following proposition characterizes the optimal strategy.

Proposition 1. The strategy that maximizes expected discounted lifetime utility can be completely characterized by three numbers $e(z)$, $u_2(z)$, and $\alpha(u_2; z)$, such that

$$V_1(z + e, u_2) \gtrless V_3(z + e, u_2) \quad \text{as} \quad e \gtrless e(z), \tag{7a}$$

$$V_2(z + e, u_2) \gtrless V_3(z + e, u_2) \quad \text{as} \quad u \gtrless u_2(z), \tag{7b}$$

$$V_1(z + e, u_2 \gtrless V_2(z + e, u_2) \quad \text{as} \quad e \gtrless \alpha(u_2; z), \tag{7c}$$
$$\text{where} \quad \partial \alpha(u_2; z)/\partial u_2 = (\rho + \mu_1)/(\rho + \mu_2).$$

Proof. The claims follow directly from the equations of (5).

The above claims imply (a) employment is preferred to nonparticipation if and only if the current utility flow when employed is at least $z + e(z)$, (b) unemployment is preferred to nonparticipation if and only if the utility flow when unemployed is at least $u_2(z)$, and (c) employment is preferred to unemployment if and only if, for given u_2, the utility flow when employed is at least $z + \alpha(u_2; z)$. These results are used in Figure 5.1 to illustrate the acceptance sets $A_i(z)$, $i = 1, 2, 3$.

So far we have considered the optimal strategy of an individual with human capital wage z. We now demonstrate how the acceptance sets change as individuals with different human capital wages are considered. From (3) it follows that

$$\frac{\partial V_1(z + e, u_2)}{\partial z} = \frac{1}{\rho + \mu_1}\left\{1 + \frac{dT(z)}{dz}\mu_1\right\} \tag{8a}$$

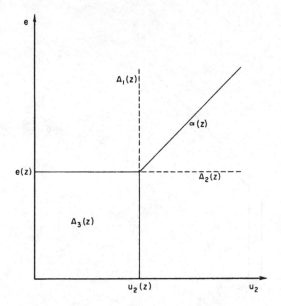

Figure 5.1. Acceptance regions.

and

$$\frac{\partial V_i(z + e, u_2)}{\partial z} = \frac{\mu_i}{\rho + \mu_i} \frac{dT(z)}{dz}, \qquad i = 2, 3. \tag{8b}$$

Since $\partial V_i(z + e, u_2)/\partial z$ is independent of e and u_2, let

$$\partial V_i(z + e, u_2)/\partial z = \partial V_i(z)/\partial z,$$

$i = 1, 2, 3$. Using (4) we have

$$\frac{\partial V_i(z)}{\partial z} > \frac{dT(z)}{dz} > 0 \tag{9}$$

for at least one i, $i = 1, 2, 3$. However, inspection of (8b) reveals (9) is not satisfied for i equal to 2 or 3. Thus,

$$\frac{\partial V_1(z)}{\partial z} > \frac{\partial V_i(z)}{\partial z}, \qquad i = 2, 3. \tag{10}$$

Further, since it was assumed in (1) that $\mu_2 > \mu_3$,

$$\frac{\partial V_2(z)}{\partial z} > \frac{\partial V_3(z)}{\partial z}. \tag{11}$$

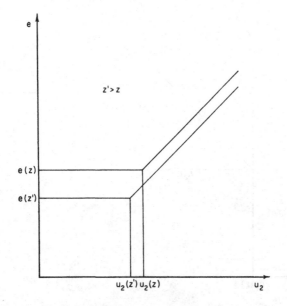

Figure 5.2. Effect of human capital wage on acceptance sets.

The following proposition is an immediate consequence of (9) and (10) on the function defined by the equations of (7).

Proposition 2

$$\frac{de(z)}{dz} < 0, \qquad \frac{du_2(z)}{dz} < 0, \qquad \frac{\partial \alpha(u_2; z)}{\partial z} < 0, \qquad \text{and} \qquad \frac{\partial^2 \alpha(u_2; z)}{\partial u_2 \, \partial z} = 0.$$

Figure 5.2 illustrates the claims made in Proposition 2. Note also that Proposition 2 and (10) imply that $A_1(z) \subset A_1(z')$ and $A_3(z) \supset A_3(z')$ if $z > z'$. Hence, an individual with a greater human capital wage is more likely to choose employment and less likely to choose nonparticipation after an event occurs. Without imposing more restrictions, the probability of choosing unemployment after an event may increase or decrease with an increase in z.

So far we have considered the optimal strategies of different individuals. It will now be shown that these strategies imply that any individual's labor market history can be described by a Markov process. Given Proposition 1, it follows that if state i is currently occupied, the instantaneous probability flow that state j will next be occupied, $\lambda_{ij}(z)$, can be written as

$$\lambda_{ij}(z) = \mu_i \pi_j(z), \qquad i, j = 1, 2, 3, i \neq j, \tag{12}$$

where

$$\pi_j(z) = \int_{A_j(z)} dF(\bar{e}, \bar{u}_2). \tag{13}$$

The escape rate, or hazard, $\lambda_i(z)$, associated with state i is

$$\lambda_i(z) = \sum_{j=1, j \neq i}^{3} \lambda_{ij}(z), \qquad i = 1, 2, 3. \tag{14}$$

Hence, the duration of any particular spell in state i is an exponential random variable with an expectation equal to $1/\lambda_i(z)$, $i = 1, 2, 3$. From Proposition 2, (10), (11), and (12) it is possible to establish the following claims.

Proposition 3

- (a) $\partial\lambda_{12}(z)/\partial z = ?$
- (b) $\partial\lambda_{13}(z)\partial z < 0$
- (c) $\partial\lambda_{21}(z)/\partial z > 0$
- (d) $\partial\lambda_{23}(z)/\partial z < 0$
- (e) $\partial\lambda_{31}(z)/\partial z > 0$
- (f) $\partial\lambda_{32}(z)/\partial z = ?$

The instantaneous transition rates defined above can be used to construct a continuous time three state Markov chain. Let $M(z) = \{\lambda(z)\}_{ij}$, $i, j = 1, 2, 3$, denote the instantaneous transiton matrix associated with this Markov chain where $\lambda_{ii}(z) = 1 - \lambda_i(z)$, $i = 1, 2, 3$. Let $p_i^0(z)$ indicate the probability the individual occupies state i at time zero, $i = 1, 2, 3$, and let $p^0 = (p_1^0, p_2^0, p_3^0)$. Using standard results from the theory of Markov chains it can be shown that mild regularity conditions imply $p'(z) \rightarrow p_i^*(z)$ as $t \rightarrow \infty$, for any initial $p^0(z)$. Thus, $p_i^*(z)$ can be interpreted as the expected proportion of the individual's life spent occupying state i. Alternatively, $p_i^*(z)$ can be thought of as the proportion of a large number of identical workers who will occupy state i in the long run. Under the latter interpretation it appears reasonable to think of $p_2^*(z)/(p_1^*(z) + p_2^*(z))$ as the natural rate of unemployment for a group of workers with human capital wage z. Similarly, $p_1^*(z) + p_2^*(z)$ can be thought of as the long run labour-force participation rate.

Given a steady state vector $p^*(z)$ exists, the flow into a state will equal the flow out of that state, i.e.

$$\sum_{i=1, i \neq j}^{3} \lambda_{ij}(z)p_i^*(z) = \lambda_j(z)p_j^*(z), \qquad j = 1, 2, 3, \tag{15a}$$

whereas

$$\sum_{i=1}^{3} p_i^*(z) = 1. \tag{15b}$$

Solving the above system of equations and then substituting in (12) yields the following result.

Proposition 4. The steady state proportions satisfy

$$p_1^*(z) = \mu_2\mu_3\pi_1(z)/R(z), \tag{16a}$$
$$p_2^*(z) = \mu_1\mu_3\pi_2(z)/R(z), \tag{16b}$$
$$p_3^*(z) = \mu_1\mu_2\pi_3(z)/R(z), \tag{16c}$$

where $R(z) = \mu_2\mu_3\pi_1(z) + \mu_1\mu_3\pi_2(z) + \mu_1\mu_2\pi_3(z)$.

How will these steady state proportions change as a group of workers with a different human capital wage is considered? Taking the derivatives of the equations of (16) yields the next proposition.

Proposition 5

$$\frac{\partial p_1^*(z)}{\partial z} = \frac{\mu_2\mu_3}{R(z)^2} \{\partial\pi_1(z)/\partial z[R(z) + \mu_3(\mu_1 - \mu_2)\pi_1(z)]$$
$$- \pi_1(z)\mu_1(\mu_2 - \mu_3)\partial\pi_3(z)/\partial z\},$$

$$\frac{\partial p_3^*(z)}{\partial z} = \frac{\mu_1\mu_2}{R(z)^2} \{\partial\pi_3(z)/\partial z[R(z) + \mu_1(\mu_3 - \mu_2)\pi_3(z)]$$
$$- \pi_3(z)\mu_3(\mu_2 - \mu_1)\partial\pi_1(z)/\partial z\},$$

$$\frac{\partial p_2^*(z)}{\partial z} \gtreqless 0 \qquad \text{as} \qquad |\partial p_1^*(z)/\partial z| \gtreqless |\partial p_3^*(z)/\partial z|. \tag{17c}$$

Hence, $\partial p_1^*(z)/\partial z > 0$ and $\partial p_3^*(z)/\partial z < 0$.

The model analysed above is Markov in the following practical sense. Suppose a statistician collects information on an individual's labour market history up to, and including, time t. Let X_t denote a vector describing such information, i.e. X_t contains information on which state was occupied at each moment in time, and what wage was earned during each spell of employment. This vector X_t with z can be used to specify the instantaneous probability flow for movements from state i directly to state j, given state i is currently occupied. Let $\theta_{ij}(z, X_t)$ denote this probability flow. In the model constructed above $\theta_{ij}(z, X_t) = \lambda_{ij}(z)$ for any X_t. Thus, knowledge about how long the current state has been occupied, which states have previously been occupied, etc. have no effect on the transition rates. Significant alterations to the model will imply this Markovian property will not hold. Below, we show that dropping Assumptions 1 and 2 in turn leads to the loss of Markovian property.

First, suppose the arrival rate of events depends on the duration of the current spell in the state occupied, or on the age of the worker, or on the wage faced when employed, etc. Let $\mu_i(t)$ denote the arrival rate of events when state i has currently been occupied for duration t, $i = 1, 2, 3$. Given that $\mu_i(t)$ changes with duration, it is straightforward to show that the optimal strategy for the individual will be conditioned on the state occupied and on the duration in the state. An example will demonstrate the point. Suppose $\mu_3(t) = 0$ for all $t > \bar{t}$, and $\mu_3(t) = b > 0$ otherwise. Obviously, all individuals who occupy state 3 for more than time $\bar{t}$ will not leave this state in the future, whereas those who have been in state 3 for less than time t may leave it in the future.

Second, suppose Assumption 2 is replaced with the restriction that the current realization of the utility flow triple will influence the next realization. To be more specific we briefly consider a variant of a model considered by Burdett et al. (1980) and by Flinn and Heckman (1982). This model is the same as the one presented above with the exception that $T(z)$, defined in (3), is replaced by

$$T_1(e, z) = E \max\{\max_{k=1,2,3}(V_k(z + \bar{e}, \bar{x}_2)), V_1(z + e, \bar{x}_2)\}$$

when the individual is in state 1. Thus, it is assumed that an employed worker can select to hold on to his previous utility flow when employed after an event has occurred. In this case it is simple to show that knowledge of the individual's current wage when employed will influence the transition rates. For example, suppose there are two wage offers an individual can receive, w^h and w^l, $w^h > w^l$. Further, assume that the individual either obtains utility flow u^h or u^l when unemployed, $u^h > u^l$. It is known that if wage offer w^h is received, then employment is always preferred whereas unemployment is preferred when u^h is faced when unemployed and w^l when employed. Nonparticipation is never preferred by this worker. In this example it follows that the worker will never leave employment when offer w^h has been received.

5.3   Estimation

The model developed above provides a conceptually simple framework for examining individual labour market histories. The focus of attention will be on the duration of time spent in each state and on the frequency of each possible transition. From the hazard function, $\lambda_i(z)$, defined in (14), it is possible to specify the distribution function associated with the duration of any spell in state i: $F_i(t \mid z) = 1 - \exp(-t\lambda_i(z))$, $i = 1, 2, 3$.[2] Using (12) and (13) it can be seen that the conditional probability that state j will be the new state after a completed spell in state i, $i \neq j$, is $\lambda_{ij}(z)/\lambda_i(z)$. Thus, the probability density function associated with a completed spell in a status when the origin state is i and j is the destination state, $f_{ij}(\cdot \mid z)$ can be written as

$$f_{ij}(t \mid z) = \frac{\lambda_{ij}(z)}{\lambda_i(z)} f_i(t \mid z) = \lambda_{ij}(z)(1 - F_i(t \mid z)), \qquad (18)$$

$i, j = 1, 2, 3$, $i \neq j$. Therefore the log likelihood for a sample of $k = 1, 2, 3, \ldots, K$ spells can be expressed as

$$\ln L = \sum_{k=1}^{K} \{d_k \ln \lambda_{i_k j_k}(z_k) - T_k \lambda_{i_k}(z_k)\}, \qquad (19)$$

where d_k equals unity if the spell is completed and equals zero otherwise, i_k and j_k denote the origin and destination states respectively, z_k indicates the human capital wage of the individual involved in the spell, and T_k indicates the length of the spell. Note that left and right censored spells are treated symmetrically. This is appropriate only because our specification implies an exponential distribution of durations.

To implement the model a functional form for the $\lambda_{ij}(z)$ must be chosen. Though the theoretical model focused on the effect on transition functions of the human capital wage, or what we now term the expected wage, z, in practice we expect that the transition functions may also differ among individuals according to characteristics such as age, education, race, etc. Let x denote a vector of such characteristics as well as z, for each individual and spell (and subscript by k). In the present case a convenient functional form is $\lambda_{ij}(z) = \exp(x\beta_{ij})$, a specification that has been widely used. Previous economic applications include Lancaster (1979), Tuma

[2] See Kalbfleisch and Prentice (1980), p. 6.

and Robbins (1980), and Lundberg (1981). With this specification the log likelihood function becomes

$$\ln L = \sum_{k=1}^{K} \left\{ d_k x_k \beta_{i_k j_k} - T_k \sum_{n=1, n \neq i_k}^{3} \exp(x_k \beta_{i_k n}) \right\}. \tag{20}$$

The additive separability and global concavity of the log likelihood function make this specification particularly attractive from a computational point of view. The results that follow were obtained by maximizing (20) using Newton's method with analytic first and second derivatives within SAS's MATRIX procedure, a method that was fast even using starting values of zero. Asymptotic standard errors were obtained by inverting the negative of the Hessian of the log likelihood function.

5.4   The DIME data

To obtain estimates of the transition functions described above it is necessary to have information on the labour market histories of individuals. In the ideal situation, the data would consist of information on a representative sample. Unfortunately, the two most familiar longitudinal data sets, the National Longitudinal Survey (NLS) and the Michigan Income Dynamics Survey, do not have the requisite information on labour market transitions, whereas the Current Population Survey (CPS), which does have the relevant information, follows individuals only for a few months. One data set that contains a reasonable span of time for different demographic groups is the Denver Income Maintenance Experiment data (DIME). We describe this data set briefly.[3]

The Denver Income Maintenance Experiment was one of the largest programs designed to measure the effects of a negative income tax on labour supply. The sample was stratified by race and family type. The Public Use Files are organized in a monthly format with data covering 48 months. They contain sufficient information to reconstruct histories of labour market status – employment, unemployment, and nonparticipation – using CPS definitions. We focus on households not receiving financial "treatments," and we organize the data with spells in each state as the units of observation. Attached to each spell was the length of the spell, whether or not it was completed, and the demographic variables relating

---

[3] For a detailed description see Lundberg (1981).

Table 5.1. *Means by age/sex groups: DIME data – all transitions*

	Young males	Adult males	Young females	Adult females
Education	10.6	11.1	11.0	11.7
% Black	34.5	29.5	31.6	37.0
% Hispanic	31.7	36.2	28.3	28.5
ln Wage	4.6	5.5	4.3	4.8
Age	18.2	31.7	18.5	31.8
Assets/1,000	0.4	0.2	0.3	0.2
No. of children	0.3	1.0	0.5	0.9
Black × ln wage	1.5	1.63	1.3	1.8
Hispanic × ln wage	1.4	2.0	1.2	1.3
N = number of separate transitions	1,119	1,571	1,138	2,524
P = number of persons in each group in 1973	260	660	326	946

to the individual involved. The means of these variables, by age group, are given in Table 5.1. Most of these variables are self-explanatory, the exceptions using the asset and wage variables. Assets were constructed from information on the value of stocks, cash in checking accounts, equity value in house or cars, etc., which were available in each periodic interview. Linear interpolations were used to produce asset values for the intervening months between interviews. The wage variable used is derived from the reported wage on the longest job worked in a given month. Wages are defined only for employed individuals. Nevertheless, this information is used to construct an instrument for expected wages by regressing the natural logarithm of wages on age, age squared, education, and race for each of the age/sex groups. This procedure was done by quarters, resulting in a maximum of sixteen predicted wage rates for each individual. Each labour market spell was matched to the predicted wage appropriate to the quarter in which the spell began. All wage rates were deflated by the Denver area CPI for each of the years 1971–1974. All wages are entered in logarithms.

5.5   Estimates

Tables 5.2–5.5 present the estimates of the transition functions for the different age and sex groups considered. The effects of controlling for various factors such as age, education, sex, etc. are not the subject of this study. Our interest is in (a) ascertaining if the predictions made about

Table 5.2. *Transition function estimates: males 21 and under*

	E → U	E → N	U → E	U → N	N → E	N → U
Constant	-15.4691	10.9978	-15.9207	-8.9033	-16.6377	-17.7792
	(1.49)	(1.17)	(1.66)	(0.56)	(2.47)	(1.81)
Education	-0.3583	0.0444	-1.0010	0.1058	0.1074	-0.0987
	(5.09)	(0.51)	(0.01)	(0.69)	(1.62)	(0.95)
Age	1.9148	-1.1447	1.1493	1.0758	1.1582	1.3800
	(1.71)	(1.10)	(1.11)	(0.64)	(1.56)	(1.26)
$Age^2/100$	-4.9368	2.7047	-2.9876	-2.4367	-2.3284	-3.7750
	(1.63)	(0.96)	(1.09)	(0.53)	(1.13)	(1.20)
Assets/1,000	-0.0066	0.0821	-0.0562	0.0102	-0.0143	0.0064
	(0.10)	(1.95)	(1.52)	(0.19)	(0.51)	(0.16)
Children	0.0572	-0.1529	0.0999	0.2191	0.0851	0.0868
	(0.44)	(0.97)	(0.87)	(1.11)	(0.78)	(0.52)
Black	1.1915	2.9494	1.4850	1.9201	0.5389	2.2017
	(1.23)	(3.62)	(0.78)	(0.61)	(0.30)	(0.82)
Hispanic	2.0258	2.6893	3.2149	-0.4751	2.1706	-3.0469
	(2.02)	(2.77)	(1.75)	(0.12)	(1.25)	(1.03)
ln Wage	-0.4096	-0.5442	0.7625	-1.4597	0.0377	0.6200
	(2.82)	(4.07)	(2.07)	(1.72)	(0.09)	(0.87)
B ln Wage	-0.2124	-0.6396	-0.4048	-0.3297	-0.2508	-0.3714
	(1.07)	(3.53)	(1.01)	(0.47)	(0.64)	(0.61)
H ln Wage	-0.3695	-0.5463	-0.7143	0.1743	-0.5970	0.6910
	(1.78)	(2.61)	(1.86)	(0.23)	(1.61)	(1.07)
ln(L)	-851.43	-739.03	-606.77	-289.80	-819.31	-515.19

Note: Numbers in parentheses are asymptotic *t*-statistics.

Table 5.3. *Transition function estimates: males 22 and over*

	$E \to U$	$E \to N$	$U \to E$	$U \to N$	$N \to E$	$N \to U$
Constant	1.6264	4.2304	-6.9535	-7.7707	-18.0220	-15.1749
	(1.60)	(3.53)	(2.20)	(0.88)	(4.22)	(1.84)
Education	0.0186	-0.0001	0.0066	0.0596	-0.0952	-0.0319
	(0.79)	(0.00)	(0.26)	(1.00)	(2.72)	(1.32)
Age	-0.1346	-0.2331	-0.1866	-0.1543	-0.2312	-0.1149
	(3.11)	(4.46)	(3.33)	(1.50)	(3.64)	(1.10)
Age^2/100	0.1442	0.2933	0.2126	0.2466	0.2472	0.1083
	(2.40)	(4.19)	(2.81)	(1.93)	(3.04)	(0.82)
Assets/1,000	-0.9922	-0.3346	0.3923	-0.3209	0.1963	-0.3998
	(5.02)	(2.07)	(4.32)	(0.56)	(1.87)	(1.05)
Children	0.0693	-0.0342	0.1188	0.1002	0.0006	-0.1879
	(1.27)	(0.44)	(2.14)	(0.69)	(0.01)	(1.35)
Black	2.4180	0.1911	-5.0105	4.0144	-7.3915	-8.4390
	(2.75)	(0.17)	(1.14)	(0.36)	(1.17)	(0.73)
Hispanic	0.7259	2.8305	-10.5040	-1.1940	-2.1147	1.9822
	(0.73)	(2.89)	(2.26)	(0.11)	(0.37)	(0.20)
ln Wage	-0.5539	-0.8277	1.6299	1.081	3.8086	2.7149
	(4.58)	(6.47)	(2.70)	(0.66)	(4.67)	(1.75)
B ln Wage	-0.4322	-0.0431	0.8110	-0.7539	1.3109	1.5087
	(2.67)	(0.20)	(1.04)	(0.39)	(1.18)	(0.75)
H ln Wage	-0.0902	-0.4941	1.8027	0.2288	0.3953	-0.2642
	(0.50)	(2.69)	(2.21)	(0.12)	(0.40)	(0.15)
ln (L)	-2087.77	-1255.98	-1038.09	-323.23	-783.38	-357.22

Note: Numbers in parentheses are asymptotic *t*-statistics.

Table 5.4. *Transition function estimates: females 21 and under*

	E → U	E → N	U → E	U → N	N → E	N → U
Constant	-20.2854	-25.2351	1.0345	-11.9666	-5.8334	17.6153
	(2.22)	(3.99)	(0.09)	(0.69)	(0.68)	(1.50)
Education	-0.3731	-0.1972	-0.0078	-0.2321	0.0269	-0.1674
	(4.15)	(3.18)	(0.09)	(1.75)	(0.43)	(1.87)
Age	2.5252	2.9890	-0.1918	1.6489	-0.0323	-2.5754
	(2.54)	(4.40)	(0.14)	(0.82)	(0.03)	(1.82)
Age²/100	-0.0665	-0.0777	0.6363	-4.3313	-0.3274	6.2507
	(2.50)	(4.32)	(0.18)	(0.83)	(0.12)	(1.70)
Assets/1,000	-0.0454	-0.0640	0.1064	0.0778	0.0301	-0.1020
	(0.89)	(1.36)	(2.36)	(.68)	(0.93)	(0.85)
Children	-0.6992	0.0009	-0.3123	-0.1781	-0.2151	-0.2272
	(3.82)	(0.01)	(2.12)	(1.08)	(1.99)	(1.46)
Black	-0.3313	-1.6977	-6.8361	-0.2206	-1.2658	-0.3549
	(0.36)	(2.82)	(2.97)	(0.06)	(0.97)	(0.24)
Hispanic	-1.8682	-1.3201	-1.4145	-2.2939	-0.8853	-3.2725
	(1.65)	(2.09)	(0.59)	(0.61)	(0.67)	(1.68)
ln Wage	-0.5485	-0.8049	0.2861	1.8527	1.0261	1.4518
	(3.35)	(7.89)	(0.69)	(1.01)	(2.42)	(2.34)
B ln Wage	0.1381	0.3284	1.3809	0.1282	0.3024	0.3191
	(0.68)	(2.47)	(2.71)	(0.15)	(1.00)	(0.91)
H ln Wage	0.4703	0.2443	0.2165	0.5832	0.1781	0.8300
	(1.90)	(1.67)	(0.41)	(0.67)	(0.57)	(1.79)
ln(*L*)	-582.11	-918.98	-456.16	-303.58	-1275.23	-704.51

Note: Numbers in parentheses are asymptotic *t*-statistics.

Table 5.5. *Transition function estimates: females 22 and over*

	E→U	E→N	U→E	U→N	N→E	N→U
Constant	3.0943	2.3540	-2.3364	-7.8167	-10.3372	-17.1868
	(3.09)	(3.71)	(1.08)	(2.56)	(6.46)	(5.79)
Education	-0.0458	-0.0687	-0.1353	-0.2117	-0.1667	-0.2658
	(1.41)	(3.38)	(2.48)	(3.12)	(4.24)	(4.35)
Age	0.2049	-0.0846	-0.3555	-0.1651	-0.3338	-0.4084
	(4.87)	(2.97)	(4.60)	(1.68)	(6.47)	(5.18)
Age^2/100	-0.2090	-0.0789	0.4191	0.1789	0.3227·	0.3913
	(3.86)	(2.14)	(4.53)	(1.51)	(5.57)	(4.35)
Assets/1,000	-1.0329	-0.0757	0.1038	0.0289	-0.0214	-0.0572
	(4.12)	(1.27)	(1.14)	(0.22)	(0.37)	(0.53)
Children	-0.3371	0.1280	-0.1805	0.1407	-0.2348	-0.2489
	(3.74)	(2.49)	(2.67)	(1.78)	(4.91)	(3.10)
Black	1.7380	-0.1358	-4.3931	-2.4317	0.2265	8.1160
	(2.57)	(0.39)	(1.76)	(0.73)	(0.12)	(2.61)
Hispanic	0.9845	0.1574	-3.2420	1.6755	-5.3018	5.2322
	(1.31)	(0.43)	(1.09)	(0.46)	(2.88)	(1.52)
ln Wage	-0.4547	-0.6316	1.8694	2.2820	3.3638	5.0282
	(4.16)	(12.06)	(2.64)	(2.49)	(6.14)	(5.69)
B ln Wage	-0.3286	-0.0679	0.7237	0.3936	-0.1364	-1.5789
	(2.35)	(0.92)	(1.44)	(0.59)	(0.37)	(2.51)
H ln Wage	-0.2161	-0.0150	0.6309	-0.3685	1.0724	1.0632
	(1.35)	(0.19)	(1.03)	(0.49)	(2.83)	(1.49)
ln(L)	-1371.15	-2740.44	-946.48	-722.92	-3139.44	-1345.19

Note: Numbers in parentheses are asymptotic *t*-statistics.

increases in human capital wage are satisfied, and (b) determining whether the Markovian specification is satisfactory.

Judging by the relative values of the "t"-statistics in the tables, the influence of expected wages on labour market status is important. A more insightful view can be obtained by looking at these results in the light of Proposition 3, which (loosely) states that (i) individuals with higher expected wages have higher transition rates into employment and lower transition rates out of employment, and (ii) individuals with higher expected wages have lower transition rates into nonparticipation and higher transition rates out of that state.

Considering (i) first, it can be seen from inspection of the tables that this claim is confirmed in all cases except for nonwhite male teenagers from nonparticipation to employment. Even here the negative effects are small and not significantly different from zero. The transition rates out of employment decline with higher expected wages for all the groups considered. Evidence on claim (ii) above is less clear cut. Unambiguously the transition rates out of nonparticipation increase with rises in expected wages. Further, the transition rates from employment to nonparticipation decrease with increases in expected wage for all groups with the possible exception of hispanic female teenagers. The evidence on the influence of expected wages on the transition rate from unemployment to nonparticipation is mixed. It was predicted that this transition rate should decline with higher expected wages. Nevertheless, for adult males the coefficient is positive, but insignificant, whereas for adult females it is positive and significant. Thus, adult females appear to be more likely to leave unemployment for nonparticipation the higher their expected wage.

To explain the discrepancy between the theory and the results on adult females noted above, an alternative model would need to be used for this group. For example, it could be argued that for adult females the difference between unemployment and nonparticipation is not significant. The arrival rate of events may be higher for females who claim to be nonparticipants than those who claim to be unemployed. If this were the case for adult women, then the discrepancy between theory and results would disappear. Another alternative explanation is that for adult women the arrival rate of events declines with expected wages. Again this alternative restriction will lead to the prediction required.

The empirical results presented above provide substantial evidence that variations in personal characteristics, particularly wages, are associated with variations in labour market behaviour. Nevertheless, the estimates

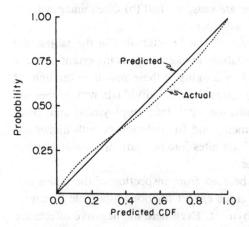

Figure 5.3. Cumulative distribution function of unemployment duration (transformed), young males.

obtained depend on the Markovian structure imposed. Below, some checks of this specification assumption are noted.

Clark and Summers (1979) and Kiefer and Neumann (1979, 1980) have suggested that there is duration dependence in the transition rates out of unemployment. Of course, the lack of duration dependence is equivalent to assuming an exponential distribution of completed spell lengths. One way to see the effects of divergence from this assumed distribution is to examine the cumulative probability plots of time spent in a spell in a status. Specifically, from (18) we have that the cumulative distribution of a spell, say unemployment, is

$$z_i = F_2(t_i \mid x) = 1 - \exp(-t_i\{\exp(x_i\beta_{21}) + \exp(x_i\beta_{23})\}). \qquad (21)$$

It is well known (see Kendall and Stuart (1973) for details) that the distribution of Z is uniform on the unit interval. Thus, the Z's can be sorted and plotted against a 45 degree line (the cumulative distribution function of the uniform distribution) and a visual diagnostic check can be made.[4] Alternatively, a formal distributional test such as the Kolmogorov–Smirnov test or a chi-square test can be applied to check the goodness of fit. One could describe the distribution of spell lengths in this manner for each of the states; we focus here on unemployment spells. The cumulative residual functions are displayed in Figures 5.3–5.6 for each age and sex group.

[4] It should be noted that our specification analysis cannot separate out "true" nonstationarity from unmeasured population heterogeneity (see the discussion in Lancaster and Nickell (1980)).

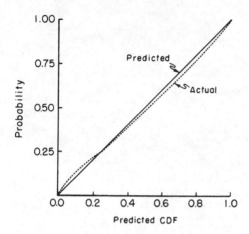

Figure 5.4. Cumulative distribution function of unemployment duration (transformed), young females.

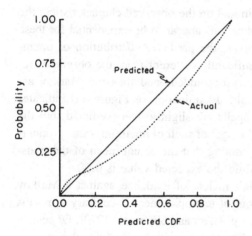

Figure 5.5. Cumulative distribution function of unemployment duration (transformed), adult males.

For young males and for females of both age groups, the predicted and actual distributions line up very nicely. The Kolmogorov–Smirnov (K–S) statistics are: 1.30 for older females, 0.72 for young females, 1.32 for young males (the 5% critical value is obtained from the asymptotic distribution of the K–S statistic and it turns out to be 1.36). Thus, on this basis, we cannot reject the hypothesis that the distributions are the

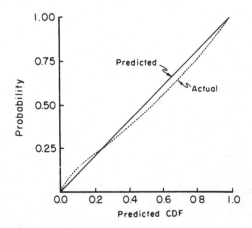

Figure 5.6. Cumulative distribution function of unemployment duration (transformed), adult females.

same.[5] This implies that, conditional on the observed characteristics, the distributions of unemployment durations appear to be exponential for these groups. For adult males, however, the predicted distribution of unemployment spell lengths are significantly different from the observed, regardless of the number of regressors added, and thus the Markov assumption does not appear to hold. Examination of Figure 5.5 indicates that very short and very long spells are slightly over-predicted, but the major problem is the "average" length of spell of unemployment is underpredicted. This can be seen by noting that the actual mean of the transformed observations is 0.43 while the expected value is 0.50.

The absence, except for adult males, of evidence against a Markov Process governing transitions out of unemployment is contrary to results which use more aggregate data, e.g. Clark and Summers (1979). Of course, the use of aggregate data requires that measurable individual heterogeneity, that is differences in education, expected wages, and so forth, be

[5] It should be noted that the K–S statistics used here are conditional on the estimated parameters. As Durbin (1973) has shown, the nominal K–S significance levels are not correct in this situation – in essence, one must correct for degrees of freedom. Nevertheless, the statistic is a useful summary measure of the distance between the predicted and actual c.d.f.s. The reader who is fond of significance levels, and too impatient to look at residual plots, is warned that comparison of our statistics with nominal significance levels will probably lead to a conservative test, in the sense that the size will be overstated. Chi-squared tests, based on grouping the data into deciles (arbitrarily) lead to qualitatively similar results – i.e. some doubt is cast on the specification as applied to adult men.

Table 5.6. *Kolmogorov–Smirnov statistics corresponding to alternative specifications of transition functions*

Age/sex group	Regressors included[a]		
	Constant only (1)	All except wages (2)	All (3)
Adult males (22–59)	3.93	3.00	2.68
Young males (16–21)	1.42	1.31	1.30
Adult females (22–59)	2.32	1.95	1.34
Young females (16–21)	1.53	0.66	0.73

[a]All regressors include: Education, Assets, Age, Age^2, Number of children less than six, Race dummies, Wages and Race–Wage interactions.

ignored. This induces spurious duration dependence, as is well known. It is of some interest therefore to examine the contribution of the measurable factors included in the transition functions. Table 5.6 contains the K–S statistic for alternative specifications. When only a constant is entered, all test statistics are greater than the nominal critical values and the graph of the cumulative duration distribution shows substantial underprediction of long spells of unemployment. With all the regressors except expected wage rates included (as shown in column 2), the statistics are improved substantially. Finally, when expected wages are entered, the behaviour of three of the four groups is consistent with the Markov assumption. Thus, with the exception of adult males, we conclude that the appearance of a declining hazard rate for the unemployment status is due to differences in measurable characteristics across individuals, particularly expected wages.

5.6   Steady state analysis

Given the estimates reported in the last sections, Propositions 4 and 5 can be used to calculate how the steady state employment, unemployment, and nonparticipation rates vary with expected wages. Table 5.7 presents the average duration of a spell in each state for each of the sex and race groups considered. The expected wage elasticities of the steady state unemployment and labour force participation rates are also presented in Table 5.7. In what follows our attention will be focused on the steady state unemployment rates.

The time spent in the labour force consists of spells of both employment and unemployment. Although unemployment is often viewed as an

Table 5.7. *Steady state spell lengths and wage rate elasticities*

Group	Average spell length (months)			Wage elasticity of	
	Employ. (1)	Unemploy. (2)	Nonpart. (3)	Unemploy. rate (4)	Labour force part. rate (5)
Young males					
Black	5.9	3.8	9.0	−0.36	0.69
Hispanic	6.6	3.5	9.9	−0.17	0.44
White	8.8	2.9	6.9	−0.51	0.24
Adult males					
Black	33.3	3.5	5.7	−2.95	0.33
Hispanic	25.6	3.3	5.5	−3.68	0.51
White	37.0	2.4	5.6	−2.11	0.27
Young females					
Black	8.1	4.0	10.0	−0.70	0.71
Hispanic	7.9	3.8	15.2	−0.13	0.95
White	7.7	2.8	13.7	−0.38	0.97
Adult females					
Black	19.6	4.1	13.2	−2.72	1.03
Hispanic	13.2	4.5	27.0	−2.74	1.67
White	14.9	2.6	16.9	−1.63	1.68

indication that the labour market is not clearing, the expected wage elasticities shown in column 4 in Table 5.7, and the graphs of the steady state employment rates shown in Figures 5.7–5.10, support an intertemporal allocation of time interpretation. Indeed, in the case of adults, the elasticities of unemployment with respect to expected wages are particularly large.

Inspection of Figures 5.7–5.10, reveals that unemployment rate differences by race would be dramatically reduced if the different races faced the same expected wage. Nevertheless, for youths the differences remain large in the relevant wage range. One notable feature of these responses is that they mirror the behaviour of national unemployment rates during the seventies, i.e. downward shocks in expected real wages induce significant increases in adult unemployment rates, but rather small changes in the unemployment rates for youths. Furthermore, to the extent that real wage rates across races move together, unemployment rate differences become exaggerated as the real wage level falls.

It should be noted that the theory presented does not require a negative relationship between the unemployment rate and the real wage across individuals. Only a positive association between the fractions of a lifetime

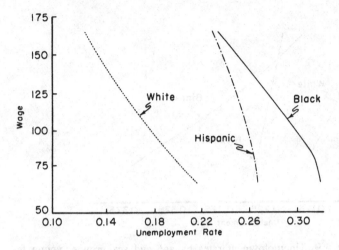

Figure 5.7. Unemployment rates by age and sex groups, young males.

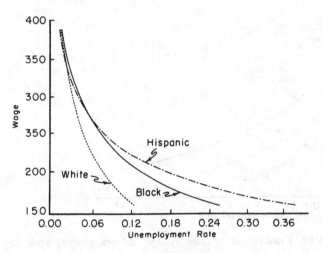

Figure 5.8. Unemployment rates by age and sex groups, adult males.

spent participating and employed is implied. A negative elasticity in the case of unemployment is a reflection of the empirical fact that the positive proportional response in employment exceeds the effect on participation.

5.7 Conclusions

Viewing the individual as experiencing "shocks" from time to time in the available wage offer and the value of time yields two behavioural

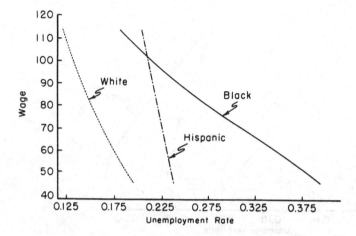

Figure 5.9. Unemployment rates by age and sex groups, young females.

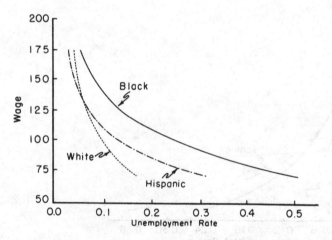

Figure 5.10. Unemployment rates by age and sex groups, adult females.

propositions: (1) Higher earnings are associated with longer employment spells and more frequent transitions to employment. (2) To the extent that a worker is actively searching while unemployed, higher expected earnings are associated with shorter spells of nonparticipation and less frequent transitions out of the labour force. The model is a marriage of a dynamic generalization of classic participation theory and of wage search theory wherein movements between activities, work, search and "leisure" are explicitly modelled.

The empirical findings generally support the theory and accord well with existing evidence on cross section studies of labour supply. The one anomaly is the apparent positive relationship between the expected wage and movements from unemployment to out of the labour force in the case of adult women. The labour force participation rates implied by the estimated models are positively related to earnings for all age, sex and race groups, as expected. The demonstration that the elasticities of the unemployment rates for all groups with respect to expected wage rates are negative and large in absolute value in the case of adults is an original finding. While the role of the wage in the allocation of time is not novel, the existing neoclassical labour literature uses static labour supply models to interpret participation rate studies and search and related models of labour supply dynamics to explain unemployment patterns. The fact that these two approaches can be successfully married both theoretically and empirically is a significant finding.

Acknowledgments

An earlier version of this chapter was circulated in 1980 with the title "A Dynamic Model of Employment, Unemployment and Labor Force Participation: Estimates from the DIME data." This work has been presented at the University of Chicago, Queen's University, the University of Warwick, the University of Aarhus, the Bank of Denmark and the Research Triangle Institute. We thank participants in these workshops for their comments and suggestions. This research was partly supported by the National Science Foundation and by the National Commission on Employment Policy.

References

Bartel, A. (1975), "Job Mobility and Earnings Growth" (NBER Working Paper No. 117).

Becker, G. S. (1965), "A Theory of the Allocation of Time," *Economic Journal, 75,* 493–517.

——— (1975), *Human Capital* (New York: NBER).

Blackwell, D. (1965), "Discounted Dynamic Programming," *Annals of Mathematical Statistics, 36,* 226–235.

Burdett, K., Kiefer, N. M., Mortensen, D. T., and Neumann, G. R. (1980), "A Dynamic Model of Employment, Unemployment and Labor Force Participation: Estimates from the DIME Data" (manuscript).

Burdett, K., and Mortensen, D. T. (1978), "Labor Supply Under Uncertainty," in R. G. Ehrenberg (ed.), *Research in Labour Economics,* Vol. 2, (Greenwich, Connecticut: JAI Press), 109–158.

(1980), "Search Layoffs and Labor Market Equilibrium," *Journal of Political Economy*, 88, 652–672.

Clark, K. B., and Summers, L. H. (1979), "Labor Market Dynamics and Unemployment: A Reconsideration," *Brookings Papers on Economic Activity*, 13–60.

Durbin, J. (1973), *Distribution Theory for Tests Based on the Sample Distribution Function*, SIAM Regional Conference Series, in Applied Mathematics, No. 9 (Bristol, England: J. W. Arrowsmith, Ltd.).

Flinn, C., and Heckman, J. (1982), "New Methods for Analyzing Structural Models of Labor Force Dynamics," in J. Heckman and B. Singer (eds.), *Annals of Applied Econometrics*, 119–168.

Hall, R. E. (1970), "Why Is the Unemployment Rate so High at Full Employment?" *Brookings Papers on Economic Activity*, 369–402.

Heyman, D. P., and Sobel, M. J. (1982), *Stochastic Models in Operations Research*, Vol. I (New York: McGraw-Hill).

Kalbfleisch, J. D., and Prentice, R. L. (1980), *The Statistical Analysis of Failure Time Data* (New York: John Wiley and Sons).

Kendall, M., and Stuart, A. (1977), *The Advanced Theory of Staitstics*, Vol. 1, 4th ed. (London: Charles Griffin and Co.).

Kiefer, N., and Neumann, G. (1979), "An Empirical Job Search Model, with a Test of the Constant Reservation Wage Hypothesis," *Journal of Political Economy*, 87(1), 89–108. Chapter 3 in this volume.

(1981), "Individual Effects in Nonlinear Models: Explicit Treatment of Heterogeneity in the Empirical Job-Search Model," *Econometrica,49*. Chapter 4 in this volume.

Lancaster, T. (1979), "Econometric Methods for the Durations of Unemployment, *Econometrica*, 47, 939–956.

Lancaster, T., and Nickell, S. (1980), "The Analysis of Re-Employment Probabilities for the Unemployed," *Journal of Royal Statistical Society, Series A*, 143, 555–666.

Lucas, R., and Prescott, E. (1974), "Equilibrium Search and Unemployment," *Journal of Economic Theory*, 7, 188–209.

Lundberg, S. (1981), *Unemployment and Household Labor Supply* (unpublished Ph.D. dissertation, Northwestern University).

Marston, S. T. (1976), "Employment Instability and High Unemployment Rates," *Brookings Papers on Economic Activity*, 169–203.

Mincer, J., and Jovanovic, B. (1981), "Labor Modibility and Wages," in Sherwin Rosen, (ed.), *Low Income Labor Markets* (Chicago: University of Chicago Press).

Mortensen, D. T. (1978), "Specific Capital and Labor Turnover," *The Bell Journal of Economics*, 572–586.

Robbins, L. (1930), "Note on the Elasticity of Demand for Income in Terms of Effort," *Economica*, 10, 123–129.

Tobin, J. (1972), "Inflation and Unemployment," *American Economic Review*, 62(1), 1–18.

Tuma, N. B., and Robins, P. K. (1980), "A Dynamic Model of Employment Behavior: An Application to the Seattle and Denver Income Maintenance Experiments," *Econometrica*, 48(4), 1031–1052.

CHAPTER 6

Choice or chance? A structural interpretation of individual labor market histories

Recently survival analysis has made its debut in econometrics as a technique for modeling the observed labor force experience of individuals over time. Although continuous-time theoretical models of optimal dynamic labor force participation are available, little use of them has been made in the empirical literature. Recent papers by Burdett et al. (1982), by Flinn and Heckman (1982) and by Olsen and Farkas (1982) are exceptions. Burdett et al. develop a continuous-time Markov decision model of an individual worker's labor force participation decision problem and use the model to interpret their empirical estimates of what can be regarded as "reduced form" relationships between rates of transition between states – employment, unemployment, and non-participation – and worker characteristics. Flinn and Heckman present a different but related participation model and discuss the problem of empirically identifying its "structure." Finally, Olsen and Farkas suggest an econometric method of estimating the "structure" of continuous-time Markov chain models. This chapter makes three contributions. First, a general dynamic continuous-time discrete choice model is set down which includes those of all three papers as special cases. Second, the problem of identifying the structure of special cases of the model is studied. Third, the method suggested by Olsen and Farkas is used to estimate the structure of the Burdett et al. model.

In all three papers, "choice" is a dichotomous decision made by the individual from time to time to be in one of a finite number of mutually exclusive states. The time between decision dates is a random interval with a distribution that depends on the state occupied. The length of the interval is thought of as the waiting time required for "news" to arrive that affects preferences over states. A new choice of state is made at each

This chapter was written by Dale T. Mortensen and George R. Neumann. It is reprinted from *Studies in Labor Market Dynamics*, edited by G. R. Neumann and N. C. Westergaard-Nielsen (1984), by permission of Springer-Verlag.

information arrival date. "Chance" enters as the determinant of when state choices are made.

As in the existing models of discrete choice, the probability that an individual will opt for a particular state at the moment of decision depends on observed characteristics of the choice, the decision maker and the environment. It is the probability that some random component of the individual's utility index is such that the specified choice is preferred. This well known framework is generalized in the three papers reviewed above to a dynamic context by regarding the time to the next arrival of a new realization of the random component as a random exponential variable with expectation that may depend on the state currently occupied and the observed explanatory variables. Standard survival models allow one to estimate the association between instantaneous state to state transition rates and a set of explanatory variables. However, because a transition rate is the product of the expected rate at which new information arrives in the origin state and the probability that the new information will induce a choice of the designated destination state, the total effect is the sum of the effect on "choice" and the effect on "chance." The problem of identification in this context is the problem of obtaining separate empirical estimates of the association between an explanatory variable and the information arrival rate on the one hand and the choice probability on the other.

As in the Burdett et al. study, the substantive relationships of interest in this chapter are those between the transition probabilities and the wage a worker can expect to receive when employed. Their empirical evidence, obtained from an analysis of labor market histories drawn from the Denver Income Maintenance Experiment (DIME) data, suggests strong positive relationships in the cases of transitions to employment and from non-participation and negative relationships in the cases of transitions from employment and to non-participation. Are these relationships explained by the hypothesis that high earners prefer employment and are adverse to non-participation? Or are they explained by the possibility that high earners obtain employment opportunities more frequently when not employed and are less likely to receive new information that would induce them to leave employment. Both explanations are consistent with the observations reported by Burdett et al.

The theoretical case for "choice" as an explanation is well developed in the static theory of labor force participation. Those who participate do so because employment opportunities for them are relatively more attractive. The static theory obviously has nothing to say about "chance" arrival of information about such opportunities. However, search theory does suggest that workers who face relatively more attractive employment opportunities have the incentive to seek out an acceptable one more quickly. By analogous reasoning, employers should allocate more resources to the recruitment of workers for jobs that offer relatively greater profit opportunities. To the extent that higher profit and higher earnings are associated with those job–worker matches that offer greater match specific capital, one should observe that those who can expect to earn more will receive employment opportunities more frequently. For the same reason one should also observe less frequent separations.

The empirical results obtained in this chapter imply that the observed relationships between state to state transition rates and the wage individuals can expect are explained by both "choice" and "chance." However, the evidence also suggests that the association between the expected wage and information arrival rates may be more important than that between the choice probabilities and the wage. In sum, "chance" may dominate "choice" as an explanation of participation behavior over time.

6.1   The dynamic random utility model

The idea to be modeled is that a worker moves among the states of employment, unemployment and non-participation over time in response to changes in employment opportunities and the opportunity cost of work. These changes are viewed as random shocks that arrive at random intervals. Given "news," a change in the disturbance, the worker faces a discrete choice problem – the state to occupy. The worker is assumed to select that state which yields the highest expected present value of future utility conditional on current information, the current state and realized value of the disturbance. These ideas are formalized in this section as a dynamic generalization of the random utility model of discrete choice by assuming that the disturbance arrival process is Poisson and that the sequence of disturbances is distributed independent of the time required for new information to arrive. Under these assumptions, the individual's participation problem is a Markov decision process in continuous time which has a well defined solution. The decision models developed by Burdett et al. and by Flinn and Heckman are special cases of the general formulation.

At any point in time a worker can be found in one of three states –

employment, unemployment, or non-participation. Denote these three states as E, U, and N respectively. Associated with each worker is a stationary characteristic vector $\mathbf{x}$ and a vector of random transitory characteristics ε. The vector of characteristics, $\mathbf{x}$, might be interpreted as a two element vector containing the individual's mean wage offer, w, and mean expected value of non-market time, v, and ε can be regarded as a vector of disturbances. In other words, $\mathbf{x} + \varepsilon$ can be interpreted as the currently realized wage offer and value of non-market time pair. A worker's current instantaneous utility $u_i(\mathbf{x} + \varepsilon)$ depends on this vector and the state occupied.

The disturbance ε is regarded as a random variable that changes from time to time at random intervals. Given a change in the disturbance, "news", the worker reassesses his or her state occupancy. By assumption the individual chooses the state that can be expected to yield the highest present value of the future utility flow.

Let $\tilde{t}_i$ denote the random time to arrival of new information in state i and let $\tilde{\varepsilon}_i$ denote the new disturbance given that state i is occupied. Assume that $\tilde{t}_i$ has a negative exponential distribution characterized by the "hazard" $\eta_i(\mathbf{x})$, the information arrival rate, which is independent of all past and current disturbances. Let $F_i(\tilde{\varepsilon}; \varepsilon)$ denote the distribution of $\tilde{\varepsilon}_i$ given the current realized value of the disturbance and the worker's characteristics. The expected present value of future utility associated with state i can be expressed as a function $V_i(\mathbf{x}, \varepsilon)$ of the current disturbance and the worker's stationary characteristics. Indeed,

$$V_i(\varepsilon, \mathbf{x}) = E\left\{ \int_0^{\tilde{t}_i} u_i(\mathbf{x} + \varepsilon)e^{-\rho s}\, ds + e^{-\rho \tilde{t}_i} \max_k V_k(\mathbf{x}, \tilde{\varepsilon}_i)\, \varepsilon \right\}$$

$$= \frac{u_i(\mathbf{x} + \varepsilon)}{\rho + \eta_i(\mathbf{x})} + \frac{\eta_i(\mathbf{x})}{\rho + \eta_i(\mathbf{x})} \psi_i(\varepsilon, \mathbf{x}), \tag{1}$$

where ρ is the subjective rate of time discount and

$$\psi_i(\varepsilon, \mathbf{x}) = \int \max_k V_k(\tilde{\varepsilon}, \mathbf{x})\, dF_i(\tilde{\varepsilon} \mid \varepsilon) \tag{2}$$

is the expected value of the future optimal state choice when in state i given that the current disturbance is ε. As (1) and (2) define the vector of functions $[\Psi_i(\cdot)]$ as the fixed point of a contraction mapping by virtue of Blackwell's Theorem (1965), existence and uniqueness of the value functions are guaranteed.

The first term on the right side of (1) is the expected present value of the utility enjoyed prior to the arrival of new information. The second term is the expected present value of the optimal state choice to be made when new information arrives given the worker's current state and information. The value functions derived from this dynamic formulation of the participation choice problem are indirect utility indicators of the worker's preferences over states conditional on the current disturbance. Let

$$A_j(\mathbf{x}) = \{\varepsilon : V_j(\varepsilon, \mathbf{x}) = \max_k V_k(\varepsilon, \mathbf{x})\} \tag{3}$$

denote the set of disturbances such that state j is preferred (weakly), hereafter referred to as the acceptance set of state j. The probability that state j will be preferred at the next information arrival date given the current state and disturbance is

$$\pi_{ij}(\varepsilon, \mathbf{x}) = \int_{A_j(\mathbf{x})} dF_i(\bar{\varepsilon} \mid \varepsilon). \tag{4}$$

the conditional probability that the next disturbance will fall in the acceptance set $A_j(\mathbf{x})$. Since the instantaneous probability that new information will arrive in state i is $\eta_i(\mathbf{x})\, dt$, the instantaneous probability of a transition from state i to a different state $j \neq i$ given ε is $\lambda_{ij}(\varepsilon, \mathbf{x})\, dt$, where

$$\lambda_{ij}(\varepsilon, \mathbf{x}) = \eta_i(\mathbf{x})\pi_{ij}(\varepsilon, \mathbf{x}), \qquad j \neq i, \tag{5}$$

defines the state to state transition rates. Since (3) and (4) imply $\Sigma_j \pi_{ij} = 1$ for every origin state i, the conditional hazard rate associated with the distribution of spell lengths in state i given ε is

$$\lambda_i(\varepsilon, \mathbf{x}) = \sum_{j \neq i} \lambda_{ij}(\varepsilon, \mathbf{x}) = \eta_i(\mathbf{x})(1 - \pi_{ii}(\varepsilon, \mathbf{x})). \tag{6}$$

As presented in equations (1) through (6), the model is an abstraction. To give it content as a formulation of the worker's dynamic participation problem requires restrictions. For this purpose, we interpret $(\mathbf{x} + \varepsilon) = (w + \varepsilon_1, v + \varepsilon_2)$ as the current realization of the wage offer and value of non-market time pair, where w and v are their respective means, and view $u_i(\mathbf{x} + \varepsilon)$ as the instantaneous utility currently realized from the pair. The following restrictions are imposed both by Burdett et al. and by Flinn and Heckman:

$$\frac{\partial u_E(\cdot)}{\partial(w + \varepsilon_1)} > \frac{\partial u_U(\cdot)}{\partial(w + \varepsilon_1)} = \frac{\partial u_N(\cdot)}{\partial(w + \varepsilon_1)} = 0, \tag{7a}$$

$$\frac{\partial u_N(\cdot)}{\partial(v + \varepsilon_2)} > \frac{\partial u_U(\cdot)}{\partial(v + \varepsilon_2)} = \frac{\partial u_E(\cdot)}{\partial(v + \varepsilon_2)} = 0. \tag{7b}$$

The first assumption simply reflects the fact that the current wage offer is "enjoyed" by the worker only when employed. The second assumption reflects the search theoretic interpretation of unemployment. Specifically, non-market time must be foregone while searching for work as well as while working. To be willing to forgo non-market time while searching, the worker must receive a return. A return exists if, and only if, the expected time to arrival of the next choice opportunity is shorter when searching than not; i.e.

$$\eta_U(\mathbf{x}) > \eta_N(\mathbf{x}). \tag{8}$$

Given these assumptions, the Burdett et al. specification is simply the special case in which the disturbance is sequentially independent. By virtue of (4), the transition choice probabilities are independent of the current disturbance. Given sequentially independent disturbances, the transition rates are

$$\lambda_{ij}(\mathbf{x}) = \eta_i(\mathbf{x})\pi_{ij}(\mathbf{x}), \quad j \neq i. \tag{9}$$

In this case, the six transition rates associated with a particular worker's characteristics define the worker's participation experience over time as a continuous-time Markov chain on the three states. Conceptually, any continuous-time Markov chain is a stochastic process that moves from state to state according to an embedded Markov chain, which in our case is characterized by the probability matrix of transition choice probabilities $P = [\pi_{ij}]$. Each time state i is visited the process remains there for a random time, which in our case is the time required for new information to arrive. The waiting time has a negative exponential distribution, which in our case has an expected length equal to $1/\eta_i$.

These two components of the process, the matrix of state to state choice probabilities on the one hand and the vector of expected waiting times on the other, correspond respectively to what is meant in this chapter by "choice" and "chance."

To rigorously demonstrate how choice and chance interact to determine participation behavior in the model, one can solve for the steady state probability distribution over states in terms of the choice probabilities and the expected waiting times. The steady state probabilities $p = (p_E, p_U, p_N)$, which solve the equations:

$$\lambda_j(\mathbf{x})p_j(\mathbf{x}) = \sum_{j \neq i} p_i(\mathbf{x})\lambda_{ij}(\mathbf{x}) \qquad \text{for each } j, \tag{10a}$$

$$\sum_j p_j(\mathbf{x}) = 1, \tag{10b}$$

have two equivalent interpretations. Since the conditions require that the probability density flows into and out of each state balance, $p_j(\mathbf{x})$ is both the unconditional probability of finding the worker in state j in the long run and the expected fraction of a sample of identical workers who will eventually occupy the state. Hence, in the language of labor economics $1 - p_N(\mathbf{x})$ is the participation rate of those with characteristics $\mathbf{x}$ and $p_U(\mathbf{x})/[p_E(\mathbf{x}) + p_U(\mathbf{x})]$ is their unemployment rate.

Define $\boldsymbol{\pi} = (\pi_E, \pi_U, \pi_N)$ as the stationary probability vector associated with the embedded Markov chain; i.e., the solution to

$$\boldsymbol{\pi} = \boldsymbol{\pi}P. \tag{11}$$

If the process were in fact a discrete time chain – new information were to arrive with certainty at the same discrete points of time in all states – then the steady state probability vector would be $\boldsymbol{\pi}$. In the more natural case of random waiting times, Heyman and Sobel (1982) show that

$$p_j(\mathbf{x}) = \frac{\pi_j(\mathbf{x})/\eta_j(\mathbf{x})}{\sum_i \pi_i(\mathbf{x})/\eta_i(\mathbf{x})}. \tag{12}$$

Hence, "chance" matters as a determinant of the steady state probability distribution if and only if the information arrival rates are not identical across states. Equation (12) motivates an interest in empirically testing the hypothesis that expected information arrival times are invariant across states for workers with the same characteristics. If the hypothesis can be rejected, then one cannot infer that observed relationships between either the participation rate or the unemployment rate and worker characteristics are attributable to the relationships between choice probabilities and the characteristics.

The essential structure of the Flinn and Heckman model is captured as a special case of sequentially dependent disturbances. Although they assume that a new realization of either the wage offer or the value of non-market time is independent of the old one, the arrival of each is governed by a separate process. Hence, only one element of the disturbance vector changes at any information arrival date. Since one does not know which kind of information will arrive next, this structure is mathematically equivalent to one in which there is a single information arrival process but a distribution of the next disturbance which depends on the current realization.

Specifically, let $\eta_{i1}(\mathbf{x})$ and $\eta_{i2}(\mathbf{x})$ represent the arrival rates of the wage offer and value of non-market time processes respectively. Let the $F_{ik}(\bar{\varepsilon}_k)$ denote the distribution of the next realization of the disturbance given that the new information will be of type $k = 1$ or 2. With this notation in hand, the rate at which new information about either the wage offer or the value of non-market time arrives is simply the sum of the two information arrival rates:

$$\eta_i(\mathbf{x}) = \eta_{i1}(\mathbf{x}) + \eta_{i2}(\mathbf{x}). \tag{13a}$$

The probability that the wage offer will change at the next information arrival date is η_{i1}/η_i and the probability that the value of non-market time will change is η_{i2}/η_i. Therefore, the joint distribution of the next two component disturbance vector, $\bar{\varepsilon}$, given the current one, ε, is

$$F_i(\bar{\varepsilon}|\varepsilon,\mathbf{x}) = \begin{cases} \dfrac{\eta_{i1}(\mathbf{x})}{\eta_i(\mathbf{x})}F_{i1}(\bar{\varepsilon}_1,\mathbf{x}) & \text{when } \bar{\varepsilon}_2 = \varepsilon_2 \\[2ex] \dfrac{\eta_{i2}(\mathbf{x})}{\eta_i(\mathbf{x})}F_{i2}(\bar{\varepsilon}_2|\mathbf{x}) & \text{when } \bar{\varepsilon}_1 = \varepsilon_1 \\[2ex] 0 & \text{otherwise} \end{cases} \tag{13b}$$

with the interpretation of the "arrival rate" and distribution of the "next disturbance" specified in (12) and (13), the essence of the structure of the Flinn and Heckman model is as defined by equations (3)–(5). Indeed, direct substitution yields

$$\lambda_{ij}(\varepsilon, \mathbf{x}) = \eta_{i1}(\mathbf{x})\int_{A_{j1}(\varepsilon_2,\mathbf{x})} dF_{i1}(\bar{\varepsilon}_1) + \eta_{i2}(\mathbf{x})\int_{A_{j2}(\varepsilon_1,\mathbf{x})} dF_{i2}(\bar{\varepsilon}_2), \tag{14}$$

where

$$A_{j1}(\varepsilon_2, \mathbf{x}) = \{\bar{\varepsilon}_1 : V_j(\bar{\varepsilon}_1, \varepsilon_2, \mathbf{x}) = \max_k V_k(\bar{\varepsilon}_1, \varepsilon_2, \mathbf{x})\} \tag{15a}$$

is the set of wage offer disturbances such that state j is preferred given the current value of non-market time and

$$A_{j2}(\varepsilon_1, \mathbf{x}) = \{\bar{\varepsilon}_2 : V_j(\varepsilon_1, \bar{\varepsilon}_2, \mathbf{x}) = \max_k V_k(\varepsilon_1, \bar{\varepsilon}_2, \mathbf{x})\} \tag{15b}$$

is the set of non-market time values such that state j is preferred given the current wage offer.

There are two differences between this version of the general model and the specifics of Flinn and Heckman. Transitions to non-employment states can be induced by a sufficiently low realization of a new wage offer and transitions to employment can be induced by a sufficiently low realization of the value of non-market time. In Flinn and Heckman these two possibilities are respectively ruled out by assuming that an employed worker always has the option of continuing employment at the old wage when a new offer arrives and that any employment opportunity arriving while not employed must be either accepted or rejected immediately. Neither assumption is particularly realistic since the first rules out layoffs and the second rules out the recall of employment opportunities known to the worker.

6.2   An analysis of wage effects

The purpose of this section is to derive necessary and sufficient conditions under which one can sign the relationship between the probability of preferring employment (non-participation) and the expected wage offer. For this purpose, sequentially independent disturbances and the interpretive restrictions stated in (7) and (8) are assumed. An important implication of the analysis is that these conditions are generally violated when information arrival rates depend on the expected wage offer in ways suggested by search and turnover theory.

In the case of sequentially independent disturbances, equations (1) and (2) imply that the value functions satisfy

$$V_i(\varepsilon, \mathbf{x}) = \frac{u_i(\mathbf{x} + \varepsilon)}{\rho + \eta_i(\mathbf{x})} + \frac{\eta_i(\mathbf{x})}{\rho + \eta_i(\mathbf{x})} \int \max_k V_k(\tilde{\varepsilon}, \mathbf{x}) \, dF_i(\tilde{\varepsilon}) \qquad (16)$$

for each i. In other words, the conditions of (7) and (16) imply

$$\frac{\partial V_E(\cdot)}{\partial \varepsilon_1} > \frac{\partial V_U(\cdot)}{\partial \varepsilon_1} = \frac{\partial V_N(\cdot)}{\partial \varepsilon_1} = 0, \qquad (17a)$$

$$\frac{\partial V_N(\cdot)}{\partial \varepsilon_2} > \frac{\partial V_U(\cdot)}{\partial \varepsilon_2} = \frac{\partial V_E(\cdot)}{\partial \varepsilon_2} = 0. \qquad (17b)$$

Consequently, the slope of the boundary between A_E and A_N is positive, between A_E and A_U is zero, and A_U and A_N is infinite as drawn in Figure

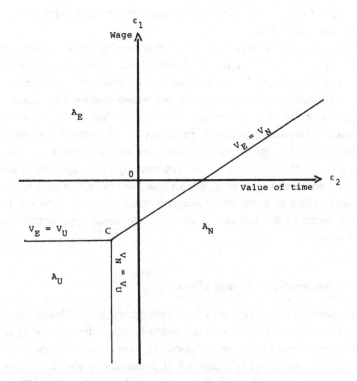

Figure 6.1. The acceptance sets.

6.1. Assumption (8) is needed to guarantee that A_U be non-empty; i.e., that there will be circumstances in which unemployment is preferred to non-participation. As drawn, the worker prefers employment when the current wage offer is relatively high, non-participation when the realized value of non-market time is relatively high, and unemployment when both are relatively low.

In the absence of information about the form of the disturbance distribution, one can obtain general qualitative results concerning the relationship between the transition choice probabilities and worker characteristics only from information on the relationship between the set of disturbances over which the designated destination state is preferred and the characteristics. By virtue of (4), the probability that state j will be chosen at the next information arrival date can be said to increase (decrease) with the characteristic in question for all disturbance distributions if and only if the correspondence $A_j(\mathbf{x})$ increases (decreases) in a set inclusion sense. Given this fact, one cannot expect sharp qualitative comparative results except in the case of severely restrictive assumptions. We proceed by first showing what properties the value functions must have in order to conclude that workers facing higher mean wage offers prefer employment and don't prefer non-participation in a probabilistic sense, holding the expected value of non-market time constant.

To determine how the set of disturbances associated with employment (A_E in Figure 6.1) varies with the mean wage offer, we use the fact that the boundaries of the set are determined by the condition:

$$V_E(\varepsilon, \mathbf{x}) = \max[V_N(\varepsilon, \mathbf{x}), V_U(\varepsilon, \mathbf{x})].$$

Given ε_2, the value of ε_1 satisfying the condition is the critical difference between the wage offer at which the worker is indifferent between employment and the next best alternative, the reservation wage, and the mean wage offer. Any wage disturbance in excess of this critical value is sufficient to induce a choice of employment by the individual. A differentiation of this condition with respect to the mean wage offer holding ε_2 constant yields

$$\frac{\partial \varepsilon_1}{\partial w} \times \frac{\partial(V_E - \max[V_N, V_U])}{\partial \varepsilon_1} = \frac{\partial(\max[V_N, V_U] - V_E)}{\partial w}. \tag{18}$$

Hence, the set A_E increases in the set inclusion sense with the mean wage offer by virtue of (17a) and (18) if, and only if, the difference between the value of employment and the value of the best alternative increases with the mean wage offer on the boundary.

Analogously, the boundary of A_N is defined by

$$V_N(\varepsilon, \mathbf{x}) = \max[V_E(\varepsilon, \mathbf{x}), V_U(\varepsilon, \mathbf{x})].$$

A differentiation of this condition, holding ε_1 constant, yields

$$\frac{\partial \varepsilon_2}{\partial w} \times \frac{\partial(V_N - \max[V_E, V_U])}{\partial \varepsilon_2} = \frac{\partial(\max[V_E, V_U] - V_N)}{\partial w} \tag{19}$$

along the boundary of the set A_N. Consequently (17b) and (19) imply that A_N decreases with the expected wage offer in the set inclusion sense if, and only if, the difference between the value of the best alternative and the value of non-participation increases with the mean wage offer.

In sum, we have established the following:

Proposition 1. $\partial \pi_E / \partial w > 0$ for every distribution of ε if, and only if,

(a) $\dfrac{\partial (V_E - V_N)}{\partial w} > 0$ when $V_E(\varepsilon, \mathbf{x}) = V_N(\varepsilon, \mathbf{x}) > V_U(\varepsilon, \mathbf{x})$

and

(b) $\dfrac{\partial (V_E - V_U)}{\partial w} > 0$ when $V_E(\varepsilon, \mathbf{x}) = V_U(\varepsilon, \mathbf{x}) > V_N(\varepsilon, \mathbf{x})$.

Proposition 2. $\partial \pi N / \partial w < 0$ for every distribution of ε if, and only if,

(a) $\dfrac{\partial (V_E - V_N)}{\partial w} > 0$ when $V_N(\varepsilon, \mathbf{x}) = V_E(\varepsilon, \mathbf{x}) > V_U(\varepsilon, \mathbf{x})$

and

(b) $\dfrac{\partial (V_U - V_N)}{\partial w} > 0$ when $V_N(\varepsilon, \mathbf{x}) = V_U(\varepsilon, \mathbf{x}) > V_E(\varepsilon, \mathbf{x})$.

Note that the sign of $\partial \pi_U / \partial w$ is generally ambiguous when all the conditions hold because the set A_U varies in a non-set inclusion sense with w.

The conditions of both propositions clearly have an intuitive appeal. However, the source of this intuition is the standard static model of participation. That model supposes that the probability of finding a worker in a given state is the probability that the worker prefers the state ($P_i = \pi_i$). As we observed in the previous section, such is a special case of the dynamic model if and only if the distribution of times between disturbance arrivals and the distribution of the disturbance itself are both independent of the state occupied. Since these conditions ($\eta_i = \eta$ and $F_i = F$) and equation (16) imply

$$V_i(\varepsilon, \mathbf{x}) - V_j(\varepsilon, \mathbf{x}) = \frac{u_i(\mathbf{x} + \varepsilon) - u_j(\mathbf{x} + \varepsilon)}{p + \eta(\mathbf{x})},$$

the conditions of both propositions hold in this case by virtue of the assumptions of (7).

In their analysis, Burdett et al. have shown that the conditions of the propositions also hold if the distribution of the disturbance is independent of the state occupied and the mean wage offer, the information arrival rates are all independent of the mean wage offfer, and the instantaneous utility functions are linear. These assumptions and the two propositions together with equations (5) and (6) imply that transition rates from either non-employment state to employment and the hazard rate associated with non-participation increase with the mean wage offer while transition rates from either participation state to non-participation and the hazard rate associated with employment all decrease with the mean wage offer. These "reduced form" implications are generally consistent with the empirical findings reported by Burdett et al. with the notable exception of a positive wage effect found for the transition from unemployment to non-participation in the case of adults.

Of course, the assumption that only "choice" matters is not the only explanation of these reduced form observations. Transition rates from employment may decrease with the wage because more highly paid workers are less likely to be laid off and transition rates to employment may increase with the mean wage offer because non-employed workers who can command higher earnings are more likely to receive offers. In other words, the possibility that "chance" matters in the sense that relationships between information arrival rates and the expected wage offer are a part of the explanation for observed relationships between transition rates and expected wage rates cannot be ruled out.

The assumption that the information arrival rates are independent of the expected wage offer is crucial to any demonstration that the conditions of Propositions 1 and 2 hold. To demonstrate the fact, we assume that the disturbance is independent of the state occupied, $\psi_i(\cdot) = \psi(\cdot)$ in equation (1), and suppose that $\eta_E(\mathbf{x})$ decreases with the mean wage offer while $\eta_U(\mathbf{x})$ increases with w. Hence one can generally find a value for the mean wage offer, w^*, such that these two information arrival rates are equal. By virtue of equation (16),

$$
\left. \frac{\partial[V_E(\cdot) - V_U(\cdot)]}{\partial w} \right|_{w=w^*} = \frac{\partial u_E(\cdot)/\partial w}{\rho + \eta_E(\mathbf{x})} - \frac{\partial u_U(\cdot)/\partial w}{\rho + \eta_U(\mathbf{x})}
$$

$$
+ \frac{\psi(\cdot) - V_E(\cdot)}{\rho + \eta_E(\mathbf{x})} \times \frac{\partial \eta_E(\cdot)}{\partial w}
$$

$$
- \frac{\psi(\cdot) - V_U(\cdot)}{\rho + \eta_U(\cdot)} \times \frac{\partial \eta_U(\cdot)}{\partial w} \tag{20}
$$

at that value of the wage. The difference between the first two terms on the right side of (20) is positive by virtue of (7a). However, the last two terms are negative for the following reasons. Along the boundary between A_E and A_U, $V_E(\cdot)$ is a constant and $V_E(\cdot) = V_U(\cdot)$ by definition. Therefore,

$\Psi - V_U = \Psi - V_E$ is a constant along the boundary. At the corner point, C in Figure 6.1, equation (16) implies

$$V_E - V_N = V_U - V_N = \frac{u_U}{\rho + \eta_U} - \frac{u_N}{\rho + \eta_N} + \left[\frac{\eta_U}{\rho + \eta_U} - \frac{\eta_N}{\rho + \eta_N}\right]\psi = 0.$$

Because search is costly ($u_U < u_N$) but offers a return ($\eta_U > \eta_N$), this equation implies $\psi - V_U = \psi - V_E > 0$ at the point C and everywhere on the boundary between A_E and A_U. Hence, the sign of (20) can be made negative by making either information arrival rate sufficiently responsive to the mean wage offer.

In sum, condition (b) of Proposition 1 will not hold. One can easily construct a similar example for which condition (b) of Proposition 2 is also violated. Hence, if the information arrival rates depend on the mean wage offer, the qualitative relationship between the probability that a state is preferred and the mean wage offer is an empirical issue.

6.3   Identifying the structure

By the structure of the model we mean the components that make up the transition rates as defined in equations (3) through (5). These include the acceptance sets, the distributions of the next disturbance and the information arrival rates. How can continuous-time observations on the labor market histories of individuals be used to obtain empirical estimates of these constructs?

In the discussion that follows, it will be useful to refer to Figure 6.1. The figure portrays a possible theoretical partition of the space of disturbances into the collection of acceptance sets. In fact, those drawn are implied by (7), (8) and the assumption of independent disturbances as noted in the previous section. Although these qualitative characteristics of the acceptance sets hold more generally, the reader is warned that the specific shapes drawn in Figure 6.1 crucially depend on the assumption of sequentially independent disturbances.

The general model

Consider a hypothetical sample of N worker histories over some common continuous interval of time of length T containing the following information: the dated sequence of realized wage offer and value of non-market time pairs experienced and the dated sequence of state spells by type for each individual in the sample. For simplicity, suppose that all individuals are known to be identical in the sense that their mean wage offer and value of non-market time pair, current state and disturbance contingent distributions of the next realization of the disturbance, and state contingent information arrival rates are the same. Hence, observed differences in experience are attributable to random differences in information arrival dates and disturbance realizations. The data in the hypothetical sample on the dated sequence of wage offer and value of non-market time pairs in conjunction with the dated sequence of spells by type and the durations of time between arrivals of new values of the pair permit direct consistent estimation of the conditional disturbance distributions and arrival rates respectively. Given the estimated mean of the pair, residuals can be calculated as estimates of the disturbance pair associated with each realization and plotted as points in Figure 6.1. If the theory is correct, the state occupied during the period of each realization for each individual should be such that the plots form an approximation to the theoretical partition of the disturbance space. The sample partition of the disturbance space is a consistent estimate of the theoretical partition, like that drawn in Figure 6.1, in the sense that the former converges to the latter as $N \times T \to \infty$. Hence, the acceptance sets can be estimated.

With these estimates of the components of the transition rates, estimates of the transition rates can be calculated using equation (5). However, the observations on the sequence of spell types and durations in conjunction with the simultaneously recorded disturbance can also be used to obtain consistent estimates of the transition rates conditional on the current state and disturbance. Hence, the model is overidentified by the information supposed to be available in our hypothetical sample.

The Flinn and Heckman model

Of course, our hypothetical sample is overly idealized as a characterization of real data. Realized disturbances that don't induce changes in state, particularly unaccepted wage offers, are not likely to be recorded. Flinn and Heckman consider the case in which the sequence of values of non-market time are observed but unaccepted wage offers and their arrival dates are not. There are three problems which complicate identification in this case. Because some arrival dates are not observed, it is not possible to consistently estimate information arrival rates directly. Second, the boundary between the acceptance sets associated with the two nonemployment states cannot be determined by the method suggested above in general because the boundary need not be vertical when the disturbance is sequentially dependent. Third, of observed accepted wage offers the set is drawn from a truncated distribution of all wage offers and the truncation point is endogenous. The first and third problems have been dealt with in the empirical wage search literature but not the second. Its presence is a consequence of the three state structure. The Flinn and Heckman model is designed to cope with all three problems.

Recall that new wage offers and new values of non-market time are assumed by Flinn and Heckman to arrive by different and independent processes. Given this assumption, the distribution of the new value of either is independent of the old. As the dated sequence of values of non-market time is supposedly observed, its own state dependent arrival rates, the η_{i2}'s, and distributions, the F_{i2}'s, can be estimated directly. Although unacceptable wage offers are not observed, the sample of observed wage offer and value of non-market time pairs approximate the theoretical set A_E. A consistent estimate of the reservation wage associated with each observed value of non-market time is the smallest such accepted wage in the sample. Hence, a curve appropriately fitted to these points is a consistent estimate of the boundary of A_E. Given this estimate of the set of truncation points and an assumed form for the wage offer distribution, the parameters of the latter can be estimated in principle with the truncated wage offer and value of non-market time data available. Finally, since a transition from employment to either non-employment state associated with no change in the value of non-market time signals the arrival of an unacceptable wage offer and since arrival dates of new acceptable wage offers are recorded even when employed, the wage offer arrival rate conditional on employment, η_{E1}, can also be consistently estimated because the information on durations between wage offer arrivals is complete.

However, neither the wage offer arrival rates in the non-employment states nor the boundary dividing the acceptance sets of the two non-employment states can be estimated directly when the unacceptable wage offer sequence and arrival dates are not observed. In our version of the Flinn and Heckman model, equation (14), observations on the sequence of state spells and their durations will not help identify these because transition rates from non-employment states depend on the current wage offer available even though unacceptable. However, if unacceptable wage offers must be responded to immediately, as Flinn and Heckman assume, then the value of non-market time at which a worker is indifferent between unemployment and non-participation and all transition rates are independent of unaccepted wage offers. Hence, if the assumption of no recall is valid, then the value of non-market time dividing A_U and A_N can be determined from the simultaneous observations on values of non-market time and state occupancy. Furthermore, the transition rates to employment, which are

$$\lambda_{iE}(\varepsilon, \mathbf{x}) = \eta_{i1}(\mathbf{x}) \int_{A_{E1(\varepsilon_2, \mathbf{x})}} dF_i(\bar{\varepsilon}_1), \qquad i = U \text{ and } N,$$

under the assumption, can be estimated using the sequence of spell types and durations. These estimates together with the estimates of A_E and wage offer distributions already discussed imply estimates of the wage offer arrival rates in both non-employed states. Hence, the model without recall is identified as Flinn and Heckman argue. In fact, it is overidentified since all components of the transition rates from employment, as defined in equation (14), can be estimated directly and independent estimates can be obtained from the observations on the sequences of state spell durations and types. This statement is true even when transitions induced by low realizations of the wage offer (layoffs) are allowed.

The Burdett et al. model

Still the supposed presence of the sequence of the values of non-market time in any sample is unrealistic. After all the "value of non-market time" is an unobservable construct which can best be proxied for by such things as the employment status of other household members, the number of children, and a potential host of other variables. Imagine a sample for which both unaccepted wage offers and the values of non-market time are not present. What kind of identification is possible in this case?

Clearly neither the acceptance sets nor the distributions of new disturbances can be estimated directly in general. Even with observations on accepted wage offers, an estimate of the boundary or A_E in Figure 6.1, the locus of reservation wages, is obtainable only in the case in which it is horizontal, which is contrary to the theory. Indeed, one cannot even use observations on spell types and durations to estimate the transition rates because they depend on the unobserved realized current disturbances in general. However, in the case of sequentially independent disturbances the transition rates can be consistently estimated, which brings us to the Burdett et al. model.

Consider a sample which contains only information on the sequence of spells by type and their durations for each individual. Assuming sequentially independent disturbances, the six transition rates defined by equation (6) can be estimated. However, because these are sufficient statistics for the sample, the three information arrival rates and the six independent transition choice probabilities cannot be uniquely inferred. Identification of the information arrival rates is possible when the disturbance is independent of the state occupied since

$$\pi_{ij}(\mathbf{x}) = \pi_j(\mathbf{x}) \qquad \text{for all } i \text{ and each } j$$

in this case by virtue of equations (3) and (4). Indeed, the model is over-identified in the sense that the six transition rates are determined by three information arrival rates and the two independent transition choice probabilities. The method suggested by Olsen and Farkas can be used to estimate this version of the model, to test for the overidentifying restrictions and to test for the state dependence of the information arrival rates.

6.4   Estimating the structure of the Burdett et al. model

The state to state transition rates defined in equation (9) completely characterize an individual's participation history as a continuous-time Markov chain. Burdett et al. use this fact and maximum likelihood methods to estimate transition rate functions that relate each transition rate to a set of worker characteristics. The estimated parameters are "reduced form" in the sense that each incorporates the association of both the information arrival rate and the probability of choosing the destination state with each explanatory variable. The purpose of this section is to present the specification and method used in the next to separate these two effects.

The data to be explained take the following form. Each individual in the sample is observed over the same time period. For each, the period is divided into spells by state type; i.e., as a spell of either employment, unemployment, or non-participation. Let K denote the set of spells completed during the observation period and let K_0 represent the set of incomplete spells, generally the last one for each individual. Each completed spell is described by its length t_k, its state i_k, the state of the next spell j_k, and the characteristic of the individual experiencing the spell x_k. Each incomplete spell is characterized by its truncated length t_k, state i_k, and characteristic of the individual x_k.

The maintained assumption is that the state history for each individual in the sample is generated by a continuous-time Markov chain with associated characteristic-contingent transitions rates

$$\lambda_{ij}(\mathbf{x}) = \eta_i(\mathbf{x})\pi_{ij}(\mathbf{x}), \qquad j \neq i, \tag{21a}$$

where η_i is the information arrival rate in state i and π_{ij} is the probability of a transition from state i to j given new information. Under this assumption, the length of a completed spell of type i is distributed negative exponential with hazard rate

$$\lambda_i(\mathbf{x}) = \sum_{j \neq i} \lambda_{ij}(\mathbf{x}). \tag{21b}$$

Given that a spell of type i has ended, the conditional probability that the transition is to a different state j is $\lambda_{ij}(\mathbf{x})/\lambda_i(\mathbf{x})$. Finally, an incomplete spell of truncated length t is a completed spell of length t or more. Consequently, the natural log of the likelihood of the sample is

$$\ln L = \sum_{k \in k} [\ln \lambda_{i_k j_k}(x_k) - t_k \lambda_{i_k}(x_k)] - \sum_{k \in k_0} t_k \lambda_{i_k}(x_k). \tag{22}$$

A common specification of the transition rate functions in applications of survival analysis and that used by Burdett et al. is the exponential

$$\lambda_{ij}(\mathbf{x}) = \exp(\mathbf{x}\gamma_{ij}), \qquad j \neq i, \tag{23}$$

where $\mathbf{x}$ is the vector of explanatory variables and γ_{ij} is the associated vector of parameters. Given the specification, which guarantees that the non-negativity condition is satisfied, the log likelihood of the sample is additively separable into components each of which is a strictly concave function of the parameter vector of one and only one of the transition rates. This fact facilitates computation of the unique maximum likelihood estimates of the parameters.

It is useful to point out again that (21) imposes no structure beyond that implied by the continuous-time Markov chain assumption. Specifically, any such process can be interpreted as composed of an exponential distribution of waiting time until the next transition for each state and an embedded Markov chain. However, the exponential specification of the transition rate functions, equation (23), together with (21) implies that the transition choice probabilities are of the logit form. Conversely, if the logit form,

$$\pi_{ij}(\mathbf{x}) = \frac{\exp(\mathbf{x}\beta_{ij})}{\sum_j \exp(\mathbf{x}\beta_{ij})}, \tag{24}$$

is imposed, then the only specification of the information arrival rates which is consistent with (23) is

$$\eta_i(\mathbf{x}) = \exp(\mathbf{x}\alpha_i) \times \sum_j \exp(\mathbf{x}\beta_{ij}).$$ (25)

This specification, which Olsen and Farkas suggest and implement in their study, yields the following relationship between "reduced form" and "structural" parameters:

$$\gamma_{ij} = \alpha_i + \beta_{ij}, \qquad j \neq i.$$ (26a)

Without loss of generality, one can choose

$$\beta_{in} = 0,$$ (26b)

where n is any one of the states.

However, the structural parameter vectors, the three α_i's and the six free β_{ij}'s in the case of three states, are not identified by the sample information, the six reduced form parameter vector estimates. Observations on the information arrival dates are needed to identify the general model, as was noted in the previous section. However, identification can be obtained in the special case in which the distribution of the disturbance is independent of the state occupied. That restriction, $\pi_{ij}(\mathbf{x}) = \pi_i(\mathbf{x})$ for all i and each j, is equivalent to

$$\beta_{ij} = \beta_j \qquad \text{for all } i \text{ and each } j$$ (27)

given the specification. Overidentification obtains in the case of three or more states. Namely, the three α_i's and the two free β_j's determine the six reduced form parameter vectors.

The specification (24) and (25) has several advantages. First, because the likelihood of the sample expressed as a function of the reduced form parameters is strictly concave and the restrictions (26) and (27) are linear, the maximum likelihood estimates of the identified structural model are unique. Second, the overidentifying restrictions can be tested by comparing the likelihoods of the restricted and unrestricted reduced form models. Third, the hypothesis that the information arrival rates are state independent, i.e., that only choice matters, is equivalent to $\alpha_i = \alpha$ and can be easily tested. The principal disadvantage, implicit in the logit specification of the transition probabilities, is the assumption that the disturbance inducing changes in state is distributed extreme value. At this stage of research on the problem, the advantages would seem to outweigh this disadvantage.

Finally, note that the specification of the likelihood function (22) proceeds conditionally on the initial state occupied, i_0. As is well known (Cox and Lewis (1966), Flinn and Heckman (1982)) the distribution of completed first spells is not, in general, the same as the distribution of all completed spells from a particular state. This is so because the initialization of the experiment catches persons in mid-spell; hence longer spells are more likely to be sampled. The probability of observing a person in state i at the start of the observation period depends on the entire pre-observation history. However, the assumption of a continuous-time Markov chain that has been operating sufficiently long that the steady-state distribution is reached characterizes the probability distribution completely. Specifically, the probability of observing a person with characteristics $\mathbf{x}$ in a particular state is that presented in equation (12) above.

For the three state case the solution is

$$\text{(a)} \quad P_E^* = \frac{\lambda_{31}(\lambda_{21} + \lambda_{23}) + \lambda_{32} \cdot \lambda_{21}}{\Delta}$$

$$\text{(b)} \quad P_U^* = \frac{\lambda_{32}(\lambda_{12} + \lambda_{13}) + \lambda_{31} \cdot \lambda_{12}}{\Delta} \tag{28}$$

$$\text{(c)} \quad P_N^* = 1 - P_E^* - P_U^*$$

where

$$\Delta = \lambda_{12}(\lambda_{23} + \lambda_{32}) + \lambda_{13}(\lambda_{21} + \lambda_{23} + \lambda_{32}) + \lambda_{31}(\lambda_{21} + \lambda_{23}) + \lambda_{32} \cdot \lambda_{21}.$$

Given the exponential specification of the transition functions, the restriction (27) implies that these probabilities are logits, i.e.,

$$P_i(\mathbf{x}) = \frac{\exp\{(\beta_i - \alpha_i)\mathbf{x}\}}{\Sigma_j \exp\{(\beta_j - \alpha_j)\mathbf{x}\}}. \tag{29}$$

6.5 Empirical results

In this section we present estimates of the reduced form and structural parameters implied by (23) and by (27). As we noted above, the likelihood of the sample data depends upon the distribution of individuals in the initial state even if the duration distribution is exponential as in the Markov case. One solution to this problem is to discard the first spell for all individuals since, as Billingsley (1961) notes, its contribution to the likelihood function becomes negligible asymptotically. However, in samples of finite length, which are the norm in social science applications, such treatment will generate a selectivity bias whenever the marginal distribution of state occupancy is not independent of the transition process. When the initial distribution across states is independent of the transition process, as, for example, in random assignment, inclusion of the first spell causes no bias. An alternative strategy is to assume that the distribution of initial state occupancy is completely characterized by the parameters of the transition process; in particular, that it is the steady state distribution.

Neither of these options seems particularly realistic and each has an effect on the decomposition of transition rates into arrival rates and preferences. For example, ignoring the initial distribution of states implies that incomplete spells contribute primarily to inferences about arrival rates. Since in the data we use 23% of the males were continuously employed during the observation period, and 13% of the females were non-participants for the same period, the difference between the two strategies may not be inconsequential.

With these considerations in mind we proceed cautiously by providing results using both strategies; readers may choose to place greater weight on one or the other of the estimates.

Before proceeding to the results, a description of the data is useful. As in Burdett et al. the data came from the control portion of the Denver Income Maintenance Experiment. Indeed, except that we focus here on adult (22 and over), white males and females, the data are the same as they used. Each observation is composed of a duration of time spent in a particular state, an indicator of the type of transition made, and a vector of individual characteristics defined as of the beginning of the spell. Included in the set of variables are: age, age^2, education, number of children less than six years old, the value of household assets and the natural logarithm of predicted real hourly earnings. Detailed description of the construction of the data set and its conformity with CPS definitions of employment, unemployment and non-participation are given in Lundberg (1981): Burdett et al. provide a further discussion of the differences between CPS and DIME data.

Most of the variables are of standard construction, the exception being expected earnings. Observations on the hourly wage of each individual are available for a maximum of forty-eight months, the length of the published sample. All such observations were deflated by the monthly CPI index for Denver, thus putting wages into real 1967 dollars. Monthly observations on real wages were averaged by year, resulting in a maximum of four wage observations per individual. Least squares were used to calculate annual regressions for each group. The regressor variables in all cases were the same variables included in the transition rate functions reported below and thus identification of the effect of expected wages depends *solely* upon annual variation in expected wages. To each duration observation, the appropriate one of the four predicted earnings was attached.

Two criticisms can be made of this mean wage imputation process. First, since wages are available only for those who are employed, estimated wage equations may be biased because of well-known selectivity effects (Heckman (1979)). As an empirical matter, a Mills ratio adjustment yielded insignificant changes in predicted wages and we therefore used the least squares predictions throughout. Second, the use of annual wages as the unit of observation is somewhat arbitrary since one could fit regressions to the monthly wage data. However, for some groups, particularly female, monthly regressions would have to be run on small samples, leading to unstable parameter estimates. As a practical compromise we used annual wages as it produced wage equations with significant predictive power with magnitudes and signs of coefficients in accord with the human capital literature.

Given these empirical measures of the vector $\mathbf{x}$, the sample likelihood function described by (22) and (23) was estimated separately for white males, 22 and over, and white females, 22 and over.

Although we use only about one-third of the sample, the estimates in Table 6.1 are remarkably similar to Burdett et al.'s. In particular, the result that ln wage is consistently a major determinant of transition rates, judged by the magnitude of the asymptotic "t" values, is obtained, as is the conformity of the coefficients on wages with Propositions 1 and 2. Specifically, the analysis of Burdett et al. predicts that λ_{UE}, λ_{NE}, and $(\lambda_{NE} + \lambda_{NU})$ are increasing functions of the wage and that λ_{EN}, λ_{UN}, and $(\lambda_{EU} + \lambda_{EN})$ are decreasing functions of the wage. All these predictions are confirmed in Table 6.1, with, as in Burdett et al., the notable exception of adult female transitions from unemployment to non-participation. As we have shown above, this is not necessarily a puzzle if arrival rates vary with expected earnings.

To effect the decomposition of transition rates into separate components of arrival rates and choice probabilities, we impose the restrictions implied by (26) and (27), i.e., $\lambda_{ij}(\mathbf{x}) = \alpha_i(\mathbf{x}) + \beta_j(\mathbf{x})$. These cross-transition rate conditions impose in the three state case 1 restriction for each of the independent variables. A test of the restrictions is given by

Table 6.1. Reduced form transition function estimates, $\lambda_{ij} = \exp[\beta_{ij}\mathbf{x}]$

	Transition					
	EU	EN	UE	UN	NE	NU
Adult males						
Constant	0.993	5.980	-6.874	-5.483	-20.4300	-15.401
	(0.63)	(3.31)	(2.11)	(0.61)	(4.42)	(1.77)
Education	0.008	0.036	0.047	0.142	-0.0035	-0.126
	(0.19)	(0.67)	(1.05)	(1.05)	(0.67)	(1.16)
Age	-0.084	-0.305	-0.008	0.116	-0.116	-0.279
	(1.06)	(3.62)	(0.07)	(0.45)	(3.29)	(1.28)
Age²/100	0.075	0.354	-0.034	-0.105	0.482	0.339
	(0.67)	(3.14)	(0.25)	(0.31)	(2.96)	(1.20)
Assets	-0.865	-0.019	0.473	-0.047	0.165	-0.366
	(3.27)	(0.11)	(2.73)	(0.09)	(1.39)	(0.67)
Children	0.138	-0.170	0.103	-0.131	0.167	-0.079
	(1.51)	(1.23)	(1.09)	(0.46)	(1.22)	(0.26)
ln Wage	-0.586	-0.775	1.02	-0.290	4.610	3.302
	(4.81)	(6.03)	(1.42)	(0.15)	(4.63)	(1.77)
ln L^a	-728.8	-459.6	-295.8	-81.4	-281.7	-111.9

Adult females

Constant	−0.122	2.741	1.503	−9.182	−14.903	−16.800
	(0.08)	(2.85)	(0.47)	(2.01)	(5.91)	(3.32)
Education	0.089	−0.036	0.035	−0.347	−0.391	−0.202
	(1.42)	(1.00)	(0.31)	(1.92)	(4.71)	(1.23)
Age	−0.134	−0.114	−.071	−0.526	−0.601	−0.504
	(2.33)	(2.65)	(0.38)	(1.87)	(5.54)	(2.30)
$Age^2/100$	0.145	0.092	0.073	0.601	0.594	0.518
	(2.07)	(1.63)	(0.34)	(1.84)	(4.99)	(2.16)
Assets/1,000	−0.282	0.014	0.297	−0.098	0.058	−0.551
	(1.11)	(0.33)	(1.81)	(0.29)	(0.75)	(1.78)
Children	−0.153	0.089	0.285	−0.101	−0.449	−0.338
	(0.93)	(1.04)	(2.12)	(0.54)	(5.65)	(2.05)
ln Wage	−0.497	−0.630	−0.380	4.130	5.981	5.194
	(4.51)	(11.63)	(0.26)	(1.93)	(5.51)	(2.36)
ln L^a	−453.5	−1038.8	−265.8	−171.8	−1189.1	−367.9

Note: Asymptotic "*t*"-ratios in parentheses.

[a] The number of observations by transition are for Adult males: $EU - 148$, $EN - 86$, $UE - 158$, $UN - 21$, $NE - 99$, $NU - 26$. In addition there were 211 incomplete employment, 14 incomplete unemployment, and 9 incomplete non-participation spells. For Adult females the corresponding numbers were: $EU - 86$, $EN - 260$, $UE - 106$, $UN - 54$, $NE - 296$, $NU - 67$. There were 197 incomplete employment, 15 incomplete unemployment, and 135 incomplete non-participation spells.

Table 6.2. *Likelihood ratio tests of the restrictions* $\lambda_{ij} = \alpha_i + \beta_j$

Group	Unconstrained ln L	Constrained ln L	-2Δ ln L	$\chi^2_{.05}(k)$
Adult males (7)	$-1,959.2$	$-1,961.7$	3.86	14.0
Adult females (7)	$-3,486.9$	$-3,489.3$	4.70	14.0

-2Δ ln L, which is distributed $\chi^2(k)$ asymptotically. In this application $k = 7$ for both males and females. The results of imposing these restrictions are shown in Table 6.2. The restrictions are acceptable for both groups at the 5% level; indeed the marginal significance levels of the computed test statistics are in the range of .5 so the restrictions are quite compatible with the sample data.

Table 6.3 contains estimates of the structural parameters. By convention, we set $\beta_2 \equiv 0$ so that the reported choice coefficients (β_1^*, β_3^*) are to be interpreted measuring relative preferences, i.e., $\beta_1^* = \beta_1 - \beta_2$, $\beta_3^* = \beta_3 - \beta_2$. A comparison of the structural and reduced form estimates provides material for some interesting interpretations of empirical puzzles – e.g., assets lower the arrival rate of "events," but markedly affect preferences for labor force attachment, a finding that has relevance to the poor performance of asset measures in static labor supply models – but these interpretations distract us from the central issue of disentangling choice from chance.

For males and females the effect of wages on labor market transitions appears mostly in the arrival rate of "events," not in the choice probabilities. High wage earners in both groups have lower arrival rates in the employment state, which contributes to long durations of employment, and greater arrival rates when out of the labor force. Arrival times do not differ significantly by wage rates in the unemployed state.

The effects of "choice," as measured by B_1^* and B_3^*, are imprecisely estimated for both groups. For males the results conform to intuition based on static choice models, i.e., $B_E > B_U > B_N$, although for females the results are perverse: $B_U > B_N > B_E$. Because of the imprecision of the estimates one should not put much weight on the ordering of the B_j's. Rather the data appear to indicate that wage differences manifest themselves most clearly in arrival times.

As we noted above, estimates of the α_i's and B_j's are affected by the number of individuals in a sample of finite length who do not exit a state. Heuristically, information on the choice probabilities comes from the

Table 6.3. *Structural transition function estimates,* $\lambda_{ij} = \exp\{(\alpha_i + \beta_j^*)\mathbf{x}\}$

	α_1	α_2	α_3	β_1^*	β_3^*
Adult males					
Constant	1.280	−7.217	−19.301	−0.019	4.173
	(0.83)	(1.05)	(2.80)	(0.00)	(1.85)
Education	−0.003	0.068	−0.045	−0.011	−0.014
	(0.07)	(0.69)	(0.49)	(0.11)	(0.23)
Age	−0.090	0.198	−0.214	−0.208	−0.201
	(1.16)	(1.02)	(1.19)	(1.09)	(1.86)
Age^2/100	0.076	−0.244	0.277	0.213	0.268
	(0.71)	(0.96)	(1.19)	(0.86)	(1.82)
Assets/100	−0.803	−0.529	−0.766	0.957	0.748
	(3.28)	(1.26)	(1.76)	(2.22)	(2.59)
Children	0.122	0.014	0.026	0.107	−0.257
	(1.36)	(0.06)	(0.11)	(0.45)	(1.66)
ln Wage	−0.587	0.098	3.571	0.963	−0.198
	(4.88)	(0.07)	(2.41)	(0.65)	(1.14)
ln L	−1961.1				
Adult females					
Constant	−0.084	−7.382	−20.804	6.871	2.847
	(0.06)	(1.98)	(5.44)	(1.76)	(1.90)
Education	0.094	−0.021	−0.332	−0.025	−0.133
	(1.78)	(0.16)	(2.53)	(0.18)	(2.33)
Age	−0.140	−0.287	−0.658	0.079	0.027
	(2.58)	(1.47)	(3.83)	(0.55)	(0.42)
Age^2/100	0.147	0.171	0.084	−0.157	−0.143
	(2.01)	(1.51)	(0.24)	(0.56)	(0.98)
Assets/1,000	−0.275	−0.362	−0.597	0.652	0.281
	(1.24)	(1.32)	(2.26)	(2.44)	(1.29)
Children	−1.031	−0.239	−0.357	−0.089	0.182
	(0.74)	(1.40)	(2.41)	(0.56)	(1.19)
ln Wage	−0.486	2.039	6.914	−1.363	−0.150
	(4.54)	(1.24)	(4.16)	(0.81)	(1.26)
ln L	−3489.3				

Note: Asymptotic "t"-statistics in parentheses.

"modal" splits, i.e., the fractions going into state j rather than j' from state i. If, as is true in these data, continuously employed individuals have higher wages than those who make a transition, this will be reflected in the arrival rate parameters but not in the choice probabilities. Essentially, the absence of transitions for such individuals creates a form of selection bias. To focus on this issue we have reestimated the parameters without conditioning on the initial state. We treat the initial distribution as a draw-

Table 6.4. *Structural transition function estimates: stationary state initial conditions*, $\lambda_{ij} = \exp\{(\alpha_i + \beta_j^*)x\}$

	α_1	α_2	α_3	B_1^*	B_3^*
Adult males					
Constant	1.312	−7.146	−19.200	−.019	4.064
	(0.97)	(1.04)	(2.80)	(0.00)	(1.76)
Education	−0.002	0.074	−0.054	−0.009	−0.021
	(0.06)	(0.72)	(0.50)	(0.08)	(0.26)
Age	−0.113	0.214	−0.203	−0.195	−0.207
	(1.31)	(1.21)	(1.04)	(1.10)	(1.88)
Age^2/100	0.073	−0.314	0.236	0.249	0.267
	(0.71)	(1.00)	(1.20)	(0.91)	(1.82)
Assets/100	−0.777	−0.549	−0.871	0.981	0.885
	(2.27)	(1.46)	(1.81)	(2.41)	(2.64)
Children	0.121	0.010	0.024	0.113	−0.269
	(1.36)	(0.05)	(0.09)	(0.45)	(1.73)
ln Wage	−0.483	0.043	3.579	1.016	−0.247
	(4.62)	(0.03)	(2.62)	(1.04)	(1.98)
ln *L*	−2170.00				
Adult females					
Constant	−0.091	−7.111	−20.413	6.703	2.856
	(0.07)	(1.99)	(5.02)	(1.72)	(1.94)
Education	0.096	−0.031	−0.312	−0.026	−0.136
	(1.81)	(0.18)	(2.43)	(0.19)	(2.32)
Age	−0.142	−0.291	−0.631	0.771	0.024
	(2.56)	(1.48)	(3.76)	(0.51)	(0.51)
Age^2/100	0.147	0.179	0.076	−0.149	−0.150
	(2.02)	(1.52)	(0.28)	(0.54)	(1.00)
Assets/1,000	−0.281	−0.366	−0.602	0.652	0.280
	(1.24)	(1.32)	(2.33)	(2.44)	(1.28)
Children	−1.032	−0.227	−0.364	−0.091	0.179
	(0.76)	(1.21)	(2.47)	(0.61)	(1.20)
ln Wage	−0.473	1.987	6.587	−1.101	−0.168
	(4.47)	(1.19)	(4.07)	(0.67)	(1.41)
ln *L*	−3610.4				

Note: Asymptotic "t"-statistics in parentheses.

ing from the ergodic distribution, as described in (28) and (29). Thus the log likelihood function is that given by (22) plus the term

$$\sum_{i=1}^{N} \ln P_{i0}(\mathbf{x}).$$

As the reduced form estimates are not of great interest we present only the estimates of the α's and B's in Table 6.4.

Comparison of the coefficients in ln Wage in Table 6.4 with those in

Table 6.3 indicates only a small effect on the choice probabilities. The effect of wages on choice is slightly more pronounced in the manner that static labor market models suggests, but the effect on arrival rates still dominates by a large margin.

As a further check on these findings, logit specifications of the choice of destination state were estimated. For both males and females the results were the same as in Tables 6.3 and 6.4: wage rates do not explain the destination state.

To sum up, these data indicate that wage rates have a significant influence on the length of time spent in a particular state, but that this influence is due primarily to differences in the arrival rate of new events rather than to differences in preferences for particular labor market states. In other words, chance dominates choice in explaining dynamic labor market behavior.

6.6   Summary

This chapter has examined the problems of influence that arise in dynamic models of labor market activity. To account for observed movements of individuals among the states of employment, unemployment, and non-participation, previous research (Burdett et al. (1982), Flinn and Heckman (1982)) has modeled the process as the outcome of a random arrival time of "events" – changes in market and non-market opportunities – and a discrete choice of labor market state given that an event has occurred. Intuition based on the static models of labor supply suggests that labor force participation will increase if wages rise, because individuals will have greater preferences for participation. In the model developed here this intuition is shown to be correct only in the special case where arrival times of "events" are independent of labor market status. In general, the probability of observing a person in a particular state depends upon both the arrival rate and the choice probabilities, which we have called choice and chance. Hence, unlike the simple static model of labor supply, one cannot directly infer preferences from observed labor force frequencies. Necessary and sufficient conditions for inferring preferences are developed, but these conditions are generally violated whenever arrival rates depend upon market wages. It is therefore an empirical matter whether choice or chance dominates as an explanation of labor market activity.

Disentangling the separate effects of choice and chance raises an important identification issue. Flinn and Heckman's analysis of identification is examined and found to hold only if observations on the value of non-market time are available, a condition that is unlikely to ever be satisfied in a data set. For the case of serially uncorrelated events the method of Olsen and Farkas is shown to solve the identification problem provided the number of discrete choices is at least three. This method was applied to the data used by Burdett et al. to obtain estimates of the arrival rates and choice probabilities. The estimates indicated that although the transition rates across states were responsive to wages in the manner suggested by static models, the effects of higher wages were concentrated in the arrival rates rather than the choice probabilities. In sum, for these data chance dominates choice.

References

Billingsley, Patrick, *Statistical Inference for Markov Processes,* University of Chicago Press, Chicago (1961).

Blackwell, David, "Discounted Dynamic Programming," *Annals of Mathematical Statistics,* vol. 36 (1965), pp. 226–235.

Burdett, Kenneth, Nicholas M. Kiefer, Dale T. Mortensen and George R. Neumann, "Earnings, Unemployment, and the Allocation of Time Over Time," *Review of Economic Studies,* vol. 51 (1984), pp. 559–578. Chapter 5 in this volume.

Cox, David R., and P. A. Lewis, *The Statistical Analysis of Series of Events,* Methuen Co.: London (1966).

Flinn, Christopher, and James Heckman, "New Methods for Analyzing Structural Models of Labor Force Dynamics," *Journal of Econometrics,* vol. 18 (1982), pp. 115–168.

"Models for the Analysis of Labor Force Dynamics," in G. Rhodes and R. Basmenn, eds., *Advances in Econometrics.* JAI Press: London, Conn. (1982).

Heckman, James, "Sample Selection Bias as a Specification Error," *Econometrica,* vol. 47, no. 1 (1979), pp. 153–162.

Heyman, Daniel P., and Matthew J. Sobel, *Stochastic Models in Operations Research,* vol. 1, McGraw-Hill Book Co., New York (1982).

Lundberg, Shelly J., *Unemployment and Household Labor Supply,* unpublished doctoral dissertation, Northwestern University (1981).

Olsen, Randall J., and George Farkas, "Utility Maximization and Dynamic Employment Models: Black Youth Employment in the Public and Private Sectors," Ohio State University, mimeo (1982).

CHAPTER 7

Layoffs and duration dependence in a model of turnover

7.1 Introduction

The purpose of this chapter is to analyze and estimate a model of labor market turnover in which there is duration dependence. To achieve this goal a semi-Markov model of an individual's labor market history is constructed. Preliminary results presented here appear to support the claim that the particular semi-Markov specification derived in this study is preferred to the Markov specification.

Previous work on turnover in the context of behavioral models includes papers by Burdett et al. (1980) and Flinn and Heckman (1982). Recent empirical and theoretical work on turnover in the labor market has often emphasized a Markov model as the base case. The assumptions necessary to generate a Markov process for transitions between labor market states are discussed in Burdett et al. (1984). Heuristically, a Markov model requires conditions that guarantee that the probability an individual changes state depends only on the state currently occupied. Thus, restrictions are imposed which rule out that this individual's previous labor market history plays any role.

The Markov model is a natural extension of previous work done on job search. With job search models, however, only the transition from unemployment to employment is considered. The vast majority of job search models presented to date imply that the transition rate from unemployment does not depend on the duration in that state. Matching such a job search model with a simple model of job separation (in which the separation rate does not depend on the duration of employment) generates a Markov model of labor market turnover.

Relaxing the Markov specification, while maintaining an empirically tractable model, is no simple task. Often, if a model is specified which

This chapter was written by Kenneth Burdett, Nicholas M. Kiefer, and Sunil Sharma. It is reprinted from the *Journal of Econometrics*, vol. 28 (1985), by permission of Elsevier Science Publishers.

allows for the transition rates to depend on more than the state currently occupied, then these rates depend on all the individual's labor market history. In the present study a model will be specified in which the transition rate from unemployment to employment does not depend on the duration of unemployment. The transition rate from employment to unemployment, however, does depend on the duration of the current spell of employment. The basic reason for this duration dependence of the employment transition rates is that layoffs are often generated on the 'first in, last out' principle. It will be shown that an individual's reaction to this institutional constraint generates duration dependence in the employment transition. It should be noted that the reason for this duration dependence is quite different from that presented by Jovanovic (1984) or Mortensen (1984) where uncertainty about ability plays the major role.

After analyzing the theoretical model and obtaining predictions, some preliminary results are obtained based on the DIME data. Although reduced form estimates are obtained, a detailed structural analysis, following Mortensen and Neumann (1984) in separating acceptance rates from arrival rates (arrivals of layoffs or new offers), remains a topic for further study. Nevertheless, our results do indicate that our semi-Markov approach (with duration dependence in the employment transition rate) is an improvement over a purely Markov specification.

7.2   The model

At each instant in time the individual under consideration must occupy one of two labor market states: employment (state 1) or unemployment (state 2). The choice made at a moment will depend on the prevailing conditions. As these conditions change, however, he or she may choose to go to the other state. Some movements, such as being laid off when employed, are forced on the individual, whereas a new job offer when unemployed leaves open the option of changing state. Below a model of such decisions is outlined and analyzed.

Suppose an individual faces an infinite life span and attempts to maximize expected discounted lifetime income. Anytime he is unemployed, income flow u is received at each instant. The wage rate faced when employed, w, however, changes from time to time. Specifically, events occur (such as a promotion, a new job offer, a layoff, etc.), which implies a new wage rate will be faced when employed.

The arrival rate of events may depend on the state currently occupied and the duration of time in that state during the current spell. Below it will be assumed that the arrival rate of new job offers depends only on the state currently occupied, whereas the arrival rate of a layoff may also depend on the time spent in employment. Formally, suppose the arrival rate of a new job offer in state i can be described by a Poisson process with parameter α_i, $i = 1, 2$. Thus, the probability a new offer is received in small interval of time h whenever state i is occupied is $\alpha_i h + o(h)$, $i = 1, 2$. The arrival rate of a layoff may well depend on the duration of time since last unemployed. For example, many labor contracts negotiated stipulate that the last workers employed will be laid off first. Let the function $\mu(\cdot)$ describe the arrival rate of a layoff when employed so that $\mu(s)$ is the arrival rate at time s since last unemployed. It will be assumed that $\mu(\cdot)$ is a decreasing function. Obviously, the arrival rate of a layoff when unemployed is zero.

Given a new wage offer has been received, let $F(\overline{w}; X)$ indicate the probability that w is less than $\overline{w}$ on a particular draw, where X is a vector describing the individual's fixed characteristics such as his or her race, sex, date of birth, education, etc. Thus, $F(\cdot; X)$ is a cumulative distribution function. For mathematical convenience, it will be assumed that a worker who has been laid off faces a wage rate of minus infinity. This completes the description of the environment faced by the worker.

Consider first the situation where the worker is unemployed. As the arrival rate of new job offers is independent of the duration in unemployment, an unemployed worker faces essentially the same problem at each instant. Let $V_2(X)$ denote the expected discounted lifetime income when unemployed. Letting r denote the discount rate, and u the utility flow when unemployed, it follows for a small time interval, h, that

$$V_2(X) = \frac{1}{1 + rh} [uh + \alpha_2 hT(0; X) + (1 - \alpha_2 h)V_2(X)] + o(h), \tag{1}$$

given

$$T(t_1; X) = \int \max\{V_2(X), V_1(\tilde{w}, t_1; X)\} \, d\tilde{F}(w; X), \tag{2}$$

where $V_1(w, t; X)$ denotes the maximum expected discounted lifetime income of a worker who has been continuously employed for time t_1 and currently faces wage rate w (later conditions will be imposed to guarantee the existence of such a maximum). Dividing (1) by h, manipulating, and then letting h go to zero yields

$$V_2(X) = \frac{u + \alpha_2 T(0; X)}{r + \alpha_2}. \tag{3}$$

The situation is not so simple when the worker is employed, as the arrival rate of a layoff may vary with duration. Suppose the individual has been employed in the current spell for time t_1 and currently faces wage rate w. Any future this individual may face if he continues to remain employed can be fully represented by an infinite sequence of doubletons, $\tau = ((w_1, a_1), (w_2, a_2), (w_3, a_3), \ldots)$, where w_k denotes the wage faced after the kth event (from now), and a_k indicates the time from now when the kth event will occur. Let Ω denote the space of all such sequences.

The probability laws generating such possible futures can be constructed. Specifically, α_1, $\mu(\cdot)$, and $F(\cdot; X)$ can be used to specify the probability measure $\Phi_x(\cdot; t_1)$ on possible futures given X, and that the duration in the current spell is t_1. When should he or she leave employment for unemployment? Any possible strategy to quit employment can be characterized by a stopping time function $s(\cdot)$. Any function $s(\cdot)$ is a stopping time function if

(a) $s(\tau) \geq 0$ for all $\tau \in \Omega$, and
(b) if τ and τ' have same first m elements and $s(\tau) \leq a_m$, then $s(\tau) = s(\tau')$.

Condition (b) above implies that any strategy used can only be based on what the individual has observed and the underlying probability laws. The space of all such functions, $s(\cdot)$, is indicated by S.

Let $\Gamma(w, t_1, s; X)$ denote the worker's expected discounted lifetime income, given duration of employment in the current spell is t_1, the wage rate faced is w, vector X, and stopping time function $s(\cdot)$. It follows that

$$\Gamma(w, t_1, s; X) = \int \theta(\tau, w, \ s; X) \, d\Phi_x(\tau; t_1), \tag{4}$$

where

$$\theta(\tau, w, t_1, s; X) = \int_0^{a_1} we^{-rt} \, dt + \sum_{j=1}^{k-1}$$
$$\times \int_{a_j}^{a_{j+1}} w_j e^{-rt} \, dt + \int_{a_k}^{s(\tau)} w_k e^{-rt} \, dt$$
$$+ e^{-s(\tau)r} V_2(X), \tag{5}$$

given

$$a_k \leq s(\tau) < a_{k+1}.$$

Using standard techniques [see, for example, DeGroot (1970)], for any given w and t_1, there exists $s^*(\cdot; X)$ such that

$$\Gamma(w, t_1, s^*; X) = \max_{s \in S} \Gamma(w, t_1, s; X). \tag{6}$$

Let $V_1(w, t_1; X) = \Gamma(w, t_1, s^*; X)$, i.e., $V_1(w, t_1; X)$ is the maximum expected discounted lifetime income (given w, t_1, and X). It follows immediately that the individual will choose to be employed if and only if

$$V_1(w, t_1; X) > V_2(X).$$

Some properties of $V_1(\cdot; X)$ can now be stated.

Proposition 1

(a) $V_1(w, t_1; X) \geq V_2(X)$ for all w and t_1 [if $s^*(\tau; X) = 0$ for all $\tau \in \Omega$, then $V_1(w, t_1; X) = V_2(X)$].

(b) $V_1(\cdot; X)$ is (strictly) increasing in w [if $s^*(\tau; X) > 0$ for some $\tau \in \Omega$].

(c) $V_1(\cdot; X)$ is (strictly) increasing in t_1 [if $s^*(\tau; X) > 0$ for some $\tau \in \Omega$ and $\mu(\cdot)$ is strictly decreasing]. $V_1(\cdot; X)$ is independent of t_1 if $\mu(\cdot)$ is a constant.

(d) For any given w and t_1, $s^*(\cdot; X)$ is such that the individual will only quit employment immediately after an event occurs. (Obviously, a layoff event always implies the individual will quit employment.)

Proof. To establish (a) note that if $s(\cdot) = 0$ for all $\tau \in \Omega$, then $\Gamma(w, t_1, s; X) = V_2(X)$. Claim (b) follows from inspection of (5). To establish claim (c) note that if $\mu(\cdot)$ is strictly decreasing, then $\Phi_X(\cdot; t_1)$ is such that $\Pr(w_m = -\infty, m = 1, 2, \ldots | t_1)$ is strictly decreasing with respect to t_1. It also follows that if $\mu(\cdot)$ is a constant, then $\Phi_X(\cdot; t_1)$ is such that $\Pr(w_m = \infty, m = 1, 2, \ldots | t_1)$ is constant with respect to t_1. As the individual will only select to be employed if $V_1(w, t_1; X) > V_2(X)$, he will always regret being laid off and thus $V_1(\cdot; X)$ is a (strictly) increasing function of t_1 [if $\mu(\cdot)$ is strictly decreasing]. Claim (d) follows directly from the previous claims.

Given claim (d) in Proposition 1, the maximum expected discounted lifetime income when employed, $V_1(\cdot; X)$, can be constructed (without loss of generality) assuming he or she will only leave employment immediately after an event. Thus, for small enough h ($h > 0$) we have

$$V_1(w, t_1; X) = \frac{1}{1 + rh} [wh + \alpha_1 h\{J(t_1, h)V_2(X)$$

$$+ (1 - J(t_1, h))T(t_1 + h; X)\}$$

$$+ (1 - \alpha_1 h)\{J(t_1, h)V_2(X)$$

$$+ (1 - J(t_1, h))V_1(w, t_1 + h; X)\}] + \bar{o}(h^2), \quad (7)$$

where $J(t_1, h)$ indicates the probability the individual will be laid off in the time period $[t_1, t_1 + h]$, i.e.,

$$J(t_1, h) = \mu(t_1)h - \int_0^h \{[\mu(t_1) - \mu(t_1 + m)]/m\} \, dm. \quad (8)$$

Manipulating (7) and (8), and then letting h go to zero yields

$$V_1(w, t_1; X) = \frac{w + \mu(t_1)V_2(X) + \alpha_1 T(t_1; X) + V_1'(w, t; X)}{\mu(t_1) + \alpha_1 + r}, \quad (9)$$

where $V_1'(\cdot)$ denotes the derivative of $V_1(\cdot)$ with respect to t. The major properties of the individual's optimal strategy can now be stated without proof as they follow directly from Proposition 1, (3) and (9).

Proposition 2. Suppose the individual has been employed for time t_1 in the current spell ($t_1 = 0$, if presently unemployed) and faces wage rate w. The strategy that maximizes this individual's expected discounted lifetime income can be characterized by the function $z(t_1; X)$ such that he or she will choose to be employed if and only if $w > z(t_1; X)$. Further, $z(\cdot; X)$ (strictly) decreases with t_1 [if $\mu(\cdot)$ is strictly decreasing]. If $\mu(\cdot)$ is a constant, then $z(\cdot; X)$ is a constant.

From Proposition 2 it is straightforward to establish that the individual's labor market history can be described by a semi-Markov process. A two-state semi-Markov process can be completely characterized by two numbers, p_1 and p_2, and two distribution functions, $H_1(\cdot)$ and $H_2(\cdot)$, such that

(a) p_i denotes the probability state i will be left anytime it is occupied, $i = 1, 2$, and

(b) $H_i(t_i)$ denotes the probability state i will be left no later than t_i conditional on leaving, $i = 1, 2$.

A two-state Markov process is a semi-Markov process with the added restriction that $H_i(\cdot)$, $i = 1, 2$, is an exponential distribution function. Note that if $p_i = 1$, $i = 1, 2$, then $H_i(t_i) = 1$ as t_i goes to infinity. An intuitive explanation of the above technical definition can be presented as follows. Let $\pi_i(w, t_i, D, X)$ denote the transition rate (which in a two-state model is the same as the hazard rate) from state i given (a) w is the wage faced when employed, (b) t_i is the duration of the current spell in state i, (c) D is a vector describing the individual's labor market history to date, i.e., wage rate faced at each instant in the past, dates jobs were obtained and lost, etc. (but not w or t_i), and (d) X is the vector describing the fixed characteristics of the individual described above. The vector X determines the opportunities to be faced in the labor market. The individual's labor market history can be described by a two-state semi-Markov process if

$$\pi_i(w, t_i, D, X) = \pi_i(w, t_i, D', X) \qquad \text{for all } D, D', \qquad i = 1, 2, \quad (10)$$

i.e., previous labor market history plays no role. Further, his or her labor market history can be described by a Markov process if

$$\pi_i(w, t_i, D, X) = \pi_i(w, t_i', D', X) \qquad \text{for all } D, D', t_i, t_i',$$
$$i = 1, 2, \qquad \qquad (11)$$

i.e., previous labor market history and duration in the current state play no role.

Let $\pi_i(\cdot)$ (defined above) indicate the transition rate in state i in the model specified above. It follows that

$$\pi_1(w, t_1, D, X) = \alpha_1 F(z(t_1; X); X) + \mu(t_1), \qquad (12)$$

and

$$\pi_2(w, t_2, D, X) = \alpha_2[1 - F(z(0); X)]. \qquad (13)$$

Note that both transition rates are independent of D and w. Further, $\pi_1(\cdot)$ is a decreasing function of t_1, whereas $\pi_2(\cdot)$ is independent of t_2. Thus, to simplify the notation, let $\pi_i(t_i; X) = \pi_i(w, t_i, D, X)$. Restrictions will now be used to guarantee the individual continues to change state, i.e., $p_i = 1$, $i = 1, 2$. This is the more interesting case to consider although the extension to the situation where $p_i < 1$ is straightforward. Assume $z(\cdot)$ is such that $0 < F(z(t_i); X) < 1$. In this case $p_i = 1$, $i = 1, 2$. The next proposition is stated without proof as it follows directly from Proposition 2, (12), and (13).

Proposition 3. Given the model outlined above, the individual's labor market history can be described by a two-state semi-Markov process such that

$$H_i(t_i; X) = 1 - \exp\left\{ -\int_0^{t_i} \pi_i(m, X)\, dm \right\}, \qquad i = 1, 2, \qquad (14)$$

where $H_2(\cdot; X)$ is an exponential distribution function. Further, if $\mu(\cdot)$ is a constant, then the individual's labor market history can be described by a two-state Markov process, i.e., in this case $H_1(\cdot; X)$ is also an exponential distribution function.

In the final part of this section different individuals will be considered. To obtain results two simplifications will be made to the model presented above. First, it will be assumed that the vector of fixed characteristics associated with an individual, X, can be fully described by a real number, x, which we will interpret as his or her human capital wage. Second, assume the actual wage faced by an individual at a moment in time, w, can be written as $w = x + e$, where e is the realization of a random variable. Suppose this random variable is distributed independently of x and has zero mean. Let $G(\cdot)$ indicate the distribution function associated with e. Given these restrictions $V_1(w, t_1, X)$ can be written as

$$V_1(e, t_1, x) = \frac{x + e + \mu(t_1)V_2 + \alpha_1 T(t_1, x) + V_1'(e, t_1, x)}{(r + \mu(t_1) + \alpha_1)}. \qquad (15)$$

Further, the reservation wage, $z(t_1, X)$, can be rewritten as $z(t_1, X) = x + \bar{e}(t_1, x)$. With the above construction we now demonstrate how the transition rates change as individuals with different human capital are considered.

Given the restrictions made above, the transition rates (or hazard rates) can be written as

$$\pi_1(t_1, x) = \alpha_1 G(\bar{e}(t_1, x)) + \mu(t_1), \qquad (16a)$$

and

$$\pi_2(t_2, x) = \alpha_2[1 - G(\bar{e}(t_1, x))]. \qquad (16b)$$

The final proposition can now be stated.

Proposition 4. The transition rate out of employment (given any particular duration, t_1) decreases as the human capital wage increases. Further, an increase in the human capital wage increases the transition rate from unemployment.

Proof. From (16a) and (16b) it can be seen that the claims made above will hold if $d\bar{e}(t_1, x)/dx < 0$. To establish that this condition holds note that

$$\frac{d\bar{e}(t_1, x)}{dx} = \frac{\partial V_2(x)/\partial x - \partial V_1(z(t_1, x), x)/\partial x}{\partial V_1(z(t_1, x))/\partial e}. \tag{17}$$

As it is straightforward to show that the numerator on the right-hand side of (17) is negative, the claims are established.

This result implies that the wage coefficient in the employment to unemployment transition, holding duration constant, should be negative, and that the coefficient in the unemployment to employment transition should be positive. Signs of the estimated coefficients can then be used as the basis of an informal specification check.

7.3   Estimation

The model presented provides a conceptual framework for studying individual labor market histories. The empirical implication of the model is that only two observable characteristics of an individual, state currently occupied and duration of time in current state since last change of state, determine the probability of transition between states. In order to specify the likelihood function for a sample of K spells, we focus on the duration of time spent in each state and the frequency of these transitions.

We identify four types of spells:

(1)   completed unemployment spell,
(2)   incomplete unemployment spell (right or left censored); since the duration distribution in unemployment is exponential, left and right censored spells can be treated symmetrically.
(3)   completed employment spells, and
(4)   incomplete employment spells (right censored only); the left censored incomplete spells were ignored because of the problem of initializing the spells, i.e., the problem of determining the length of time spent in the spell before the individual is observed.

The contribution of each type of spell to the likelihood function is

(1) $\pi_2 \exp\{-\pi_2 \cdot t\}$,

(2) $\exp\{-\pi_2 \cdot t\}$,

(3) $\pi_1(t) \exp\left\{ - \int_0^t \pi_1(\tau) d\tau \right\}$, and

(4) $\exp\left\{ - \int_0^t \pi_1(\tau) d\tau \right\}$.

The likelihood function for a sample of K spells can be written as

$$\prod_{i_1=1}^{K_1} \pi_2^{(i_1)} \exp\{-\pi_2^{(i_1)} t_{i_1}\} \cdot \prod_{i_2=1}^{K_2} \exp\{-\pi_2^{(i_2)} t_{i_2}\},$$

$$\prod_{i_3=1}^{K_3} \pi_1^{(i_3)}(t_{i_3}) \exp\left\{ - \int_0^{t_{i_3}} \pi_1^{(i_3)}(\tau) \, d\tau \right\},$$

$$\prod_{i_4=1}^{K_4} \pi_1^{(i_4)}(t_{i_4}) \exp\left\{ - \int_0^{t_{i_4}} \pi_1^{(i_4)}(\tau) \, d\tau \right\},$$

where $K_1 + K_2 + K_3 + K_4 = K$, and K_j indicates the number of spells of type j, listed above.

The model is implemented by assuming functional forms for $\pi_j(t)$, $j = 1, 2$. We expect that the hazard rates among workers will differ, depending on individual characteristics such as race (black, white, hispanic), age, education, etc. Let X_i be the vector of characteristics for the ith individual. The observable vector X_i is related to the instantaneous probability of leaving each state using Cox's proportional-hazard framework. In this framework, the hazard is assumed to factor into a function of time and a function of the observable X_i. For the ith individual we have $\pi^{(i)}(t) = \psi(t_i)\phi(X_i)$, where t_i is the duration in the current state. A natural assumption for $\phi(X_i)$ is $\exp(X_i\beta)$, where β is a vector of parameters, because it ensures the non-negativity of $\pi^{(i)}(t)$. Since the unemployment hazard is independent of time, we specify $\pi_2^{(i)}(t) = \exp(X_i\beta)$, i.e., $\psi(t) = 1$. This implies an exponential duration distribution in unemployment with mean $\exp(-X_i\beta)$. The time dependence of the employment hazard is captured by specifying $\pi_1^{(i)}(t) = \lambda t_i^{\lambda-1} \exp(X_i\beta)$. This specification implies a Weibull distribution for the durations in employment, and has been widely used in statistics, biostatistics and more recently economics. It is sufficiently flexible to allow for negative or positive duration dependence. If $\lambda < 1$ the hazard decreases with duration, if $\lambda > 1$ it increases with duration, and if $\lambda = 1$ we get the exponential hazard.

Consider the estimation of the parameters of the employment to unemployment transition. Suppose we have data on N employment spells of which N_1 are complete and N_2 are right censored. The Weibull specification implies that the density function is $\lambda t^{\lambda-1} \exp[X\beta - t^\lambda e^{X\beta}]$ and the survivor function is $\exp[-t^\lambda e^{X\beta}]$. The loglikelihood can be written as

$$
\begin{aligned}
l &= \sum_{i=1}^{N_1} \{\ln \lambda + (\lambda - 1) \ln t_i + X_i\beta - t_i^\lambda e^{X_i\beta}\} + \sum_{j=1}^{N_2} \{-t_j^\lambda e^{X_{ji}\beta}\} \\
&= \sum_{i=1}^{N_2} \{\ln \lambda + (\lambda - 1) \ln t_i + X_i\beta\} + \sum_{j=1}^{N} \{-t_j^\lambda e^{X_{ji}\beta}\} \\
&= \sum_{i=1}^{N} [\delta_i \{\ln \lambda + (\lambda - 1) \ln t_i + X_i\beta\} - \{t_i^\lambda e^{X_i\beta}\}],
\end{aligned}
$$

where δ_i is 0 if spell is censored, and 1 if spell is complete.

The loglikelihood function was maximized using the Newton–Raphson method. Let $\gamma = [\lambda\beta']'$, where β is a $m \times 1$ vector of parameters, corresponding to the m covariates in vector X_i (which includes a constant term).

$$
\frac{\partial l}{\partial \gamma} = \begin{bmatrix} \sum_{i=1}^{N} \left[\delta_i\left\{\frac{1}{\lambda} + \ln t_i\right\} - \{t_i^\lambda \ln t_i \exp(X_i\beta)\} \right] \\ \sum_{i=1}^{N} [\delta_i X_{im} - t_i^\lambda \exp(X_i\beta)X_{im}] \end{bmatrix}
$$

$$
\frac{\partial l^2}{\partial \gamma\, \partial \gamma'} = \begin{bmatrix} \dfrac{\partial l}{\partial \lambda\, \partial \lambda} & \dfrac{\partial l}{\partial \lambda\, \partial \beta'} \\ \dfrac{\partial l}{\partial \beta\, \partial \lambda'} & \dfrac{\partial l}{\partial \beta\, \partial \beta'} \end{bmatrix},
$$

where

$$
\frac{\partial l}{\partial \lambda\, \partial \lambda} = \sum_{i=1}^{N} \left[\delta_i\left\{\frac{-1}{\lambda^2}\right\} - \{t_i^\lambda(\ln t_i)^2 \exp(X_i\beta)\} \right],
$$

$$
\frac{\partial l}{\partial \lambda\, \partial \beta'} = \sum_{i=1}^{N} - t_i^\lambda \ln t_i \exp(X_i\beta)X_i',
$$

$$
\frac{\partial l}{\partial \beta\, \partial \beta'} = \sum_{i=1}^{N} - t_i^\lambda \exp(X_i\beta)X_i'X_i.
$$

The iterative procedure used was

$$\gamma_{s+1} = \gamma_s - \left[\frac{\partial^2 l}{\partial \gamma\, \partial \gamma'}\right]^{-1}_{\gamma=\gamma_s} \left[\frac{\partial l}{\partial \gamma}\right]_{\gamma=\gamma_s}.$$

The convergence criterion used was that the sum of the squared deviations in the individual elements of γ_{s+1} and γ_s not exceed 10^{-3}. Convergence was always achieved. The matrix $[-\partial^2 l/\partial \gamma\, \partial \gamma']^{-1}$ was taken as the estimated asymptotic covariance matrix of the parameter estimates.

7.4   Specification diagnostics

In this section we develop a statistic for testing functional form misspecification in the employment duration distribution. For ease of exposition, the subscripts are dropped and the hazard function and density function written as

$$\pi = \lambda t^{\lambda-1} \exp(X\beta), \qquad g(t; X) = \lambda t^{\lambda-1} \exp(X\beta) \exp\{-t^\lambda \exp(X\beta)\}.$$

Suppose that the individual characteristics in the vector X do not sufficiently control for heterogeneity. The actual hazard function is

$$\pi = \lambda t^{\lambda-1} \exp(X\beta + v),$$

where v is an unobserved random variable whose distribution is not known. One interpretation of v is that the population sampled is heterogeneous with respect to the constant term in X. (It could also be interpreted as arising out of the effect of measurement error in X or t.)

Let the distribution of v across spells be given by the density function $q(v)$. The duration density of t, given X and v, is

$$g(t; X, v) = \lambda t^{\lambda-1} \exp(X\beta + v) \exp\{-t^\lambda \exp(X\beta + v)\},$$

while the duration density conditional on X only, which is relevant for data analysis, is

$$g(t; X) = \int_{-\infty}^{+\infty} g(t; X, v) q(v)\, dv.$$

Given a constant term in vector X, without loss of generality, we can assume $E(v) = 0$. The density $q(v)$ is not known, and hence we need a test-statistic which does not require knowledge of v.

The null hypothesis is that there is no misspecification, which can be viewed as asking whether σ^2, the variance of v, is zero. With the alternative hypothesis of small misspecifications we approximate $g(t; X, v)$ with a Taylor expansion around $v = 0$, and since $E(v) = 0$, neglecting terms of higher order than two, we can write

$$g(t; X, v) \approx g(t; X, 0) + v \left[\frac{\partial g(t; X, v)}{\partial v} \right]_{v=0} + \frac{v^2}{2} \left[\frac{\partial^2 g(t; X, v)}{\partial v^2} \right]_{v=0}.$$

Integrating with respect to $q(v)$ gives

$$g(t; X) = g(t; X, 0) + \frac{\sigma^2}{2} \left[\frac{\partial^2 g(t; X, v)}{\partial v^2} \right]_{v=0}.$$

Twice differentiating $g(t; X, v)$ with respect to v and evaluating at $v = 0$, the second derivative is

$$\left[\frac{\partial^2 g(t; X, v)}{\partial v^2} \right]_{v=0} = \lambda t^{\lambda-1} \eta \exp\{-t^{\lambda}\eta\}[1 - 3t^{\lambda}\eta + t^{2\lambda}\eta^2],$$

where

$$\eta = \exp(X\beta),$$

and substituting we get

$$g(t; X) = \lambda t^{\lambda-1} \eta \exp\{-t^{\lambda}\eta\} + \frac{\sigma^2}{2} \lambda t^{\lambda-1} \eta$$
$$\times \exp\{-t^{\lambda}\eta\}[1 - 3t^{\lambda}\eta + t^{2\lambda}\eta^2].$$

The survivor function for above density is

$$\bar{G}(t; X) = \left(\frac{1 + \sigma^2}{2} \right) \Gamma(1, \eta t^{\lambda}) - \frac{3\sigma^2}{2} \Gamma(2, \eta t^{\lambda}) + \frac{\sigma^2}{2} \Gamma(3, \eta t^{\lambda}),$$

where

$$\Gamma(a, z) = \int_z^{\infty} e^{-u} u^{a-1} \, du$$

is the incomplete gamma function.

The proposed diagnostic statistic for misspecification is a score (or Lagrange multiplier) statistic for the hypothesis $\sigma^2 = 0$. The loglikelihood function for N spells, of which N_1 are complete and N_2 are censored, is

$$l = \sum_{i=1}^{N_1} \ln g(t_i; X_i) + \sum_{j=1}^{N_2} \ln \bar{G}(t_j; X_j)$$

$$= \sum_{i=1}^{N} [\delta_i \ln g(t_i; X_i) + (1 + \delta_i) \ln \bar{G}(t_i; X_i)]$$

$$= \sum_{i=1}^{N} \left[\delta_i \left\{ \ln \lambda + (\lambda - 1) \ln t_i + \ln \eta_i - t_i^{\lambda} \eta_i \right. \right.$$

$$\left. + \ln \left[1 + \frac{\sigma^2}{2} (1 - 3t_i^{\lambda} \eta_i + t_i^{2\lambda} \eta_i) \right] \right\}$$

$$+ (1 - \delta_i) \left\{ \ln \left[\left(\frac{1 + \sigma^2}{2} \right) \Gamma(1, t_i^{\lambda}, \eta_i) \right. \right.$$

$$\left. \left. \left. - \frac{3\sigma^2}{2} \Gamma(2, t_i^{\lambda}, \eta_i) + \frac{\sigma^2}{2} \Gamma(3, t_i^{\lambda}, \eta_i) \right] \right\} \right].$$

The mean score for σ^2 evaluated at $\sigma^2 = 0$ is

$$S = \frac{1}{N} \cdot \frac{\partial l}{\partial \sigma^2} \bigg|_{\sigma^2 = 0}$$

$$= \frac{1}{2N} \sum_{i=1}^{N} \left[\delta_i \{1 - 3t_i^{\lambda} \eta_i + t_i^{\lambda} \eta_i^2 \} \right.$$

$$\left. + (1 + \delta_i) \frac{\{\Gamma(1, t_i^{\lambda} \eta_i) - 3\Gamma(2, t_i^{\lambda} \eta_i) + \Gamma(3, t_i^{\lambda} \eta_i)\}}{\Gamma(1, t_i^{\lambda} \eta_i)} \right],$$

where δ_i is 0 if spell is censored, and 1 if spell is complete. The expressions derived above are evaluated at the maximum likelihood estimate of β under the null hypothesis.

Let

$$\xi_i = \left[\delta_i \{1 - 3t_i^{\lambda} \eta_i + t_i^{\lambda} \eta_i^2 \} \right.$$

$$\left. + (1 - \delta_i) \frac{\{\Gamma(1, t_i^{\lambda} \eta_i) - 3\Gamma(2, t_i^{\lambda} \eta_i) + \Gamma(3, t_i^{\lambda} \eta_i)\}}{\Gamma(1, t_i^{\lambda} \eta_i)} \right].$$

The variance of S is estimated by $(1/4N^2)\sum_{i=1}^{N}(\xi_i - \bar{\xi})^2$, where $\bar{\xi}$ is the sample mean of ξ_i. The proposed test statistic $Z = S/\sqrt{\text{var}(S)}$ is asymptotically standard normal, conditionally on the estimated values of α and β, and a one-tailed test is used to examine the null hypothesis $\sigma^2 > 0$

(corresponding locally to $S > 0$). The test proposed is consistent and, as a Lagrange multiplier test, has maximum local asymptotic power for 'small' misspecifications.

A similar test can be used for analyzing the duration distribution in unemployment. The diagnostic statistic for the exponential distribution is a special case of that developed above when $\lambda = 1$ [see Kiefer (1984)]. Lancaster (1985) shows that this 'small-σ' approach to constructing diagnostics can be applied quite generally. Lancaster estimates the unconditional variance of the test statistic, rather than conditioning on estimated parameters. Thus, Lancaster focusses on the hypothesis of heterogeneity per se, while we are more interested in the statistical adequacy of the *estimated* models, with an eye to comparing specifications. Lancaster does not consider censored data, in the interest of simplicity, though the (routine) calculations will have to be made in applications.

7.5   The data

The information on individual labor histories used in the empirical analysis comes from the Denver Income Maintenance Experiment (DIME) data set. The purpose of the experiment was to measure the effect of a negative income tax on labor supply. The families enrolled in DIME met the following criteria:

(i)   *race:* head of family had to be white, black or hispanic,

(ii) *family type:* a two-head or single-head family, with at least one dependent.

(iii) *family income:* pre-experiment earnings (in 1970–71 dollars) were under $9,000 for a family of four with one head, or under $11,000 for a two-head family.

(iv) *head of family:* age 18 to 58 years and capable of gainful employment.

The Public Use files are organized in a monthly format and contain data, covering 48 months, on demographic characteristics, employment, earnings and unemployment for each principal person (head of family). The data were used to construct histories of labor market status (number, timing and sequence of all changes in status) using Current Population Survey Definitions. The unit of observation was the length of a spell of employment or unemployment. Complete and censored spells were differentiated, and for each spell a number of individual characteristics

Table 7.1. *Summary statistics*

Variable	Mean	Standard deviation
Age	29.21	9.73
Education (in years)	11.09	2.17
Wage ($ 1970)	2.80	1.12
Employment duration (days)	520	536
Unemployment duration (days)	139.15	191.88
Black (proportion)	0.321	—
Hispanic (proportion)	0.336	—

Note: Total number of spells 3132. Data are for adult males, ages > 17.9.

and labor market variables relating to the person experiencing the spell were recorded. An instrument for expected wages was constructed by regressing the natural logarithm of wage on age, age squared, education, race and other demographic variables. [See Sharma (1985) for details.] This was done for each quarter and each unemployment spell matched to the wage instrument of the appropriate quarter. Wage rates are deflated by Denver CPI for each of the years 1971–74.

Summary statistics of the sample used are provided in Table 7.1. For a detailed discussion of experimental design, data and results, refer to SRI (1983) and Public use files compiled by MPR (1978). Lundberg (1981) has discussed the construction of data on labor market spells.

7.6   Preliminary empirical results

This section reports our results from a preliminary examination of the DIME data. These results are meant to be suggestive; for a full analysis, see Sharma (1985). The fitting of the Weibull distribution with time independent covariates shows that there is negative duration dependence in employment. This implies that the longer a worker has been employed, the smaller is the probability of transition to unemployment. Part of this duration dependence is clearly spurious because of heterogeneity (which seems to be indicated by the diagnostic statistic z), and hence the results presented in Table 7.2 must be taken merely as suggestive. The estimate of the duration dependence parameter alpha is 0.69. The signs of the covariate coefficients accord with intuition. Age initially has a decreasing effect and then an increasing effect on the probability of transition to unemployment. A more educated individual is less likely to exit the em-

Table 7.2. *Employment to unemployment transition*

Variable	Coefficient (standard error in parentheses)				
Alpha	0.659	0.689	0.692	0.693	0.693
	(0.0174)	(0.0181)	(0.0182)	(0.1745)	(0.0182)
Constant	−4.526	−1.695	−1.103	−1.290	−0.805
	(0.1181)	(0.3470)	(0.3955)	(0.4047)	(0.7930)
Age		−0.165	−0.164	−0.167	−0.164
		(0.0215)	(0.0216)	(0.0217)	(0.0221)
Age squared		0.191	0.185	0.190	0.186
		(0.0311)	(0.0316)	(0.0315)	(0.0320)
Education			−0.050	0.040	0.039
			(0.0158)	(0.0167)	(0.0167)
Black				0.125	0.124
				(0.0784)	(0.0785)
Hispanic				0.178	0.177
				(0.0813)	(0.0813)
Log wage					−0.097
					(0.1364)
Diagnostic statistic (z)	5.195	3.858	3.680	3.719	3.718
Loglikelihood	−7544.8	−7477.4	−7472.8	−7469.8	−7469.6

Note: 1707 spells in employment were considered, of which 986 were complete.

ployment state. The positive signs on the dummy variables for race indicate that the incidence of unemployment is likely to be higher for blacks and hispanics. The addition of the (economic) variable wage does not significantly improve the fit.

Table 7.3 gives the estimates of the parameters in the unemployment duration distribution. The effect of age is initially positive and then negative. Higher education leads to a higher exit rate from the unemployment state. Blacks and hispanics are likely to have longer unemployment spells. Predicted wage has a positive effect.[1]

The diagnostic statistic in both the tables indicates the presence of misspecification. Also, since z takes approximately the same value across specifications, choice of regressors is left open. The results represent a first attempt at estimation and one needs to 'correct' for other characteristics such as whether an individual is married, has kids, is a welfare recipient, what his assets are and whether he is a member of a two-head family. More detailed specifications will presumably decrease the unobserved heterogeneity.

Using the estimates of Tables 7.2 and 7.3, the steady state unemployment rates for the different race groups were calculated. The means of the covariates for the different races and their steady state unemployment rates are presented in Table 7.4.

7.7   Conclusion

The model presented provides a simple framework for analyzing the incidence and duration of unemployment. It contributes to our understanding of how unemployment is generated and why it differs across various groups in the population. In the context of the model one can examine how the demographic and economic characteristics of a particular segment of the population affect the steady state unemployment rates.

Admittedly, the model imposes a special structure on labor market transitions and the estimates must be seen in this light. Further, the model does not do justice to the demand side of the labor market. Fluctuations in demand are important determinants of turnover. One expects that the layoff policies of firms and the quit behavior of labor market participants

---

[1] As a specification check the Weibull model was fit to the unemployment to employment transition. The duration dependence parameter was estimated as 0.84, close to one (exponential) but, with a standard error of 0.019, significantly different from one by usual standards. This finding clearly requires further consideration.

7.3. *Unemployment to employment transition*

Variable	Coefficient (standard error in parentheses)			
Constant	-4.960	-6.128	-6.605	-6.451	-8.422
	(0.0308)	(0.3142)	(0.3427)	(0.3567)	(0.7527)
Age		0.094	0.086	0.088	0.079
		(0.0199)	(0.0197)	(0.0196)	(0.0198)
Age squared		-0.165	-0.147	-0.148	-0.136
		(0.0290)	(0.0288)	(0.0286)	(0.0289)
Education			0.050	0.049	0.047
			(0.0153)	(0.0160)	(0.0161)
Black				-0.366	-0.353
				(0.0760)	(0.0761)
Hispanic				-0.149	-0.155
				(0.0782)	(0.0780)
Log wage					0.391
					(0.1312)
Diagnostic statistic (z)	5.81	5.59	5.51	5.03	4.99
Loglikelihood	-6263.8	-6215.3	-6209.8	-6197.98	-6193.4

Note: 1180 spells in unemployment were considered, of which 806 were complete.

Table 7.4. *Sample by race groups*

	White	Hispanic	Black
	Means		
Age	28.698	28.783	30.199
Education	11.751	10.244	11.264
Wage	5.496	5.506	5.489
	Steady state unemployment rates[a]		
	7.69	12.83	12.29

[a]Including non-participation.

would be determined by the conditions in the labor market. When demand for workers is high relative to supply, firms will layoff workers at a slower rate (if at all) because of the difficulty of getting appropriate replacements, whereas the quit rate will be high since jobs can be easily found. In a slack labor market the reverse would be true. The layoff rate would be high and workers would not quit since jobs are difficult to come by. Also, the distinction between layoffs and quits is important. Matilla (1974) pointed out that a large proportion of quits are from one job to another without an intervening unemployment spell. Hence, for the same rate of turnover a higher proportion of layoffs would be expected to lead to a higher rate of unemployment. Existing models of labor market dynamics do not permit this separation of layoffs from those transitions which are of a voluntary character. The simultaneous modelling of demand and supply sides of the labor market in models of turnover is a topic for future research.

Acknowledgments

We would like to thank Dale Mortensen and Lars Muus and participants in the Economics Seminar at Cornell for helpful discussions. This research was partially supported by the NSF.

References

Abramowitz, M., and I. A. Stegun, eds., 1965, Handbook of mathematical functions (Dover, New York).
Burdett, K., and D. T. Mortensen, 1978, Labor supply under uncertainty, in: R. G. Eh-

renberg, ed., Research in labour economics, Vol. 2 (JAI Press, Greenwich, CT), 109–158.

Burdett, K., N. M. Kiefer, D. T. Mortensen and G. R. Neumann, 1980, A dynamic model of employment, unemployment and labor force participation. Estimates from the DIME data, Manuscript.

1984, Earnings, unemployment, and the allocation of time over time, Review of Economic Studies 51, 559–578. Chapter 5 in this volume.

Clark, K. B., and L. H. Summers, 1979, Labor market dynamics and unemployment: A reconsideration, Brookings Papers on Economic Activity, 13–60.

DeGroot, M. H., 1970, Optimal statistical decisions (McGraw Hill, New York).

Flinn, C., and J. Heckman, 1982, New methods for analyzing structural models of labor force dynamics, in: J. Heckman and B. Singer, eds., Annals of Applied Econometrics, 119–168.

Hall, R. E., 1972, Turnover in the labor force, Brookings Paper on Economic Activity, 709–756.

Jovanovic, B., 1984, Matching, turnover and unemployment, Journal of Political Economy 92, 108–222.

Kiefer, N. M., 1984, A simple test for heterogeneity in exponential models of duration, Journal of Labor Economics 2, 539–549.

Lancaster, T., 1985, Generalised residuals and heterogeneous duration models: With applications to the Weibull model, Journal of Econometrics 28, 155–169.

Lundberg, S. J., 1981, Unemployment and household labor supply, Ph.D. dissertation (Northwestern University, Evanston, IL).

Marston, S. T., 1976, Employment instability and high unemployment rates, Brookings Papers on Economic Activity, 169–203.

Mortensen, D. T., and G. R. Neumann, 1984, Choice or chance? A structural interpretation of individual labor market histories, in: G. R. Neumann and N. C. Westergard-Nielsen, eds., Studies in labor market dynamics (Springer-Verlag, Berlin).

Sharma, S., 1985, Individual labor market histories, Mimeo. (Cornell University, Ithaca, NY).

SRI International, 1983, Final report on the Seattle–Denver income maintenance experiment, Vol. 1: Design and results (U.S. Government Printing Office, Washington, D.C.).

Weiner, S. E., 1984, A survival analysis of adult male black/white labor market flows, in: G. R. Neumann and N. C. Westergard-Nielsen, eds., Studies in labor market dynamics. (Springer-Verlag, Berlin).

Applications

CHAPTER 8

Structural and reduced form approaches to analyzing unemployment durations

8.1 Introduction

Workers with low current earnings comprise two types of individuals: those whose personal characteristics lead to their being permanently in the low-wage state, and those who are, owing to some exogenous event, only transitorily in the low-wage state. This distinction is recognized implicitly in public policies designed to aid such workers. Workers who are viewed as "permanent" low wage earners are provided programs which attempt to alter their personal characteristics – e.g., manpower training programs. For those workers viewed as only transitorily in the low earning state, services provided tend to be short-term income maintenance, e.g., unemployment insurance following losses in jobs and Workmen's Compensation following debilitating work injuries. The distinction between permanent and transitory is not rigid, however, since not all workers recover from a transitory shock such as the loss of a high-wage job. Similarly, some workers with characteristics normally associated with permanent low wage earnings esape to the high-wage sector. The size of the pool of low wage at any time depends then upon the magnitudes of these inflows and outflows. Although economists cannot claim to understand fully how public programs affect all movements between the two states, a clearer picture is emerging on the effects of manpower training programs and the movement out of the low-earnings state.

Our understanding of the effect of public programs on the transition into the low-earnings state is much less precise, however, partially because we have only a limited knowledge of the adjustments individuals make to such events as job loss. Why is it, for example, that one individual will become reemployed in a short time with only minimal loss of earnings while another individual with a similar earnings history finds a

This chapter is reprinted from Sherwin Rosen (ed.), *Studies in Labor Markets*, University of Chicago Press for NBER, 1981.

new job only after a considerable period of time and then experiences a substantial decline in earnings? Is this merely an example of "bad luck," or does it indicate a systematic means whereby a transitory event leads some workers into permanent low-wage status? Although much has been written on the job search behavior of individuals, comparatively little empirical evidence exists to shed light on why some individuals succeed and others fail. Moreover, the evidence that does exist is generally of little use for exploring questions about the efficacy of alternative labor market programs. This latter problem arises because customary approaches of analyzing the outcome of the job search process – that is, the wage offer accepted and the length of time required to obtain it – produce, at best, a reduced form relationship which confounds differences in market opportunities with differences in personal characteristics. Consequently, the true effect of a particular program is difficult to determine. For the purposes of policy analysis, an identification of the underlying structural relationship is necessary if one desires to measure the effects of programs designed to affect the job search process.

In this chapter we consider the effects of two alternative labor market programs designed to smooth the transition from the unemployed state: a modified version of regular unemployment insurance and a wage subsidy program. In the data used in this study, one of these programs – the modified unemployment insurance – actually operated, and we can therefore consider variations in policy parameters. The alternative wage subsidy program was not available to any individuals, but it has attracted some attention recently as a means of reducing unemployment. While no direct evidence – that is, of the experiences of treatment and control groups – is available, we show that knowledge of the *structural* parameters – but not the *reduced form* parameters – is sufficient to identify the effects of this type of program. In examining the effects of the different programs, we contrast the policy implications that flow from the reduced form estimates and the structural estimates. These differences provide a useful insight into the gains obtainable from a precise model specification.

8.2   Outcomes of job search

Analysis of the effects of unemployment has focused on the length of time required to find employment, and the resulting wage obtained; in particular, the analysis has focused on measuring the effects of programs such as unemployment insurance (UI) on the outcome of the job search process. The theory motivating this analysis is given in the well-known papers by Mortensen (1970) and McCall (1970) on search behavior. To state this theory somewhat loosely, empirical studies proceed from the observation that anything which lowers the cost of search increases an individual's reservation wage and thereby leads to both longer durations of unemployment and higher wages upon reemployment.

Empirical efforts to measure the relationship between duration and wage change have taken two directions. The first approach, typified by Classen (1977) and Ehrenberg and Oaxaca (1976), treats the outcomes of the job search process as jointly determined and attempts to estimate a *reduced form* system. The specific model is:

$$D_i = X'_{1i}B_1 + E_{1i} \tag{1a}$$

$$W_i = X_{2i}B_2 + E_{2i} \tag{1b}$$

where D_i is the number of weeks of unemployment and W_i is reemployment wage. Parameters of the UI system, i.e., the replacement rate, are included in X_1 and X_2, and their coefficients are interpreted as the net effects of the UI system on the job search process.

An alternative approach has been taken in Kiefer and Neumann (1978, 1979a b). In this approach the job search process is viewed as a selection problem following Heckman (1979). Individuals accept employment if and only if the market wage offer exceeds their reservation wage. Expected wages are then just a drawing from a truncated distribution, with the point of truncation depending upon the reservation wage, and the expected duration of unemployment is distributed geometrically about the inverse of the per period probability of finding an acceptable job offer.[1] A difficulty encountered in the approach is that reservation wages are not observable; they must be inferred from the observed choices of individuals. This problem, which motivated the use of a reduced form solution in other papers, can be solved in the following manner (see also Kiefer and Neumann 1979b).

Assume that the wage offer distribution facing the ith individual is:

$$\ln w^o_{it} = X'_i B + f_i + \varepsilon^o_{it}$$

$$\varepsilon^o_{it} \sim \text{i.i.d. } N(0, \sigma^2_o) \,\forall\, t \tag{2}$$

where X_i represents all measured characteristics of an individual (age, education, labor market characteristics, etc.), f_i represents all unmeasured

---

[1] This result holds only for the case of constant reservation wages. The correct distribution of durations for the general case is given in equation (7) below.

characteristics, which are assumed known by the individual and potential employers, and ε_{it}^o is a random error term representing the "pure" amount of wage variability. The characterization in (2) implies that the wage offer distribution is stationary, an assumption which seems reasonable in light of the span of time covered by a typical spell of unemployment, and that observed wages have two sources of variation – systematic, but unmeasured, differences in "ability" f_i, and randomness in the wage offer process, represented by ε_{it}^o.

Facing (2), an optimal strategy is to select a reservation wage with the property that offers which match or exceed this critical value are accepted and those that fall short are rejected. The reservation wage can be shown to be of the form:

$$r_{it} = g[F(w_i^o), m, \theta, t] \tag{3}$$

where $F(w_i^o)$ is the density of wage offers, m is the direct cost of search, θ is the discount factor, and t represents the effect of state dependence – that is, reservation wages may systematically vary with the length of time searching. Using results from Kiefer and Neumann (1979a b), a first-order Taylor expansion of (3) can be shown to yield

$$r_{it} = k_i(X_i'B + f_i) + Z_i(t) \cdot \gamma \tag{3'}$$

where k_i is defined as

$$k_i = \frac{\int_{r_{it}}^{\infty} r_{it} F(w_i^o)\, dw^o}{\int_{r_{it}}^{\infty} r_{it} F(w_i^o)\, dw^o + \theta} = \frac{\alpha_i}{\alpha_i + \theta} = k_i(XB, Z\gamma, k_i)$$

Note that there is no stochastic element in (3'); individuals who search optimally in this model choose a strategy – a reservation price – which is not random, although it may vary over time as reflected in the time subscript on Z, i.e., in response to time-dependent factors which directly affect the costs of search.

Individuals accept employment if and only if the wage offer exceeds the reservation wage. Using (2) and (3'), the employment condition is that

$$s_i(t) = (1 - k_i)(X_i'B + f_i) - Z_i(t)\gamma > -\varepsilon_i^o \tag{4}$$

defining $s_i(t) = -[(1 - k_i)(X_i'B + f_i) - Z_i(t)\gamma]/\sigma$. The probability of finding a job in any period α is, for a given individual,

$$\alpha[s_i(t)|f_i] = \Pr(w_i^o > r_{it}|f_i) = 1 - \Phi[s_i(t)|f_i] \tag{5}$$

where Φ is the standard normal distribution function. The statement in (5) is the probability of an individual's finding a job in period t, conditional on his unmeasured ability f_i. Although by definition we do not have measures of f_i, an implication of the optional choice of a reservation wage is that randomness in wage offers should be independent of f_i. Hence the unconditional probability of finding an acceptable job offer is

$$\alpha[s_i(t)] = \int_{-\infty}^{\infty} [1 - \Phi(s_i|f_i)] \, d\Phi\left(\frac{f_i}{\sigma_F}\right) \tag{6}$$

where we have assumed that f_i is normally distributed with mean zero and variance σ_F^2. Using (6) and results from conditional normal theory, the probability of observing a particular outcome – that is, a wage w_i^o, and a length of unemployment D_i – is given by

$$\Pr(w_i^o, D_i) = \int_{-\infty}^{\infty} \left(\{ \Pi\Phi[s_i(t)|f_i] \} \cdot \frac{1}{\sigma_o} \phi\left(\frac{\varepsilon_i}{\sigma_o}\right) \right.$$
$$\left. \cdot [1 - \Phi(s_i|f_i]) \right) d\Phi\left(\frac{f_i}{\sigma_F}\right) \tag{7}$$

as t goes from 1 to $D_i - 1$ and $d\Phi(f_i/\sigma_F)$ goes from $-\infty$ to ∞. Subject to identification criteria discussed in Kiefer and Neumann (1979a b), all parameters in equation (7) can be estimated by maximum likelihood methods.[2] In particular one can identify B, γ, σ_o^2 (the pure variation in wage offers), and σ_F^2 (the variation in unmeasured ability).

The issues which arise in estimating the model described above are discussed at length elsewhere (see Kiefer and Neumann 1979b). For the present purposes it is sufficient to note that two structural equations relating unemployment and reemployment earnings are embedded in (7). The expected length of search for a randomly chosen individual is given by:

$$E(D_i) = \sum_{j=1}^{\infty} \int_{-\infty}^{\infty} \left(\prod_{l=1}^{j-1} \Phi[s_i(l) \mid f_i] \right)$$
$$\cdot [1 - \Phi(s_i(j)|f_i] \cdot j \, d\Phi\left(\frac{f_i}{\sigma_F}\right) \tag{8}$$

The expected reemployment wage is somewhat more cumbersome to derive. Conditional on f_i, and conditional on the length of search being D_i,

[2] The identification criteria amount to the following: some variable(s) must affect wage offers but must not directly affect reservation wages. Indirect effects – e.g., through the moments of the wage offer function – are permissible, indeed necessary.

expected reemployment earnings are:

$$E(w_i^o|f_i, D_i) = X_i' B + f_i + \sigma_o \lambda[s(D)|f_i] \qquad (9)$$

where

$$\lambda[s(D)|f_i] = \frac{\phi[s_i(D)|f_i]}{1 - \Phi[s_i(D)|f_i]}$$

If the reservation wage were constant, i.e., s did not vary with D, then unconditional expected earnings would be given by

$$E(w_i^o) = \int_{-\infty}^{\infty} E(w_i|f_i, D) \, d\Phi\left(\frac{f_i}{\sigma_F}\right)$$

$$= X_i' B + \sigma_o \int_{-\infty}^{\infty} \lambda(s_i|f_i) \, d\Phi\left(\frac{f_i}{\sigma_F}\right) \qquad (10)$$

When reservation wages vary with search time, the second term on the right-hand side on (10) must be modified to allow for differences in the probability of receiving an acceptable offer in a given period. Define the probability that an acceptable offer is received in period j as:

$$g_i(j) = \left(\prod_{l=1}^{j-1} \Phi[s(l)|f_i]\right) \cdot \{1 - \Phi[s(j)|f_i]\} \qquad (11)$$

The unconditional expected reemployment wage is then:

$$E(w_i^o) = \int_{-\infty}^{\infty} \left(\sum_{j=1}^{\infty} E(w_i^o|f_i, D = j) \cdot g_i(j)\right) d\Phi\left(\frac{f_i}{\sigma_F}\right)$$

$$= X_i'B + \sigma_o \cdot \int_{-\infty}^{\infty} \left(\sum_{j=1}^{\infty} \lambda[s_i(j)|f_i] \cdot g_i(j)\right) d\Phi\left(\frac{f_i}{\sigma_F}\right) \qquad (12)$$

Equations (8) and (12) can be thought of as the structural analogues to what we have termed the reduced form solutions of (1a) and (1b). In view of the differences between the reduced form and structural approaches it is useful to examine the merits of each. Two issues are of particular importance: interpreting changes in policy variables such as UI benefits, and drawing inferences from incomplete samples (see Johnson and Kotz 1972; Heckman, 1979).

The reduced form approach has one particular advantage – it is simple and cheap to estimate. If reservation wages are constant, the estimated coefficients have a potential interpretation as the coefficients of a Taylor expansion of the inverse of (6) for the duration equation [i.e., $E(D) = 1/\alpha(s_i)$], and as

$$B + \sigma_o \int_{-\infty}^{\infty} \frac{\partial \gamma(\cdot)}{\partial(\cdot)} \frac{\partial(\cdot)}{\partial r} \frac{\partial n}{\partial X_i} d\Phi\left(\frac{f_i}{\sigma_F}\right)$$

for the earnings equation. In this case, if both forms of the job search model were estimated on a complete sample, the only difference that should arise would be due to the inherent nonlinearity of the structural duration equation. If reservation wages vary over time as well as across individuals, then the correspondence between the two approaches is less obvious. Policies which affect the duration of unemployment also affect the distribution of accepted wages since the point of truncation varies with duration.

The use of a reduced form approach also results in problems of interpretation when certain types of policy simulations are attempted. For example, if a wage subsidy of, say, ten percent were given to all individuals in the sample, it would affect both duration and reemployment earnings, although in opposite ways. In the absence of a controlled experiment – where individuals were randomly assigned to the group receiving the subsidy – it is difficult to see how one could simulate this effect using a reduced form model. The problem is one of identification: the moments of the wage distribution do not enter explicitly into the reduced form approach. If reservation wages are constant, this problem may not be serious because of the potential interpretation of the reduced form coefficients noted above. In the more general case, however, it is not possible to infer the results of such an experiment from the reduced form estimates.

Perhaps the greatest difference between the two approaches arises when information is available only for an incomplete sample. For example, it is frequently the case that a "follow-up" survey is performed after some event has occurred. At the time of the survey some individuals will have completed their job search, but some will not. Those who have not found employment will tend to have low expected market earnings, relative to their reservation wage – hence the long period of unemployment. Since neither of the dependent variables is observed, the observations are usually excluded from the analysis.[3] For well-known reasons this is likely to

---

[3] There are other reasons why truncation would occur. Using state UI records on compensated unemployment results in a truncation of those with very short durations – less than the waiting period – and those with long durations – those whose unemployment exceeds the maximum duration period.

result in biased estimates. Apart from the question of bias, there is the question of interpreting the results of any simulation exercise since the composition of an incomplete sample is not likely to be invariant under changes in policy. Consider, for example, the effect of a shift in the mean of the wage offer distribution. Search theory implies that the expected wage should increase, and expected duration decrease, for all individuals. In an incomplete sample, the effect of such a policy would be that some individuals who previously had not found employment would become employed and hence would be included in the sample. If these individuals on average had higher durations of unemployment and lower expected earnings, then *observed* average wages would fall and duration increase, even in a carefully controlled experiment.

The importance of this effect will depend upon the location of reservation wages along the distribution of wage offers. If reservation wages are high, relative to the mean of the wage offer distribution, and if the distribution of offers has small variance, even a small shift in the mean may produce a significant change in unemployment patterns.

In noting these differences, we have only pointed out the potential problems which may exist; the severity of these problems – that is, the extent to which they lead to different policy implications – is ultimately an empirical matter. In the following section, we examine the simulated responses of a group of individuals to two plans which affect their unemployment activities.

8.3   Simulating job search: the effects of a wage subsidy plan

In this section we apply the models discussed above to a sample of unemployed male workers. This particular sample was generated from a survey of trade-displaced workers conducted by the Institute for Research on Human Resources of the Pennsylvania State University. A complete description of the data source is contained in Neumann (1978). Several features make this group particularly appropriate for discussions about low-wage workers. The sample is constructed solely of individuals who were permanently separated from employment – in most cases because the entire plant shut down. Thus we observe only job search behavior and do not have to be concerned with responses to anticipated, temporary layoffs. Moreover, the nature of the shock conforms to the idea of an exogenous shock to which some individuals adjust reasonably well, and others adjust only with great difficulty. Although many of these individ-

Table 8.1. *Sample characteristics of male workers*

	Mean	Maximum	Minimum
Education (years)	10.2	21.0	0.0
No. of dependents	1.7	9.0	0.0
Percent married	83.5	—	—
Percent union members	70.4	—	—
Local unemployment rate at layoff (%)	5.30	9.00	2.20
Age	47.8	75.0	19.0
Unemployment benefits per week ($ 1967)	62.7	117.11	0.0
Maximum benefit period (weeks)	41.5	65.6	0.0
Previous weekly earnings ($ 1967)	149.0	457.0	19.20

uals would not have been considered low-wage workers prior to displacement, the average loss in weekly earnings upon reemployment was over twenty-five percent: consequently, most would be considered low-wage earners afterward. Summary statistics on this sample are contained in Table 8.1.

Estimates of the reduced form equations for duration and reemployment earnings are presented in Table 8.2, and the structural estimates of reemployment earnings (wage offers) and reservation wages are contained in Table 8.3. Although we will not dwell on the precision of the estimates, we do note that the explanatory power of the OLS regression of unemployment duration is exceedingly small; this appears to be a common finding (see, e.g., Ehrenberg and Oaxaca 1976; Classen 1977).

Both approaches indicate an effect of UI benefits on the outcome of the job search process. The reduced form estimates imply that a ten percent increase in the replacement rate – equivalent here to an average increase of $14.9 per week in UI benefits – would lead to an increase in duration of about one-half week (.0314 × 14.9), and an increase in unemployment earnings of 0.60 percent. The effects of increased UI benefits are apparent in column 2, but the numerical values of the increases in duration and reemployment earnings depend upon the position of the reservation wage in the wage offer distribution. We calculate these effects in the simulation reported below.

Before examining the simulation results it is useful to consider one feature of the job search process. Both casual empirical evidence and some previous studies (e.g., Neumann 1978) suggest that losses due to unemployment are greatest for the long-term unemployed. Although a higher reservation wage leads to higher expected reemployment and a

Table 8.2. *Reduced form estimates of duration and reemployment wage equation*

	Duration (1)	Reemployment earnings (2)
Constant	18.1566	1.839
	(2.17)	(3.16)
Education	0.0161	0.0088
	(0.96)	(2.41)
Dependents	0.0261	0.0617
	(0.41)	(0.14)
Tenure	0.0040	−0.0069
	(1.06)	(1.92)
Marital status	0.0001	0.1139
	(0.00)	(0.60)
Unemployment rate	2.1164	−0.0461
	(1.97)	(1.27)
Age	0.0441	0.0210
	(1.40)	(1.21)
Age^2	−0.0003	−0.0002
	(0.27)	(0.06)
Ed · Age	0.0143	−0.0011
	(0.20)	(1.61)
UI benefits	0.0314	0.0004
	(1.71)	(1.30)
Maximum duration	0.0214	−0.0001
	(1.40)	(0.01)
$\ln(W_{t-1})$	−0.3118	0.5406
	(1.11)	(7.24)
R^2	.1331	.2480
F	1.478	9.012

Note: t-Statistics in parentheses.

greater length of unemployment for any individual ex ante, when one observes the outcomes of the job search process ex post, this investment aspect is swamped by variations in individual characteristics and by random errors in the process. In the present context this phenomenon is likely to be concentrated among the group of workers who had not found employment by the survey date. Since their behavior is of particular interest in any discussion of low-income workers we present simulation results separately for this group.

The simulated effects of changing UI benefits in steps of five percent on duration of unemployment and the percentage change in reemployment earnings are presented in Table 8.4. Panels A and B contain the estimates from the reduced form model [equations (1a) and (1b)] for the total sam-

Table 8.3. *Structural estimates of the job search process*

	Earnings function (1)	Reservation wage function (2)
Constant	2.8263	1.9713
	(6.24)	(3.47)
Education	0.0361	0.0101
	(1.87)	(1.27)
Dependents	—	−0.0068
		(0.47)
Tenure	−0.0078	—
	(3.68)	
Marital status	—	−0.0824
		(3.68)
Unemployment rate	0.0197	0.0161
	(1.68)	(2.89)
Age	0.0194	−0.0127
	(1.86)	(3.46)
Age^2	−0.0001	0.0001
	(0.61)	(0.84)
Ed · Age	−0.0008	−0.0003
	(1.87)	(1.71)
Unemployment benefits	—	0.0016
		(2.43)
Maximum duration	—	0.004
		(0.59)
ln W_{t-1}	0.2574	—
	(4.57)	
F_t	—	−0.0014
		(0.91)
t	—	−0.0023
		(2.01)
$\sigma^2 w^o$	0.0283	
	(2.62)	
σ_F^2	0.2493	
	(12.41)	
ln ll	−1,794.83	

Note: t-Statistics in parentheses.

ple and for those workers who remained unemployed for at least sixty-five weeks; panels C and D contain the equivalent estimates for the structural model [equations (8) and (12)]. The estimates in Table 8.4 show two pronounced patterns. Looking across each panel, we see that, for this sample at least, changes in UI benefit levels would have almost negligible effects. Increasing UI benefits by twenty percent – which for this sample

Table 8.4. *Structural and reduced form simulations of the effect of alternative levels of UI benefits*

	% Δ in UI benefits				
	0.0	5.0	10.0	15.0	20.0
	Reduced form estimates A. Total sample				
Duration (weeks)	39.31	39.41	39.51	39.61	39.72
% Δ in earnings	0.0	0.13	0.25	0.38	0.50
	B. Unemployed after 65 weeks				
Duration (weeks)	39.62	39.73	39.83	39.93	40.03
% Δ in earnings	0.0	0.13	.025	0.37	0.49
	Structural estimates C. Total sample				
Duration (weeks)	43.10	43.41	43.67	43.85	43.91
% Δ in earnings	0.0	0.17	0.29	0.46	0.54
	D. Unemployed after 65 weeks				
Duration (weeks)	47.21	47.36	47.50	47.61	47.71
% Δ in earnings	0.0	0.11	0.18	0.25	0.31

is equivalent to raising the average replacement rate by 8.4 percentage points (from 42.1 percent to 50.5 percent) – would raise reemployment earnings by only about .5 percent and increase the duration of unemployment by about one-half week. These are quite modest effects when one considers that the average reemployed worker in this sample had a decline in real weekly earnings of 26.7 percent and spent 39.1 weeks unemployed. It is interesting to note that although estimates of the precise effect of changing UI benefits would differ depending upon whether one used the reduced form or structural model, the conclusions to be drawn from the evidence would not.

Looking down the columns of Table 8.4, we observe a somewhat different picture of the differences between the two approaches to modeling the job search process. Comparison of panels A and B would seem to indicate that there is little difference between those who had not become employed within 65 weeks and those who had; panels C and D indicate the contrary. The expected duration of unemployment was estimated to be 34.7 weeks for those who became employed within 65 weeks, and 47.2 weeks for those who had not become employed by 65 weeks. This amounts to about a twelve-week difference in expected duration of unemployment between the two groups. In one sense, this difference between the two models can be considered a contrived one, since the structural model takes into account information on the characteristics and, partially, the job search outcomes, of the group of workers who had not found jobs within 65 weeks.[4] But this is precisely the purpose of a structural model, and the differences observed in Table 8.4 represent the basis for using such an approach to design policies to smooth labor market transitions. Under the reduced form approach, the similarity of the estimated duration and wage changes would lead one to conclude that the two groups are essentially the same; hence it must be random influences – luck – which determine whom the labor market assigns to each group. The structural approach, on the other hand, implies that there are real differences between the two groups and thus, at least in principle, allows the possibility of predicting in advance what types of individuals are likely to be most affected by unexpected job loss.

The results of this simulation raise strong doubts about the ability of what is essentially an income maintenance program to have a significant impact on the reemployment experience of displaced workers. Although the sample used is unique, and certainly not representative of all unemployed workers, our results, both the reduced form and structural versions, are not significantly at odds with the findings of others which are based solely on a reduced form approach. While it is difficult to generalize from a sample of one, there is at least the suggestion that returns from more precise modeling of the job search process may be important for policy purposes.

Although predicting which types of individuals will be most adversely affected by job termination is one possible gain to a structural approach, a more important gain is likely to be in terms of the number of different policy options which can be considered. As an example, we consider the option of a wage subsidy program. The basic idea of a wage subsidy is to shift the distribution of wage offers facing individuals, thereby making employment more likely. In the reduced form approach there is no obvious way to incorporate such effects, except possibly through a con-

---

[4] The estimates in the reduced form approach for the sample of workers not employed in sixty-five weeks are constructed simply by using the observed characteristics of the individual and the coefficients estimated from the sample of employed. No attempt is made to adjust the constant term such that the expected value of, say, duration reflects the obvious fact that the observed period of unemployment was greater than 65 weeks.

Table 8.5. *Structural simulations of the effect of a wage subsidy program*

	% Δ in mean wage offer				
	0.0	5.0	10.0	15.0	20.0
A. Total Sample					
Duration (weeks)	43.10	42.87	42.51	42.23	42.06
% Δ in earnings	0.0	4.91	9.84	14.72	19.6
B. Unemployed over 65 weeks					
Duration (weeks)	47.21	47.03	46.74	46.39	46.12
% Δ in earnings	0.0	4.87	9.78	14.68	19.2
C. Duration of unemployment with incomplete knowledge (weeks)					
Total sample	43.10	41.64	40.02	38.75	37.29
Unemployed over 65 weeks	47.21	45.88	44.16	42.82	41.28

trolled experiment. A structural approach allows for a direct interpretation, however, since the shift in the wage offer distribution affects an individual's expected earnings both directly – i.e., through $X_i'B$ – and indirectly through its effects on reservation wages.

In Table 8.5 we present the results of a simulation exercise with varying amounts of wage subsidy. Because these simulations, as in the case of the UI subsidy, are partial equilibrium in nature, the results are sensitive to the assumed stability of the wage offer distribution. In the present case, this amounts to assuming that a wage subsidy program will not affect the distribution of wage offers apart from the mean shift, i.e., no "extra" effects due to a substitution of labor for capital. For small programs this assumption seems tenable.

The issue also arises of how accurately this shift in the distribution is perceived by individuals. If it is fully perceived, then reservation wages rise by a fraction $\alpha/(\alpha + \theta)$ of the increase in the mean. This increase in reservation wages leads to lengthier search, and, consequently, the effect on duration of unemployment is lessened. Since some wage subsidy plans (e.g., jobs credit) work in a manner that may not be obvious to individuals, we present estimates of the effect on duration assuming full reservation wage change (panels A and B), and no reservation wage change (panel C).

In contrast to a UI subsidy, a direct wage subsidy appears to have quite significant effects on the job search process. From panels A and B we observe that a twenty percent wage subsidy would lead to an increase in reemployment earnings of about nineteen percent, and a reduction of unemployment duration of about a week, if the shift in the mean is completely perceived. The effect of the change in reservation wages can be seen clearly in panel C: if reservation wages did not adjust, expected unemployment duration would decrease by six weeks instead of one.

8.4 Conclusion

This chapter has focused on two points – the inferences which can be obtained from structural versus reduced form analysis of the outcome of the job search process, and the effects of two subsidy programs on the job search process. In regard to the former topic, it is clear that a structural model permits a wider range of possible questions. In particular, it is possible to consider, ex ante, what the likely experience of a given cohort of job searchers will be, and, in principle, to tailor different types of programs to ease their labor market transitions.

The comparison of a UI subsidy with a wage subsidy revealed significant differences. Higher levels of UI payments led, as expected, to both longer durations of unemployment and higher reemployment earnings. Both effects were quite small, however, and, at least for low-wage workers similar to the individuals in this sample, there is little reason to believe that programs which emphasize income maintenance are likely to have much impact on the types of jobs obtained. By contrast, a wage subsidy program appears to have a significant effect on reemployment earnings, and also to lead to a moderate decline in duration. This is a one-blade-of-the-scissors result of course, and it is subject to criticism on those grounds. Nonetheless, for relatively small programs, the possibilities appear to be fruitful.

References

Classen, K. "The Effect of Unemployment Insurance on the Duration of Unemployment and Subsequent Earnings." *Industrial and Labor Relations Review* 30, no. 4 (July 1977): 438–44.

Ehrenberg, R., and Oaxaca, R., "Unemployment Insurance, Duration of Unemployment, and Subsequent Wage Gain." *American Economic Review* 66 (December 1976): 754–66.

Heckman, J. "Sample Selection Bias as a Specification Error." *Econometrica* 47 (January 1979): 153–62.

Johnson, N., and Kotz, S. *Distributions in Statistics*. Vol. 4: *Continuous Multivariate Distributions*. N.Y.: John Wiley, 1972.

Kiefer, N., and Neumann, G. "Estimation of Wage Offer Distributions and Reservation Wages," in S. Lippman and J. McCall, eds., *Studies in the Economics of Search*. Amsterdam: North-Holland, 1978, pp. 171–89. Chapter 2 of this volume.

"An Empirical Job Search Model with a Test of the Constant Reservation Wage Hypothesis." *Journal of Political Economy* 87, no. 1 (February 1979a). Chapter 3 of this volume.

"Individual Effects in a Nonlinear Model: Explicit Treatment of Heterogeneity in the Empirical Job-Search Model." *Econometrica* 49 (1979). Chapter 4 of this volume.

McCall, J. "Economics of Information and Job Search." *Quarterly Journal of Economics*, February 1970, pp. 113–26.

Mortensen, D. "Job Search, the Duration of Unemployment, and the Phillips Curve," *American Economic Review* 60 (December 1970): pp. 847–62.

Neumann, G. "The Labor Market Adjustments of Trade Displaced Workers: The Evidence from the Trade Adjustment Assistance Program," in R. Ehrenberg, ed., *Research in Labor Economics*, pp. 353–81. JAI Press, 1978.

CHAPTER 9

Wages and the structure of unemployment rates

The labor market consequences of macroeconomic policy during the past decade present an uncomfortable prospect for the future. Unemployment during the seventies averaged 6 percent of the labor force, reaching a quarterly high of 8.8 percent in 1975. Among some groups, the results were even worse: teenage unemployment averaged over 16 percent for the decade. Inflation, measured by movement in the consumer price index (CPI), averaged over 7 percent and was 11.5 percent in 1979. Consumers and workers face the unpleasant prospect of having to continue to cope with rates of unemployment and inflation well in excess of those considered normal a decade ago.

One "reason" for this bleak state of affairs is that the rate of unemployment consistent with any particular level of inflation has shifted. As Perry has noted, the labor force is increasingly female and young; these groups have historically had high unemployment rates.[1] The growing numbers of these groups, even coupled with their high unemployment rates, appears to have little effect on the rate of wage inflation.[2] This combination of high unemployment rates and little or no reduction in inflation presents a dilemma that appears to be unsolvable by conventional fiscal and monetary policies. However, as Baily and Tobin have noted, selective programs of job creation or wage subsidies can reduce the measured level of unemployment attendant to any rate of inflation by reducing the slope of the inflation–unemployment trade-off in the short run and the natural rate of unemployment in the long run.[3]

This chapter is reprinted from *Workers, Jobs and Inflation*, edited by M. N. Baily (1982), by permission of the Brookings Institution.

[1] George L. Perry, "Changing Labor Markets and Inflation," *Brookings Papers on Economic Acitvity, 3:1970*, pp. 411–41. (Hereafter *BPEA*.)

[2] Robert J. Gordon, "Wage–Price Controls and the Shifting Phillips Curve," *BPEA, 2:1972*, pp. 385–421, provides evidence that the unemployment rates of women and youths have little effect on the rate of inflation.

[3] Martin Neil Baily and James Tobin, "Macroeconomic Effects of Selective Public Employment and Wage Subsidies," *BPEA, 2:1977*, pp. 511–41.

While the welfare implications of the Baily–Tobin model are subject to debate, the practical matter of the extent of the empirical possibilities of such a program may decide the issue. Would direct job creation for, say, teenagers lower their unemployment rate or would it result, through fiscal substitution and increased labor force participation, in possibly even higher levels of unemployment? Would a wage subsidy program result in greater unemployment opportunities or simply afford relatively more frequent, albeit more munificent, transitions out of the labor force?

Answers to these questions are not forthcoming from existing literature on unemployment experience, in part because of a lack of data on labor market transitions on an individual basis, but mostly because of a preoccupation with unemployment accounting. Questions about the effect of a wage subsidy or a job creation program require, in the absence of a randomized experiment, a disentangling of demand and supply responses. Without such identification it is impossible to provide evidence on the potential role of a wage subsidy or similar interventionist policy.

The purpose of this chapter is to provide evidence on one aspect of the Baily–Tobin model, namely, the effect of a wage subsidy program on steady-state rates of unemployment. Our focus is on the role of wage rates in allocating workers among being employed, unemployed, and not in the labor force. We outline a model of labor market behavior that motivates the subsequent empirical analysis and discuss its relationship to the Baily–Tobin model.

For reasons explained in the text, the customary data set for this type of analysis – gross flow data from the Current Population Survey (CPS) – is inappropriate; we therefore use a less representative sample, namely the control observations from the Denver Income Maintenance Experiment (DIME). These data have some disadvantages, which we discuss at length, but when all caveats are put forth, the net result is that these are the only data that allow a careful investigation of the Baily–Tobin or related models.

Since one of the constructs used in this chapter and other publications[4] is that of a steady-state Markov structure for transition rates, diagnostic checks are made on the issue. We use these estimated transition rate functions to calculate steady-state unemployment and labor-force participation rates for various race, sex, and age groups. In turn, these estimates are used to calculate effects of a wage subsidy program. We find significant

---

[4] Kim B. Clark and Lawrence H. Summers, "Labor Market Dynamics and Unemployment: A Reconsideration," *BPEA, 1:1979*, pp. 13–60.

responsiveness of unemployment rates to wages among adults, but little among teenagers. This is because an increase in the teenage wage increases labor force participation of this group. Thus we are led to conclude that the Baily–Tobin model's theoretical possibility for reducing the natural rate of unemployment does not seem to hold much empirical promise.

9.1 Transition rates and labor market behavior

A central theme of labor market research has been an emphasis on the dynamics of the employment process. In both theoretical and, to a lesser extent, empirical work, the role of turnover has become the critical element for an understanding of unemployment. A stylized view from this perspective is that unemployment is the result of churning among labor market states: jobs are continually being lost and created, and, in the process, individuals spend time searching for employment. One particularly important finding that emerges from this view of the labor market is that the high unemployment rates observed among some groups are not due to an inability to find employment, but rather to an inability to remain employed.[5]

This simple search-cum-turnover story of labor market dynamics, while illuminating, does not provide a complete picture of labor market dynamics. The reason is that a large number of spells of unemployment are ended by withdrawal from the labor force rather than by employment, a point that has been emphasized recently by Clark and Summers.[6] Similarly, part of the instability in employment is manifested by transitions directly from employment to withdrawal from the labor force. These movements into and out of the labor force are not typically explained in standard models of labor market behavior. To account for transitions in and out of the labor market there must be a source of randomness apart from uncertainty over wages or job availability. In a related paper, a model of labor market dynamics is presented in which individuals face

---

[5] During the period 1967–73, the highest rate of leaving employment was 21.6 percent for nonwhite male teenagers, while the lowest rate was 1.2 percent for prime-age white males. Thus the ratio of the highest to the lowest rate was 17.5. In contrast, the highest probability of becoming employed from the unemployed state was 39.03 percent for 20–24-year-old white females, while the lowest rate was 17.23 percent for nonwhite female teenagers, implying a ratio of 2.27. Stephen T. Marston, "Employment Instability and High Unemployment Rates," *BPEA, 1:1976*, pp. 169–203, especially table 1, p. 175.

[6] Clark and Summers, "Labor Market Dynamics and Unemployment," pp. 25–27.

random wage offers and random shocks to state-dependent utility functions.[7] In this model, it can be shown that transition rates between states depend upon realized wages, if employed, and on the parameters of the wage-offer distribution.

In particular, using W to denote a realized wage, $\overline{W}$ the mean of wage-offer distribution, and λ_{ij} the transition rate from state i to state j, i, $j \in \{E,U,N\}$ (here E, U, and N denote the state of employment, unemployment, and nonparticipation respectively), the following results can be obtained:

$$\frac{\partial \lambda_{NE}}{\partial \overline{W}}, \frac{\partial \lambda_{UE}}{\partial \overline{W}} \geq 0; \tag{1}$$

$$\frac{\partial (\lambda_{EU} + \lambda_{EN})}{\partial W} \leq 0; \tag{2}$$

$$\frac{\partial \lambda_{UN}}{\partial \overline{W}}, \frac{\partial \lambda_{EN}}{\partial W} \leq 0; \tag{3}$$

$$\frac{\partial (\lambda_{NU} + \lambda_{NE})}{\partial \overline{W}} \geq 0. \tag{4}$$

The intuition underlying these results is straightforward. Equation 1 indicates that higher earnings induce workers to leave unemployment faster[8] and decrease the set of random shocks that will make nonparticipation optimal. In other words, the opportunity cost of not working has risen. The second relationship states that the hazard rate of nonparticipation falls with an increase in actual earnings, and the results in equation 4 indicate the opposite side of the coin: higher wages increase the hazard rate out of nonparticipation. The only ambiguity that arises concerns transitions into and out of unemployment. Higher wages make employment more

[7] Kenneth Burdett and others, "A Markov Model of Employment, Unemployment and Labor Force Participation: Estimates from the DIME Data" (Northwestern University, February 1981). The assumptions needed to generate the results used in this chapter are essentially a Markov structure on the arrival rate of job offers and the arrival of random utility shocks. The results for transitions between unemployment and withdrawal from the labor force depend critically upon the arrival rate of job offers being no less in the unemployed state that in nonparticipation. This is equivalent to assuming that there is a real difference between being unemployed and being out of the labor force.

[8] This is a generalization of a result presented for the wealth-maximizing search model in Nicholas M. Kiefer and George R. Neumann, "Estimation of Wage Offer Distributions and Reservation Wages" in S. A. Lippman and J. J. McCall, eds., *Studies in the Economics of Search*, Contributions to Economic Analysis, 123 (Amsterdam: North-Holland, 1979), p. 171. Chapter 2 in this volume.

desirable and nonparticipation less so, and thus the net effect on transitions out of unemployment is unclear.

The relationship between wages and labor market transition rates described in equations 1–4 bears directly on the Baily–Tobin model because the transition rates characterize unemployment and labor force participation rates. For example, if the transition rates are constant, a steady state is defined by inflows matching outflows or:

$$\lambda_{NE}N + \lambda_{UE}U = (\lambda_{EU} + \lambda_{EN})E; \tag{5a}$$
$$\lambda_{EU}E + \lambda_{NU}N = (\lambda_{UE} + \lambda_{UN})U; \tag{5b}$$
$$\lambda_{EN}E + \lambda_{UN}U = (\lambda_{NE} + \lambda_{NU})N. \tag{5c}$$

Steady-state unemployment, u^*, and labor force participation rates, lf^*, can be found by solving equation 5, yielding:

$$u^* = U/(E + U) = A/(A + B) \tag{6}$$
$$lf^* = (E + U)/(E + U + N) = (1 + A/B)/(1 + A/B + D/C) \tag{7}$$

where:

$$A = \lambda_{EU} + (\lambda_{EN} \cdot \lambda_{NU})/(\lambda_{NE} + \lambda_{NU});$$
$$B = \lambda_{UE} + (\lambda_{UN} \cdot \lambda_{NE})/(\lambda_{NE} + \lambda_{NU});$$
$$C = \lambda_{NE} + (\lambda_{UE} \cdot \lambda_{NU})/(\lambda_{UE} + \lambda_{UN});$$
$$D = \lambda_{EN} + (\lambda_{UN} \cdot \lambda_{EU})/(\lambda_{UE} + \lambda_{UN}).$$

For steady-state equilibrium, equations 5a through 5c must hold for each labor market group, and thus the aggregate unemployment rate is the weighted average (by labor force share) of each group's unemployment rate, that is:

$$u^* = \sum_j \frac{L_j}{L} u_j^*.$$

Since the transition rates of each group are affected by wage rates, it is possible to change the value of u^* implied by this equation by a judicious choice of wage rates.

9.2 Data

A most natural source of data for an inquiry of this sort would be the gross flow data provided by the Bureau of Labor Statistics. These data have the advantage of being representative of the U.S. population and available monthly, and they are particularly useful for studying unemployment. Moreover, because these data have been used by a number of authors, their deficiencies are generally well known.[9] Despite these attractive features, the gross flow data, and even their source, the monthly CPS survey, are not suitable for the analysis described below. The main reason is that the nature of the CPS sampling technique (a unit is in for four months, out for eight, and then in for four months) makes inferences about long spells particularly chancy. If instability in employment or transitions out of the labor force are viewed as important factors in understanding unemployment, then the use of data composed primarily of incomplete spells may lead to serious biases. Indeed, estimates based on incomplete spells alone are entirely dependent upon functional form.[10] In our opinion, this is the most serious drawback to using CPS data for analyzing labor market dynamics, and it effectively precludes the use of matched monthly CPS samples.

As an alternative, one could use the monthly gross flow data to analyze time spent in unemployment (but not the other states). This requires the assumption that the replacement group entering in each month has identical behavior with the departing group, a dubious assumption in light of the well-documented phenomena of rotation group bias.[11] Moreover, the monthly gross flow data contain very little demographic information, eliminating the possibility of controlling for all but the grossest age-race breakdowns. Donsequently, the effects of heterogeneity are confounded with duration dependence.[12]

[9] Ronald G. Ehrenberg, "The Demographic Structure of Unemployment Rates and Labor Market Transition Probabilities," Cornell University, 1979; Clark and Summers, "Labor Market Dynamics and Unemployment"; Marston "Employment Instability and High Unemployment Rates."

[10] The essential problem is that individuals are observed for only four months, a length of time that is far too short to infer anything about employment duration for most, and probably all, groups in the labor market. This is somewhat less severe in studying unemployment and nonparticipation, depending upon the length of such spells. It should be noted that these problems could be solved at virtually no increase in cost by using a stochastic stopping rule to determine how long a unit should be included in the sample.

[11] See Hall for a discussion of this phenomenon in terms of unemployment rates. Robert E. Hall, "Why Is the Unemployment Rate So High at Full Employment?" *BPEA, 3:1970*, pp. 369–421.

[12] See J. J. Heckman and G. J. Borjas, "Does Unemployment Cause Future Unemployment? Definitions, Questions and Answers from a Continuous Time Model of Heterogeneity and State Dependence," *Economica*, vol. 47 (August 1980), pp. 247–83, for an exposition of these difficulties. In the empirical literature on labor market behavior, the problem is best illustrated in the work of Clark and Summers, "Labor Market Dynamics and Unemployment." Clark and Summers were forced to use five observations from gross flow data to estimate the distribution of exit times from unemployment by

In light of these difficulties we have used data from the Denver Income Maintenance Experiment (DIME). The major feature of this data set is that it provides continuous histories of individual labor market activities over forty-eight months. Moreover, the information available in the DIME data allows one to allocate individuals to labor market states, using the same definitions as the CPS. Because this data source is not as well known as the CPS, we comment briefly on its major features and note the problems that may arise in using it.

The Denver Income Maintenance Experiment was one of the largest programs designed to measure the effects of a negative income tax on labor supply. More than 5,000 individuals participated in DIME, and most of these individuals remained in the experiment for the full forty-eight months. This sample does not constitute a random sample of the Denver area population for two reasons. Eligibility for the program was restricted to individuals who were likely to participate in a full-scale program; excluded were families with heads over fifty-eight or under eighteen years of age at the start of the program, or those with permanently disabled heads; families of four with preexperiment earnings of $9,000 for one-earner families or $11,000 for two-earner families; and individuals who did not belong to a family.[13] An additional source of nonrandomness was that DIME experimentals also had pronounced changes in labor market status.[14]

Of these two major sources of nonrandomness, the experimental effects are the easiest to remove, since 40 percent of the participants in DIME were controls. That is, they did not receive financial guarantees nor were their wages affected. The work reported in this chapter therefore uses data on controls exclusively.

The other sources of nonrandomness are more difficult to deal with, in part because of the dynamics of the experiment. The restriction by age

sex and age. Other considerations such as race or marital status were, perforce, eliminated.

[13] The original sampling framework eligibility for participation was conditional on being in a "family," where "family" is defined as a one- or two-earner family containing at least one dependent. Subsequently, unrelated individuals (one eligible person comprising an entire family) and two-earner households with no dependents were made eligible.

[14] For evidence on the reduction of labor force attachment for DIME experimentals, see Nancy Brandon Tuma and Philip K. Robins, "A Dynamic Model of Employment Behavior: An Application to the Seattle and Denver Income Maintenance Experiments," *Econometrica*, vol. 48 (May 1980), pp. 1031–52; and Michael C. Keeley and others "The Estimation of Labor Supply Models Using Experimental Data," *American Economic Review*, vol. 68 (December 1978), pp. 873–87.

to families with heads less than fifty-eight years old excludes older workers, but since the experiment ran for four years, we actually include individuals up to sixty-two years of age. Restrictions on age for younger
individuals are of minor importance because the data includes all persons
sixteen and over who are in families, and the fraction of married individuals between sixteen and eighteen is small.

A possibly more serious hindrance to representativeness of the sample
arises because of the truncation by preexperiment income levels. As noted
above, the cutoff level for eligibility was $11,000 in 1971 income for a
two-earner family – a level that was 102 percent of the Denver median
family income in 1970.[15] This preexperiment truncation overstates the
potential bias, however, because transitory fluctuations in income made
some higher-income families eligible for the program. Ashenfelter finds
that in the first year of the experiment 22.6 percent of the control families
had incomes in excess of $11,204.[16] Ashenfelter also finds that in the
absence of truncation by income one would have expected to find 34
percent of the control families with incomes in excess of $11,000. This
result suggests that the DIME controls are not completely representative
of Denver families at the higher income levels. In consequence, since
high incomes are well known to be correlated with stable employment
patterns, these data are likely to overstate labor market transitions. Table
9.1 presents some indication of the dimensions of this problem. Unemployment rates for the DIME controls were three times the standard metropolitan statistical area (SMSA) rates over the period, although movements in the two series are closely related. Some part of this difference
is accounted for by the rising participation rate of teenagers during this
period, but most of the difference is due to the sample composition. For
example, blacks and Hispanics account for 65 percent of the sample but
only 15 percent of the Denver SMSA population in 1970.[17] If the sample
is reweighted to reflect the population weights given in this 1970 census,
the results are much closer to the SMSA experience. This is shown in
line 3 of Table 9.1. Adjusted unemployment rates average 7.9 percent,

---

[15] U.S. Bureau of the Census, *Census of Population, 1970*, vol. 1., *Characteristics of the
Population*, pt. 7, *Colorado* (Government Printing Office, 1973), table 89.

[16] Orley Ashenfelter, "Discrete Choice in Labor Supply: The Determinants of Participation
in the Seattle and Denver Income Maintenance Experiments" Princeton University Industrial Relations Section, working paper 136 (Princeton: May 1980), calculated from
data in table 1.

[17] U.S. Bureau of the Census (1970), tables 23 and 96.

Table 9.1. *Comparison of unemployment rates in the Denver standard metropolitan statistical area and the Denver Income Maintenance Experiment sample, 1971–74*

Unemployment rates	Percent			
	1971	1972	1973	1974
Denver SMSA unemployment rate	4.0	3.6	3.4	3.7
DIME controls unemployment rate	11.4	11.4	11.0	11.4
Adjusted control unemployment rate[a]	8.3	7.6	7.6	8.1

[a]See text for explanation of how this rate was calculated.
Source: SMSA unemployment rates are from *Employment and Training Report of the President,* selected years. DIME unemployment rates were calculated using BLS methods.

somewhat higher than the SMSA average of 3.7 percent, but closer than the unadjusted average of 11.3 percent.

Data elements

The DIME public-use files are organized in a monthly format with data covering forty-eight months. In addition to the standard demographic variables – race, sex, age, family status – the data contain information of sufficient detail to construct histories of labor market status – employment, unemployment and nonparticipation – using Current Population Survey definitions.[18] There are, however, two points where CPS labor market data differ from DIME labor market data. The CPS sample, being a point-in-time observation, is subject to length bias; that is, short spells of unemployment are less likely to be detected than long spells.[19]

[18] Details about the construction of these labor market histories are given in Shelly J. Lundberg, "Unemployment and Household Labor Supply" (Ph.D. dissertation, Northwestern University, August 1980). It should be noted that the public-use files require significant editing in order to make the definition of, say, unemployment conform to the BLS definition.

[19] For a discussion of this problem, see Hyman B. Kaitz, "Analyzing the Length of Spells of Unemployment," *Monthly Labor Review,* vol. 93 (November 1970), pp. 11–20; and Stephen W. Salant, "Search Theory and Duration Data: A Theory of Sorts," *Quarterly Journal of Economics,* vol. 91 (February 1977), pp. 39–57.

The DIME sample, being a longitudinal data set, does not have this problem and consequently will contain more short spells of unemployment. If unemployment spells are distributed uniformly across a month, the unemployment rate calculated from a point-in-time sample should not differ from that calculated from a longitudinal basis, so no bias should arise.[20] With regard to length of spells, however, it is obvious that a point-in-time sample will overstate the length of an average spell of unemployment.

A second point where the data may differ is in the transition from unemployment to nonparticipation states. The interview structure used in gathering the DIME data consisted of ten periodic interviews at intervals of three to four months. At each interview the subject was asked if there were any periods since the last interview that were not spent in employment. An affirmative answer resulted in a series of questions about whether the individual was looking for work during this period. An affirmative answer to this type of question resulted in the individual's being recorded as unemployed for the entire period between jobs or up to the periodic interview, whichever was less.[21] No further probing was done to inquire whether there were periods of nonparticipation mixed with unemployment. Thus most changes in labor market state from unemployment to nonparticipation, and the reverse, occurred only in months in which there was a periodic interview, and transition rates between these states are understated in these data.

Table 9.2 presents a comparison of transition rates for white males and females for the DIME and CPS data. The most notable differences are in the $U \to N$ transitions of young males and females: the CPS data indicate monthly transition rates from unemployment to nonparticipation that are about five times the rate experienced in the DIME data. The lower transition rates in the latter source are no doubt due in part to the form by which labor market status was checked, but are also due to the relatively lower turnover as a whole among DIME participants.[22] The net

---

[20] This statement presumes that the longitudinal data are being used in the same manner as the point-in-time sample; that is, unemployment rates are calculated as the number of persons unemployed on a given data divided by the number employed plus unemployed on that date.

[21] There are obvious exceptions to this such as workers on vacation or strikers, which were allocated correctly by use of other information on labor market status.

[22] If the only difference between the two sources was the timing of transitions into unemployment or nonparticipation, then collapsing the data into a two-state mode – employed versus nonemployed, or participation versus nonparticipation – should yield iden-

Table 9.2. *Average monthly transition rates, DIME and Current Population Survey data, by age and sex*

Age and sex	Employment to unemployment		Employment to nonparticipation		Unemployment to employment		Unemployment to nonparticipation		Nonparticipation to employment		Nonparticipation to unemployment	
	DIME	CPS	DIME	CPS	DIME	CPS	DIME	CPS	DIME	CPS	DIME	CPS
White males, 16–19	4.6	4.1	5.1	11.4	20.3	30.1	5.7	30.8	4.8	15.0	1.6	7.2
White males, 25–59	1.6	1.0	1.0	0.3	29.5	32.1	5.0	10.0	11.0	7.2	3.2	3.2
White females, 16–19	4.0	2.9	6.6	13.8	24.1	28.0	6.8	32.7	3.8	10.1	1.2	5.8
White females, 25–59	1.1	1.0	3.4	4.5	16.9	21.3	10.5	26.5	3.9	4.5	0.9	1.2

Note: Data are percentages.
Source: CPS data are from Ronald G. Ehrenberg, "The Demographic Structure of Unemployment Rates and Labor Market Transition Probabilities" (Cornell University, 1979), table 6, which uses nationwide CPS gross change data for the 1967–77 period. DIME statistics are authors' calculations.

import of this feature of the DIME data is that durations of unemployment and nonparticipation are likely to be longer than would be measured in the CPS data (if completed spells were available).

To the extent that short spells of nonparticipation are equivalent to "coding errors," as Clark and Summers argue, there is little effect of the DIME coding procedure.[23] However, since the transitions between unemployment and nonparticipation influence the calculation of steady-state values, the caveats noted above should be kept in mind when interpreting such calculations.

The DIME public-use files were used to construct data by labor market spells. Attached to each spell was the length of time of the completed spell and demographic variables relating to each individual as of the start of the spell.[24] The means of these variables, by age group, are given in Table 9.3. Most of these variables are self-explanatory, the exceptions being the assets and wage variables. Assets were constructed from information on the value of stocks, cash in checking accounts, or equity value in house or cars which was available at each periodic interview. Linear interpolation was used to produce asset values for the intervening months between interviews.

The wage variable used is derived from the reported hourly wage on the longest job worked in a given month. Since the period of the experiment encompasses a wide range of annual inflation rates, all nominal wage rates were deflated by the Denver area CPI for each of the years 1971–74.

Wage rates, however, are defined only for employed individuals. For individuals who are not employed, it is expected wages (more precisely, all the parameters of the wage distribution) that are important. To obtain expected wages, one could either obtain information from other data sources or, equivalently, impute values based on individual characteristics. We have chosen the latter option. The natural log of wages was regressed

tical two-state transition rates. As can be seen by aggregating the appropriate rows of Table 9.2, the CPS data indicate higher rates of employment instability than the DIME data.

[23] Clark and Summers, "Labor Market Dynamics and Unemployment," pp. 28–30.

[24] In some cases a completed spell length could not be ascertained because the individual left the sample, the spell was in progress when the experiment ended, or the spell was in progress at the beginning of the sample. Spells falling under the first two causes are examples of sample censoring, or truncation from the right, and were explicitly treated in the empirical work. Spells falling under the last cause are problems of initial conditions, or truncation from the left, are much more difficult to handle correctly, and were ignored.

Table 9.3. *Variable means for DIME participants, by age and sex*

Variable	Males 16–21	Males 22–59	Females 16–21	Females 22–59
Education (years)	10.6	11.1	11.0	11.7
Black (percent)	34.5	29.5	31.6	37.0
Hispanic (percent)	31.7	36.2	28.3	28.5
Age (years)	18.2	31.7	18.5	31.8
Age^2/100	3.4	10.9	3.4	10.9
Assets/1.000	0.4	0.2	0.3	0.2
ln(wage/p)	4.6	5.5	4.3	4.8
Number of dependent children	0.3	1.0	0.5	0.9
Black × ln(wage/p)	1.5	1.6	1.3	1.8
Hispanic × ln(wage/p)	1.4	2.0	1.2	1.3
Number of separate transitions	1,119	1,571	1,138	2,524
Number of persons in each group in 1973	260	660	326	946

Source: Authors' calculations from DIME data.

against age, age squared, education and race/ethnic status for each of the age/sex groups.[25] This procedure was done by quarters, resulting in sixteen predicted wage rates for each individual. Each labor market spell was matched to the predicted wage appropriate to the quarter in which the spell began.

This imputation of expected wages raises identification questions, both econometrically and conceptually. It is arguable that all personal characteristics that affect labor market transitions – such as age, race, sex – also affect wages and hence one should not use exclusion restrictions on certain variables to secure identification. Technical corrections to imputed wages such as the Mills ratio approach may be sufficient to identify the effects of wages, provided enough nonlinearity is induced by the correction. While this means of identification is possible, and we have exploited it in previous work,[26] a more appealing method of identification is afforded by the longitudinal nature of the data. By obtaining sixteen quar-

[25] In principle, a Mills ratio type of correction could be used in imputing predicted wages. In the DIME data, the correction for truncation appears to make little difference, and, as a practical matter, we ignored it. See James J. Heckman, "Sample Selection Bias as a Specification Error," *Econometrica*, vol. 47 (January 1979), pp. 153–61.

[26] See Kiefer and Neumann, "Estimation of Wage Offer Distributions and Reservation Wages."

terly expected wages for each individual, it is essentially intertemporal variation in wages that identifies the separate effect of wages. This approach is in the spirit of the model described earlier where tastes, measured, say, by demographic variables, are treated as constant. In the empirical work presented below, when transitions out of the employment state are being considered, ln *wage* refers to the logarithm of the actual real wage; for all other transitions, ln *wage* refers to the logarithm of the predicted real wage.

9.3   Estimation of transition rates

The estimation procedure

Availability of individual data on labor market behavior affords the advantage of determining the effect of wage rates and individual characteristics on turnover. Since transitions are discrete events and there is more than one state to move to, a simple regression strategy for analyzing data is inappropriate. We present an empirical model that handles the discreteness and multiple-state problems.[27] A procedure similar to residual analysis in regression studies can be applied as a check on the specification.

It is useful to introduce the arguments of the transition functions explicitly: $\lambda_{kj} = \lambda_{kj}(t, x)$, with t the random variable "future duration" and x a vector of characteristics. The hazard function associated with state E, that is, the rate of exit from state E at time t is given by

$$\lambda_E(t, x) = \lambda_{EU}(t, x) + \lambda_{EN}(t, x). \tag{8}$$

Hazard functions for states U and N are defined analogously.[28] Associated with the hazard function $\lambda_k(t, x)$ is the distribution function for duration in state k:

$$F_k(t, x) = 1 - \exp\left\{ -\int_0^t \lambda_k(u, x) \, du \right\}, \tag{9}$$

[27] The model and simple variations have been used previously in the economics literature by Tony Lancaster, "Econometric Methods for the Duration of Unemployment," *Econometrica*, vol. 47 (July 1979), pp. 939–56; Lundberg, "Unemployment and Household Labor Supply"; and Tuma and Robins, "A Dynamic Model of Employment Behavior."

[28] Statistical models for the analysis of duration (or "failure time") data have been widely studied. A recent treatment is John D. Kalbfleisch and Ross L. Prentice, *The Statistical Analysis of Failure Time Data* (Wiley, 1980). The decomposition of the hazard function into the sum of cause-specific hazard functions is the key to the study of "competing risks."

and subdensity associated with the time to each transition[29]:

$$f_{kj}(t, x) = \lambda_{kj}(t, x)[1 - F_k(t, x)]. \tag{10}$$

Given data (t_i, j_i, d_i, x_i) for a sample of $i = 1, \ldots, N$ independent spells, where t_i is the duration of spell i, j_i indexes the destination state, d_i is an indicator equal to one if t_i is the duration of a completed spell and equal to zero if the individual does not change states over the time of the study, and x_i is a vector of characteristics of the individual experiencing the ith spell, the likelihood function is given by

$$L_k = \prod_{i=1}^{n} \lambda_{kji}(t_i, x_i)^{d_i}[1 - F_k(t_i, S_i)].$$

The joint likelihood is given by $L_E L_U L_N$. If there are no restrictions across states on the parameters of hazard functions, then each state-specific likelihood function can be maximized separately without losing efficiency. For expositional purposes, we now concentrate on L_F.

In order to make the model applicable, a functional form for $\lambda_E(t,x)$ must be chosen. A natural and popular specification (the i subscript has been dropped) is[30]:

$$\lambda_{Ej}(t,x) = \exp x\beta_j, \quad j = U, N. \tag{11}$$

With this specification, the hazard rates are person-specific but not duration-dependent, a specification that has been widely used. Assuming that the hazard functions do not depend on duration is equivalent to assuming that transitions from state to state follow a (continuous-time) Markov process. Structural models generating such a process from optimal behavior by

---

[29] The term *subdensity* is used since:

$$\int_0^\infty f_{kj}(u, x)\, du \neq 1,$$

although

$$\int_0^\infty \left[\sum_j f_{kj}(u, x) \right] du = 1.$$

This usage follows Kalbfleisch and Prentice, *The Statistical Analysis of Failure Time Data*.

[30] P. Feigl and M. Zelen, "Estimation of Exponential Survival Probabilities with Concomitant Information," *Biometrics*, vol. 21 (December 1965), pp. 826–38, and Marvin Glasser, "Exponential Survival with Covariance," *Journal of the American Statistical Association*, vol. 62 (June 1967), pp. 561–68, are early references for this specification. D. R. Cox, "Regression Models and Life Tables," *Journal of the Royal Statistical Society*, Series B, vol. 34 (1972), pp. 187–220, provides an interesting generalization.

workers are discussed by Burdett and others.[31] With this specification, we have the log likelihood function

$$\ln L_e = \sum_{i=1}^{N} [d_i x_i \beta_{ji} - t_i (\exp x_i \beta_U + \exp x_i \beta_N)] \tag{12}$$

and corresponding log likelihood functions for estimating the parameters of transitions from the other states.

The simplicity of the likelihood function (equation 12) is in part a consequence of the Markov assumption that rules out duration dependence. Recent work suggests that this assumption may be overly strong, and hence it should be tested.[32] One way to see the potential effects of duration dependence is to examine the analogs of regression residuals. We have a series of durations t_i whose distributions depend on x_i, and we would like to transform these t_i by a function $Z_i = g(t_i)$ in such a way that the distribution of the Z_i, like the distribution of ordinary regression residuals, does not depend on the x_i. One way to do this is to choose Z_i equal to the cumulative distribution function of t_i evaluated at the observed t_i. The resulting random variables Z_i are identically distributed as uniform on the unit interval, provided the model is correct.[33] The sorted values of the Z_i can then be plotted against a 45° line (the cumulative function of the uniform distribution), and either by specific tests such as Kolmogorov–Smirnov or by eyeballing one can judge the adequacy of the model.

Empirical results

Table 9.4 contains estimates of the wage coefficients in the transition functions for the four age–sex groups being considered: males and females aged 16–21, and males and females aged 22–62. (The age is as of the date the spell began.) The variables, including the construction of an instrumental variable for wages, are discussed in detail above. The most significant aspect of these estimates is the powerful role of wage

[31] Burdett and others, "A Markov Model of Employment, Unemployment and Labor Force Participation."

[32] Clark and Summers, "Labor Market Dynamics and Unemployment"; and Nicholas M. Kiefer and George R. Neumann, "An Empirical Job Search Model, with a Test of the Constant Reservation-Wage Hypothesis," *Journal of Political Economy*, vol. 87 (February 1979), pp. 89–108.

[33] Maurice G. Kendall and Alan Stuart, *The Advanced Theory of Statistics*, vol. 1, 4th ed. (London: Charles Griffin and Co., 1977), p. 18.

Table 9.4. Wage coefficients in transition functions

Demographic group	Employment to unemployment	Employment to nonparticipation	Unemployment to employment	Unemployment to nonparticipation	Nonparticipation to employment	Nonparticipation to unemployment
Males 16–21						
ln *wage*	−0.41	−0.54	0.76	−1.5	0.038	0.62
B ln *wage*	−0.21	−0.64	−0.40	−0.33	−0.25	−0.37
H ln *wage*	−0.37	−0.55	−0.71	0.17	−0.60	0.69
Males 22–59						
ln *wage*	−0.55	−0.83	1.6	1.1	3.8	2.7
B ln *wage*	−0.43	−0.043	0.81	−0.75	1.3	1.5
H ln *wage*	−0.09	−0.49	1.8	0.23	0.40	−0.26
Females 16–21						
ln *wage*	−0.55	−0.80	0.29	−0.85	1.0	1.5
B ln *wage*	0.14	0.33	1.4	0.13	0.30	0.32
H ln *wage*	0.47	0.24	0.22	0.58	0.18	0.83
Females 22–59						
ln *wage*	−0.45	−0.63	1.9	2.3	3.4	5.0
B ln *wage*	−0.33	−0.07	0.72	0.39	−0.14	−1.6
H ln *wage*	−0.22	−0.015	0.63	−0.37	1.1	−1.1

Note: B ln *wage* and H ln *wage* are interactions between the ln *wage* variable and 0–1 variables for blacks and Hispanics, respectively.
Source: Authors' calculations. Extracted from Tables 5.2–5.5.

rates on transitions. For all four age–sex groups, higher wages uniformly lead to smaller probabilities of leaving employment and to higher probabilities of moving from unemployment to employment. Moreover, labor force participation significantly increases with the wage rate for all groups except young nonwhite males, for whom the wage effects on nonparticipation, while negative, are small compared to their standard errors (given in Tables 5.2–5.5). The empirical importance of these wages effects is highlighted by the rather substantial differences across race and sex groups. These empirical results imply that variations in personal characteristics account for substantial variations in labor market behavior. We will use these estimates to construct steady-state distributions of time spent in each labor market state.

Our interpretation of these wage effects is that they reflect real changes in dynamic labor supply. A contrary view would emphasize that the wage rate reflects a number of factors, measurable and nonmeasurable. To the extent that such factors – pluck, determination, effort – are idiosyncratic, the interpretation we give to these results would be misleading. In this view, transitions out of employment are low, not because wages are high, but because an individual is unusually reliable, say, which is reflected in the wage. Higher wages act then as a proxy for these individual fixed effects. Raising wages for a group would not lead to a change to turnover behavior because it would not alter the distribution of these individual effects.

This argument underscores the need for care in interpreting any such estimates. But in the case of transition data there is further information to rely upon. The wage variable used in the nonemployment states is not an actual wage but a predicted wage. As the projection from measurable characteristics, the predicted wage does not contain any idiosyncratic elements. Hence, if idiosyncratic factors were the motivating force in transitions, one would not expect to find a significant effect of predicted wage rates on transitions *into* employment. As Table 9.4 reveals, there are significant effects of wages in the four other transitions. Finally, if the transitions out of employment are reestimated with predicted wages replacing actual wages, the results are virtually unchanged. For these reasons we believe that the estimates do indeed reflect the effect of wage rates on supply behavior.[34]

In order for steady-state calculations to be valid, their underlying transition process must be Markov, an assumption we have exploited in the

[34] This argument was suggested to us by Isabel Sawhill, to whom we are grateful.

estimation. As a check on the empirical usefulness of this assumption, we performed a "residual analysis" as described above. An appendix available from the authors presents plots of the cumulative distribution of the duration of unemployment.[35] A formal test of the null hypotheses that the actual and predicted distributions are identical can be made by use of the Kolmogorov–Smirnov statistic. For these three groups we calculate K–S statistics of: 1.44 – older females; 0.72 – younger females; and 1.30 – younger males. The 1 percent critical value obtained from the asymptotic distribution of the K–S statistic is 1.63, and thus we cannot reject the hypothesis that the predicted and observed distributions are identical. Thus, conditional on the individual characteristics that we have included, transitions out of unemployment appear to be Markov for these groups.[36] For adult males, however, the formal test (K–S = 2.68) reveals that the predicted and actual distributions are not in very close agreement. The source of the discrepancy is that we underpredict short spells of unemployment for adult males. This suggests that our estimates of equilibrium unemployment rates for adult males may be somewhat too high.

9.4   Steady-state labor market distributions

The transition function parameters above, combined with the sample means, yield estimates of the steady-state transition rates across states, which are displayed in Table 9.5 for each of the sex and age groups and within each group by race. We have calculated an overall transition rate for each age–sex group using the overall means for the entire group. Since the transition functions are nonlinear, these overall rates are not equal to the weighted average of the corresponding race groups. Also, the overall transition rates reflect the sample proportions; they have not been reweighted to reflect the Denver SMSA.

From these transition rates, steady-state unemployment and labor force participation rates are calculated as described in equations 6 and 7 and are displayed in Table 9.6. A familiar story is evident from Tables 9.5

---

[35] In principle, one could analyze the distributions of time spent in all spells. However, since the length of time spent in employment and nonparticipation is long relative to the sample period, usefulness of this technique is lessened.

[36] When no allowance is made for individual characteristics – transition rates are assumed constant across age-sex groups – the predicted and actual distributions differ substantially. Thus it appears that the results of Clark and Summers ("Labor Market Dynamics and Unemployment") arise because of their inability to control for interindividual variation in characteristics such as wage rates.

Table 9.5. *Steady-state monthly transition rates, by age, sex, and race*

Demographic group	Employment to unemployment	Employment to nonparticipation	Unemployment to employment	Unemployment to nonparticipation	Nonparticipation to employment	Nonparticipation to unemployment
Males 16–21	6.5	7.6	22.1	7.6	8.0	4.0
Black	6.9	10.1	16.6	9.5	6.3	4.8
Hispanic	7.4	7.7	22.1	6.6	6.4	3.7
White	5.4	5.9	28.6	5.6	11.5	2.9
Males 22–59	1.7	1.4	28.2	4.7	13.7	4.3
Black	1.9	1.1	24.4	3.8	13.7	3.9
Hispanic	1.9	2.0	25.6	5.1	13.1	5.1
White	1.5	1.2	35.5	5.4	14.3	3.6
Females 16–21	4.5	8.2	20.4	9.1	4.9	3.0
Black	5.2	7.1	14.9	10.3	5.1	4.9
Hispanic	4.7	7.9	17.6	8.8	4.1	2.5
White	3.9	9.1	28.4	7.2	5.4	1.9
Females 22–59	1.8	4.7	16.6	10.6	1.0	1.4
Black	1.9	3.2	13.6	11.0	5.1	2.5
Hispanic	1.8	5.8	14.3	7.7	0.3	0.6
White	1.6	5.1	24.8	14.0	4.6	1.3

Note: Data are percentages.
Source: Authors' calculations from the estimates in Tables 5.2–5.5 and the mean values of the exogenous variables.

Table 9.6. *Steady-state unemployment and labor force participation rates, by age, sex, and race*

Demographic group	Unemployment rate	Labor force participation rate (%)
Males 16–21	25.0	61.2
Black	34.0	52.9
Hispanic	28.0	57.7
White	16.9	71.1
Males 22–59	6.1	91.8
Black	7.2	93.2
Hispanic	7.8	89.0
White	4.1	92.9
Females 16–21	22.6	48.6
Black	30.2	55.2
Hispanic	25.0	44.7
White	15.4	45.3
Females 22–59	17.9	30.2
Black	12.4	64.6
Hispanic	33.4	9.4
White	7.1	50.9

Source: Authors' calculations from Table 9.5.

and 9.6. Unemployment rates vary substantially across the population from a low of 4.1 percent for adult white males to a high of 34 percent for young black males. This is in accord with the findings of previous investigators, and it suggests that the DIME participants mirror, to a large extent, forces that exist in the national labor market.[37]

That the steady-state unemployment rates differ substantially by groups is reassuring since it is a precondition for the Baily–Tobin model to be effective. Given these differences, there is the possibility of "cheating the Phillips curve," or of altering the natural rate of unemployment, by making employment opportunities more attractive to certain groups. Whether this can be achieved depends, at least in the case of subsidized wages, on how elastic the responses of the different groups are to wages. In the previous section, we demonstrated that most of the state-specific transition functions were responsive, but as was noted above, the steady-state

[37] See Marston, "Employment Instability and High Unemployment Rates" for a discussion of steady-state differences in unemployment rates among race, sex, and age groups.

Table 9.7. *Steady-state unemployment and labor force participation rate elasticities, by age, sex, and race*

Demographic group	Elasticity of unemployment (%)	Elasticity of labor force participation (%)
Males 16–21	−0.37	0.35
Black	−0.36	0.69
Hispanic	−0.17	0.44
White	−0.51	0.24
Males 22–59	−2.07	0.30
Black	−2.95	0.33
Hispanic	−3.68	0.51
White	−2.11	0.27
Females 16–21	−0.33	0.90
Black	−0.70	0.71
Hispanic	−0.13	0.95
White	−0.38	0.97
Females 22–59	−1.51	1.77
Black	−2.71	1.03
Hispanic	−1.97	0.73
White	−1.63	1.68

Source: Authors' calculations from Tables 5.2–5.5, 9.5, and 9.6.

unemployment and participation rates depend on all six transition rates. Thus the net effect of altering wages for any one group is not immediately obvious, since it depends on both the sign of the individual response and the relative numbers in each state. To find the sensitivity of the steady-state rates, we differentiated the unemployment and labor force participation rates and expressed the changes in elasticity form, as shown in Table 9.7

There are two messages in these numbers. Unemployment rates are sensitive to wage rates in all groups: the effect of a 10 percent increase in wages ranges from a reduction of adult Hispanic males' unemployment rates by 2.9 percentage points (7.8 percent to 4.9 percent) to a low of 0.3 percentage point (25.0 percent to 24.7 percent) for young Hispanic females. In general, however, the greatest sensitivity of unemployment rates is found among the groups with the highest labor force participation rate. This means that significant changes in the aggregate unemployment rate would require large subsidies to groups that would otherwise have high unemployment rates. The dilemma presented by these findings can be seen in the labor force responses of teenagers. Using the elasticities of the two columns in Table 9.7 and labor force weights reflecting the composition of the U.S. labor force results in a teenage aggregate unemployment elasticity of -0.35 and a labor force participation elasticity of 0.61. A relatively modest policy goal of reducing the teenage unemployment rate by 1.5 percentage points – a 10 percent decline – would require a 28.6 percent change in wage rates. The large increases in labor force participation – in this case 17.5 percent, primarily by females and minorities – is what makes even such a modest goal so difficult to attain. As long as the labor market participation decision is sensitive to wages, efforts to reduce unemployment are not likely to appear successful, even though they may have real employment effects.

9.5   Conclusions

This chapter has examined the effect of wage rate variation on labor market transitions. The evidence presented indicates that labor market transition rates are dependent upon earnings and that, because of this relationship, so too are unemployment rates. Finding such an effect is essential for designing policies that attempt to "cheat the Phillips curve" or to reduce the natural rate of unemployment. The major finding of this chapter is that, despite the existence of conditions that make a tax-based employment policy possible, the evidence suggests that the effects on the aggregate unemployment rate are likely to be minor. Essentially, the problem is that an increase in actual or expected earnings for one group induces a large flow into the labor market, which reduces the change in unemployment for that group, while the opposite happens for the group that bears the tax. Although there are several ways to interpret this result, the conclusion that emerges is that this variant of the Baily–Tobin model does not offer great opportunities for reducing unemployment. The offer of more remunerative terms of employment to broadly targeted groups will result in sufficiently greater labor force participation to minimize the unemployment-reducing aspect of the program. If, however, the goal of policy is to improve the employment status of young people and the hard-to-employ, then this chapter shows that such a policy could succeed.

Acknowledgments

This revised version of a paper presented at the Conference on Labor Market Tightness and Inflation, Brookings Institution, Washington, D.C.,

1980, reflects the comments of the official discussants, Isabel Sawhill, and Christopher Flinn. We also have benefited from comments made by Martin Neil Baily, Kim Clark, Shelly Lundberg, Olivia Mitchell, Melvin Reder, and Lawrence Summers. Support from National Science Foundation Grant SOC 79-12406 is gratefully acknowledged. Research assistance of David Miller, Ralph Shnelvar, and Caroline Jumper is also acknowledged.

CHAPTER 10

How long is a spell of unemployment?
Illusions and biases in the use of
CPS data

10.1 Introduction

Despite decades of intense interest in the sources and nature of unemployment, the answer to the simple question, How long do spells of unemployment last? has remained elusive. This is surprising, since economists are often tempted to interpret short spells of unemployment as a frictional (or normal) component of unemployment about which policymakers need not be concerned and long-term (or chronic) unemployment as a disequilibrium component embodying most of its socially wasteful aspects. Hall (1972) and Marston (1976) pointed out that this is not a particularly useful distinction, since the high unemployment rates of many disadvantaged groups seem to be related to employment instability or frequent unemployment spells rather than lengthy individual spells. Nevertheless, the observation that the average spell of unemployment is relatively short has been used to support the position that most unemployment is essentially "voluntary." Conversely, the inability of some individuals to locate a job over a period of several months is considered to be evidence of labor market malfunctioning. As a prelude to analyzing changes in the ratio of long-term to short-term unemployment. Green et al. (1978) stated in the *Monthly Labor Review*, "The length of time that workers remain unemployed is an important indication of the severity of the Nation's unemployment problem" (p. 12).

The duration data used to study unemployment comes almost exclusively from the Census Bureau's monthly Current Population Survey (CPS), the only representative sample obtained on a continuing basis. Despite the attractive features of CPS data that make it an invaluable tool in many research applications, the data cannot be used to answer even rather simple questions concerning unemployment durations. The CPS is a point-

This chapter was written by Nicholas M. Kiefer, Shelly J. Lundberg, and George R. Neumann. It is reprinted from the *Journal of Business & Economic Statistics*, vol. 3, no. 2 (April 1985); © 1985 by the American Statistical Association.

in-time survey and thus cannot measure important aspects of phenomena that persist over time. For example, the CPS records as duration of unemployment the average duration of unemployment spells in progress as of the survey date, rather than the duration of completed spells. Moreover, as Kaitz (1970) noted, the point-in-time sampling of the CPS understates the frequency of short spells of unemployment, since longer spells are more likely to be recorded in the survey.

In spite of these difficulties, CPS data has been "the only game in town" for analyzing unemployment durations, and thus the trend in recent work has been to glean more information from the CPS by exploiting the quasi-panel nature of the data – an individual is in the sample for four months, out for eight, and then in again for four months – and by imposing additional restrictions on the underlying distribution of spell durations. These restrictions are then used to compute descriptive statistics of the duration distribution – typically, the mean and the upper deciles. These statistics, in turn, form the basis for almost all informed discussion regarding the duration of unemployment spells.

Obviously, these empirical characterizations of unemployment spells are only as good as the statistical assumptions they are based on; yet within the confines of CPS data, there is no way to check their validity. Providing such a check is the major purpose of this chapter.

We have departed from the current trend by introducing a new sample of *completed* unemployment spells obtained from panel data. We applied CPS sampling and reporting techniques, including the censoring of long spells, to this data to replicate the type of data used by other researchers. We then applied conventional statistical analysis to the CPS-like data and censored versions of the actual duration data and used the results of that analysis to characterize the duration distribution as researchers before us have done. Comparisons of predicted with actual distributions were then made for several statistical models and applied to five different sets of duration data. In this way, we distinguished the impact of point-in-time sampling from that of censored reporting of durations, since reporting techniques can be altered more readily.

Our results suggest that point-in-time sampling, by introducing considerable error into the measurement of unemployment durations, leads to unreliable estimates of the duration distribution. When data derived from continuous monitoring are used, both applying more general parametric forms and using more information on very long spells lead to significantly better predictions. This is not the case for CPS-like data; censored data perform nearly as well as uncensored data, and the simplest parametric forms frequently provide the best fits. The best inferences that can be made about the actual distribution using CPS-like data are seriously biased. Mean durations are underestimated by 2–3 weeks, and the fraction of spells lasting more than 28 or 52 weeks are substantially understated. Based on these findings, we are skeptical about the value of CPS duration data in the study of unemployment, even with substantial changes in reporting procedures.

10.2 Estimating unemployment duration from CPS data

Inferences about completed spells of unemployment depend crucially on the type of data available. We begin by using "perfect" data to characterize the duration distribution. Assume that a homogeneous population has been continuously monitored. At each moment of time, the number of persons with elapsed duration in unemployment s is known. Denoting calendar time by t, let the distribution of exit times from unemployment be given by $F_t(s)$.

Suppose that a particular date, T_0, is chosen to analyze the unemployment records and we wish to estimate the distribution of completed unemployment durations. Denote the flow into unemployment at date t as $p(t)$. The probability that an individual who entered the unemployed state at date $t \leq T_0$ is still unemployed at date T_0 is $1 - F_t(T_0 - t) = 1 - F_t(s)$. The density of elapsed durations at the interview date T_0 is

$$h(s; T_0) = \frac{p(t)[1 - F_t(s)]}{\int_{-\infty}^{T_0} p(u)[1 - F_u(T_0 - u]\,du}. \tag{1}$$

In general, this density will depend on the entire previous history of the process, as the denominator of (1) makes plain.

The essential question is, Can we estimate the time-dependent distribution functions, $F_t(S)$? Clearly, one cross-sectional "snapshot" alone is not sufficient, even though $p(t)$ is known. With perfect data, however, we can obtain estimates of $F_t(s)$ by observing the durations of unemployment for all cohorts of the unemployed, which by assumption are observed over time. (We ignore here and throughout this chapter any distinction between a "true" escape-rate distribution and that produced by the mixture of a true distribution with a distribution generated by unobserved population heterogeneity. For the purpose of estimating the distribution of completed unemployment spells, this distinction is irrelevant.

Similarly, except where specifically noted, we assume that all data pertain to an observationally homogeneous group of individuals.) In this manner, it is possible to produce estimates of duration distributions that differ by time period and compare unemployment behavior in booms and in troughs.

The assumption of a perfect data set is, of course, counterfactual. Consequently, researchers have had to restrict the general form of (1). Two approaches are possible – the first based on cross-sectional data and the second on gross flows. If only a snapshot of elapsed durations is available but the $p(t)$'s are known, one can estimate the parameters of the distribution of exit times provided that the distribution is known up to a vector of parameters and is unchanging over time. (By unchanging over time, we mean that the form of the distribution function and its dependence on variables such as aggregate demand are known. This dependence on external covariates is not completely general, since it cannot encompass pure cohort effects.) This is known as the synthetic cohort method. In this case we have

$$h(s; T_0) = \frac{p(t)[1 - F(s; \phi)]}{\int_{-\infty}^{T_0} p(u)[1 - F(T_0 - u; \phi)] \, du}, \tag{1'}$$

where by $F(s; \phi)$ we indicate specifically the requirement that F be known up to the parameter vector ϕ.

Maximum likelihood estimates of ϕ can be used to calculate functions of ϕ, such as the average duration of a completed spell or the upper percentage points of F. The major advantage of this method is that it allows one to deal explicitly with nonstationarity. Indeed, if ϕ contains an element related to demand pressure, it is feasible to examine whether the exit distribution varies with the business cycle.

Despite the attractiveness of this specification, it has rarely been implemented in the economics literature. Unpublished papers by Luckett (1978) and Smith (1982) and the article by Bowers and Harkess (1979) are the only studies that discuss or implement this approach, to our knowledge. [Bowers and Harkess 1979 do not directly estimate the parameters of the exit distribution based on likelihood construction. Instead, they use $L(s) = U[s, T_0]/p(T_0 - s)$, the empirical survivor function, and fit smooth curves to these data. Since $L'(s)$ is not guaranteed to be nonpositive, smoothing by regressing $L(s)$ on s is necessary to produce a well-behaved survivor function. In principle, this smoothing amounts to assuming a specific form for $F(s)$.]

The more common method of using cross-sectional data is to assume that the stochastic process generating the exit times is Markov or semi-Markov. The ergodic property of regular Markov processes implies that the inflow $p(t)$ converges to $\bar{p}$, and thus $(1')$ converges to

$$h(s) = \frac{\bar{p}[1 - F(s)]}{\bar{p} \int_{-\infty}^{T_0} [1 - F(T_0 - u)] \, du} = \frac{1 - F(s)}{\bar{D}}, \tag{1''}$$

where $\bar{D} = \int_0^{\infty} [1 - F(s)] \, ds$ is the mean of completed spells. This is the result of Kaitz (1970) and Salant (1977), though obtained in a different manner. (See also Akerlof and Main 1980, Bjorklund 1981, Cripps and Tarling 1974, Frank 1978, Marston 1976, and Silcock 1954.) Typically, a parametric form of F is chosen such that $1 - F(s)$ and $\bar{D}$ can be expressed as functions of a few parameters. It should be stressed that $(1'')$ holds only in the stationary state and even relatively minor departures from stationary inflows can have large consequences for the estimates. In particular, reporting a time series of estimated functions that are based on period-by-period stationarity assumptions is likely to be of little value. [European authors, following Cripps and Tarling 1974, are more sensitive to the effect of nonstationary-state stocks on estimates of the exit distribution and tend to report moments of the exit distribution only when a "stationary position (of the register) has been reached" (p. 301). American writers (e.g., Akerlof and Main 1980) produce estimates of average durations in conditions when the steady-state stocks of the unemployed could not possibly be reached, even if the distribution function were invariant to economic conditions. Such estimates tell us nothing about the length of an average spell of unemployment.]

The second approach to estimating the distribution of exit times from unemployment is available when entry and possibly exit times are known for all individuals. (See Clark and Summers 1979 for an application of this approach.) If all entry and exit times are known, we have the perfect data described earlier. CPS data have only a quasi-panel structure; when individuals are observed for four months, only some of the labor market flows will be observed for each cohort. Aggregate flow data for successive periods, however, allow one to calculate the empirical hazard rate:

$$\lambda_t(s) \cdot \Delta h = \frac{U[s, t] - U[s + \Delta h, t + \Delta h]}{U[s, t]}, \tag{2}$$

where $U[s, t]$ is the stock of unemployed with elapsed duration s at time t and Δh is the length of the sampling window. The fundamental relationship between hazard functions and distribution functions,

$$\lambda(s) = f(s)/(1 - F(s)) \tag{3a}$$

and

$$F(s) = 1 - \exp\left\{ -\int_0^s \lambda(x)\, dx \right\}, \tag{3b}$$

provides the link between observed behavior and the hypothesized underlying distribution of completed-spell lengths (Kalbfleisch and Prentice 1980). In practice, $\lambda(s)$ is not observed for all values of s. Some simple curves are therefore fit to the data, and the complete distribution is inferred from these estimates. In this regard, it is worth remarking that nonnegativity throughout the range of s is an essential requirement for any hypothesized hazard function. Moreover, it is a requirement that

$$\lim_{s \to \infty} \int_0^s \lambda(x)\, dx = \infty \tag{4}$$

so that the distribution function in (3b) be nondefective. Although defective distributions can be of use in some problems (e.g., mover–stayer models), the intended purpose of estimating hazard rates – extrapolation to unobserved values – argues strongly against considering distributions with $F(\infty) < 1$. In other words, some hazard functions that appear to fit the data well may be objectionable on an a priori basis.

In principle, estimated parameters of the exit-time distribution obtained from gross flow methods should be identical to those obtained from the point-in-time sampling methods described in (1′) and (1″), provided the restrictions on admissible forms of λ are satisfied. Both approaches allow for nonstationary behavior in the entrance rates into unemployment, and although neither can encompass pure cohort effects on the exit distribution, each can treat fluctuation in the exit distribution as a function of aggregate economic conditions. The major advantage of gross flow data is that one may ignore the relatively cumbersome weighting shown in (1′).

Despite the close relationship between the sample data function – either the elapsed-duration distribution in the point-in-time sample or the hazard function in the gross flow approach – and the distribution of completed spells, there are serious problems associated with using CPS data in either of these manifestations to estimate duration distributions. A primary difficulty is that the reported data are presented as grouped data in intervals of 0–4, 5–6, 7–10, 11–14, 15–26, or more than 27 weeks of elapsed unemployment. Since these categories are not integer multiples of the sampling window (one month), it is not possible to obtain the exact weight, $p(t)$, needed to calculate (1′) in the synthetic cohort approach. (This problem is not insurmountable. The existing gross flow data are available monthly, and one can form weighted averages of the monthly flows, assuming that the entry rate is uniformly distributed within a month.)

Grouping of the data also causes difficulties for the gross flow approach. Since interviews are one month apart and we do not know when during the month the transition out of unemployment occurred, actual completed durations lie in the intervals 0–8.3, 5–10.3, 7–14.3, 11–18.3, 15–30.3, and 27+ weeks. As the overlapping of these intervals suggests, we know completed durations from gross flow data with very little precision. (There are further problems with the gross flow data that hinder their usefulness for the analysis of unemployment; for example, the reported flows do not add up to the current stocks. See Abowd and Zellner 1982 for a discussion of these issues.)

Other difficulties follow from the CPS reporting procedures. Usable data are censored at about six months. Only five of the reported intervals can be used to fit hazard functions, since the longer spells of unemployment in the open-ended final category must be excluded. Furthermore, since many short spells of unemployment are missed altogether – the length bias problem in sampling discussed by Kaitz (1970) – the fit of the estimated distribution depends on behavior in both the lower and upper tails being consistent with the assumed functional form.

Despite the frailties of the CPS data for purposes of estimating duration distributions, it is currently the only sample with representative coverage of all labor market participants and is thus potentially the most informative. It is therefore very important to know whether despite all of these problems, the duration distributions estimated from CPS data are reasonably accurate.

10.3   The Denver Income Maintenance Experiment data

Our new sample of completed unemployment spells comes from surveys conducted in the course of the Denver Income Maintenance Experiment (DIME). A principal advantage of these data is that they provide a continuous employment history for each individual in the sample for up to 48 months. Thus the completed duration of each unemployment spell is known, with the exception of a very small number of spells that overlap the beginning or end of the sample period. The periodic interviews are retrospective, so we have accurate information on the timing of each transition into and out of employment.

The DIME sample has been discussed extensively elsewhere (see Keeley et al. 1978 and Tuma and Robins 1980), as have the employment histories constructed from the basic DIME Public Use Files (see Lundberg 1980 and Kiefer and Neumann 1982). A few characteristics of the data, however, are particularly relevant to the application at hand, since they limit the comparability of our results with those of CPS-based studies. Specifically, the sample selection criteria for DIME families and the imprecision of recorded transitions between unemployment and nonparticipation in employment interviews may limit our ability to draw conclusions about the general population from this study.

Sample selection

The CPS sample is representative of the U.S. population; the DIME sample is not. The Denver experiment was designed to measure the effects of a negative income tax (NIT) on labor supply. So that the sample would correspond as closely as possible to the target population of a future NIT program, the 2,657 families initially enrolled in the experiment had to satisfy a number of eligibility requirements. These included restrictions concerning age, family structure, and ability to work, but most important, all families with preexperiment "normal" earnings above a specified level were excluded. Eligible families were allocated in a nonrandom fashion among 11 financial treatments and a control group containing 40% of the total sample.

The most obvious problem in using this sample to study unemployment is that the support guarantees and varying tax rates faced by financial-treatment families distort labor supply decisions. This is easily avoided, however, by restricting the analysis, as we do, to the control group, which received only token payments for reporting their work histories.

The earnings truncation of the DIME sample presents a more serious difficulty. We would expect families who experience lower incomes prior to the experiment to contain members with an unusual propensity to experience long or frequent spells of unemployment. It is not obvious how restricting our analysis to individuals in low-income families will affect the distribution of unemployment-spell durations, but we might expect long spells to be more prevalent than in the population as a whole.

The unemployment–nonparticipation distinction

In general, the information available in the DIME Public Use Files permits individuals to be classified as employed, unemployed, or nonparticipating according to the CPS definitions of these labor market states.

A problem concerning the identification of transitions between unemployment and nonparticipation arose, however, during the construction of employment histories. The data were collected via 10 periodic interviews, which were administered at intervals of 3–4 months. At each interview, all spells of employment and unemployment since the last interview were identified. After this, a series of questions relating to each spell were asked, including probes for search activity during each spell of unemployment.

This procedure had two unfortunate results. First, between periodic interviews, any transitions between unemployment and nonparticipation are not identified. As a consequence, transition rates between these two states will be underestimated (documented in Kiefer and Neumann 1982). Second, all observed transitions between these states will occur during months in which periodic interviews took place and will be placed at the end of a month in the raw data. There will thus be some error in the timing of recorded transitions. These problems suggest that some caution be exercised in interpreting results from DIME data, but given the deficiencies of CPS data, they do not seem to warrant abandoning the use of such special samples.

The appropriate way to assess these difficulties, of course, is to compare the characteristics of DIME data with those of the alternative, CPS data. It must be noted, then, that the exact date on which a transition between unemployment and nonparticipation takes place is not available from CPS gross flow data either. In fact, for *any* recorded transition, we know only that a change in labor force status has occurred at some point during the month. Thus the error in the reported duration of unemployment spells beginning or ending in nonparticipation will be larger in DIME data than in CPS data; and for spells beginning or ending in employment, it will be smaller. In addition, Woltman (1980) suggested that simple response variability results in inflated CPS gross flow data, and that this problem is particularly serious for movements into and out of the labor force. This implies that part of the discrepancy between the unemployment–nonparticipation transition rates in DIME and CPS may be due to the existence of spurious transitions in the latter.

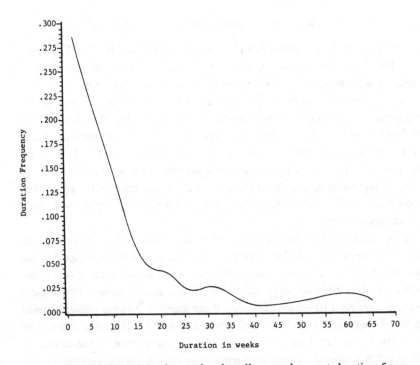

Figure 10.1. Actual completed-spell unemployment duration frequencies, adult males.

Continuous monitoring and CPS-like unemployment data

To perform the comparisons described in Section 10.1 we first constructed the true distribution of completed unemployment spells. The middle years of the sample (1972 and 1973) were used as the sampling frame. All spells of unemployment occurring during this period were included. A small fraction of these spells were censored because of sample attrition – about 1.5% for adult men and less than 1% for women – but in the main, the sample consists of about 700 completed spells of unemployment for men and women over 21 years of age.

Figures 10.1 and 10.2 display the sample density functions of unemployment duration for adult men and women, respectively. These graphs were constructed by fitting a cubic spline function through the observed frequencies to obtain smoothness. Some relevant characteristics of the sample distributions are given in Table 10.1.

Both male and female distributions exhibit skewness of the sort com-

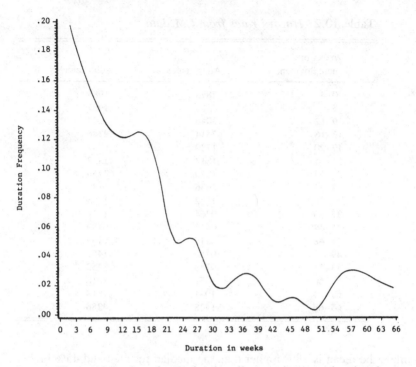

Figure 10.2. Actual completed-spell unemployment duration frequencies, adult females.

Table 10.1. *Characteristics of unemployment duration data from DIME*

	Adult males	Adult females
Mean (weeks)	14.2	18.4
Median (weeks)	8.0	12.7
Proportion of spells		
<8 weeks	51.0	35.3
<28 weeks	84.5	81.9
<52 weeks	90.7	91.3
Number of observations	355	343

monly thought to be characteristic of unemployment: most spells are quite short, but the distribution has a long skew to the right. (See Burdett et al. 1984, Kiefer and Neumann 1982, and Salant 1977 for other evidence of unemployment-spell length and its distribution.) For example, in this

Table 10.2. *Hazard rates from CM data*

Weeks of unemployment	Adult males	Adult females
0–4	.2873	.1983
5–8	.3581	.1927
9–12	.3046	.1937
13–16	.2314	.2346
17–20	.1720	.2847
21–24	.1818	.1837
25–28	.1270	.2250
29–32	.1636	.1129
33–36	.1522	.1455
37–40	.0764	.1915
41–44	.0417	.0789
45–48	.0417	.1143
49–52	.0758	.1452
53–56	.0758	.1452
57–60	.1071	.1818
61–64	.1071	.1818
65–68	.1428	.4286

sample the mean is 78% higher than the median for men and 45% higher for women. For men the sample-density function looks rather like an exponential function, at least up to about the 20th or 25th week, and the density of completed spell lengths for women does not resemble any textbook form of which we are aware.

From this sample of all spells of unemployment, we constructed hazard functions after grouping the data, separately by sex, into 4-week intervals. These are reported in Table 10.2. Hazard functions could be estimated for smaller intervals from these data, but we wished to keep the analysis close to the practical limits of what could be obtained by using CPS data. Furthermore, we have avoided using intervals of unequal length, as the CPS uses, to eliminate inessential complications. The effects of censoring duration data at 28 or 52 weeks can be determined by using only the first 7 or 13 hazard rates.

Construction of CPS-like data required an entirely different procedure. The CPS interviews individuals at one point of each month, determines the current labor market state, and then matches observations in consecutive months to give the gross monthly flows among states. [We are ignoring the complications brought about by movement into and out of CPS

Table 10.3. *Hazard rates from CPS-like data*

Weeks of unemployment at initial interview	Adult males	Adult females
0–4	.3760	.2317
5–8	.3025	.2550
9–12	.3396	.2697
13–16	.2466	.2632
17–20	.3137	.2632
21–24	.2571	.2728
25–28	.1600	.2000
29–32	.2222	.2903
33–36	.2222	.3462
37–40	.1292	.1250
41–44	.2054	.1765
45–48	.1052	.0751

due to sample rotation. Users of the CPS have generally assumed that there is no rotation effect (even though it is known to exist), and we do not attempt to reproduce the problem in our sample.] We produced CPS-like data (or when there is no possibility of confusion, simply CPS data) by matching observations on the individual's state on the first day of adjacent months, indexed by elapsed duration. The resulting gross flow data are used to produce exit probabilities grouped into duration categories at 4-week intervals. These are reported in Table 10.3. This grouping corresponds closely, but not exactly, to the one used by the CPS in reporting both gross flow and elapsed-duration distributions. In what follows, we refer to the data obtained by using the full-panel nature of the data as continuous monitoring (CM) data, whether censored or uncensored. CPS data were censored at 28 or 52 weeks.

In principle, these data could be used to estimate the distribution of exit times by either the synthetic-cohort or the gross flow approach. As a practical matter, the number of spells of unemployment recorded during the two-year period was about 350 each for men and women; consequently, the number of persons unemployed at any one time is relatively small, and the grouped duration distribution will have sparse cells at any point in time. Hence it does not appear feasible to apply the synthetic cohort approach to these data. Because labor market conditions, however, were stable during the 1972–1973 period, as measured by both the Denver Standard Metropolitan Statistical Area (SMSA) unemployment rate

Table 10.4. *Parametric models of the hazard rates*

Form	Specification	Restriction
Exponential	$\ln \lambda(d) = B_0$	$-\infty < B_0 < \infty$
Weibull	$\ln \lambda(d) = B_0 + B_1 \ln(d)$	$-1 < B_1 < \infty$
Gompertz	$\ln \lambda(d) = B_0 + B_1 d$	$0 \leq B_1 < \infty$
Log-linear	$\lambda(d) = B_0 + B_1 \ln(d)$	$0 \leq B_0 < \infty$
Generalized	$\ln \lambda(d) = B_0 + B_1 \ln(d)$	$0 \leq B_1 < \infty$
Weibull	$+ B_2(\ln(d))^2$	$0 \leq B_2 < \infty$
Generalized Gompertz	$\ln \lambda(d) = B_0 + B_1 d + B_2 d^2$	$0 \leq B_2 < \infty$

and the unemployment rates of DIME controls, it seems reasonable to treat the completed spells of unemployment as observations from a single exit-time distribution, which allows us to use the gross flow approach. [The Denver SMSA unemployment rate was 3.6% in 1972 and 3.4% in 1973; for DIME controls the equivalent unemployment rates were 7.6% in each year (Kiefer and Neumann 1982, p. 334).] The empirical work that follows focuses solely on this approach.

10.4   Fitting parametric forms to CM and CPS-like data

In this section, we report the results of fitting several specific distribution functions to the five sets of data described in Section 10.3. CM data will be referred to as CM28, CM52, or CMall to identify the censoring limit; and CPS-like data will be denoted CPS28 or CPS52. We consider six functional forms for the hazard function, described in Table 10.4, as candidates for fitting the data. These include the most commonly used failure-time models but are obviously only a subset of the family of distributions that could be considered. [Obviously, the menu of potential functional forms is broader than the six we examined. We have not investigated other functional forms (e.g., the gamma function), but it does not seem likely that the general results would change much.]

Users of actual CPS gross flows are presented with censored data on unemployment spells, from which they wish to infer moments, or functions of moments, of the full distribution. Excluding the open-ended final duration interval, censoring occurs at about 26 weeks, leaving only five observations on grouped data. This limits the choice of the distribution function substantially, and we have restricted our set of hazard functions to those that are estimable within the confines of actual CPS data. By

Table 10.5. *Parameter estimates for alternative hazard function models: maximum likelihood estimates, adult men*

Parameters	CM data			CPS-like data	
	28 weeks	52 weeks	None	28 weeks	52 weeks
	Exponential				
B_0	−2.2008	−2.3833	−2.6959	−2.5017	−2.5562
	(.0584)	(.0563)	(.0539)	(.0681)	(.0659)
	Weibull				
B_0	−2.3185	−2.2343	−2.2380	−2.9961	−2.7207
	(.0188)	(.0190)	(.0180)	(.0189)	(.0189)
B_1	−.1242	−.2182	−.2138	.2572	.0806
	(.0096)	(.0088)	(.0075)	(.0086)	(.0082)
	Gompertz				
B_0	−2.6564	—	—[a]	−2.6805	—[a]
	(.0426)			(.0218)	
B_1	.0368	—	—	.0187	—
	(.0016)			(.0018)	

Note: Standard errors are given in parentheses. 28 weeks, 52 weeks, and None are censoring points.
[a]Converged at inadmissible parameter values ($B_1 < 0$).

increasing the number of parameters above our upper limit of three, one can always find a functional form that will fit the first t (i.e., the uncensored) observations perfectly. Our primary interest, however, is in how well the fitted distributions enable us to extrapolate durations beyond the censoring limit.

We have estimated the six functional forms described in Table 10.4 by maximum likelihood, using the data reported in Tables 10.2 and 10.3. [For the CM data, elapsed duration is set at the midpoint of each 4-week interval. For CPS data, elapsed duration-to-date takes on the values of 4.15, 8.65, 12.65, 16.65, 20.65, and 24.65, the midpoint of the prior month duration category plus the sampling window (4.3 weeks).] Tables 10.5 and 10.6 contain these estimates for the first three candidate distributions. All estimates for the generalized Weibull and generalized Gompertz distributions violate the restriction $B_2 \geq 0$, which is required of a proper distribution function. Failure to satisfy this restriction implies that $F(\infty) < 1$, so sensible estimates of upper-tail probabilities are impossible. (Clark and Summers 1979, for example, did not impose these restrictions

Table 10.6. *Parameter estimates for alternative hazard function models: maximum likelihood estimates, adult women*

Parameters	CM data			CPS-like data	
	28 weeks	52 weeks	None	28 weeks	52 weeks
			Exponential		
B_0	−2.5100	−2.6883	−2.9217	−2.7593	−2.7658
	(.0600)	(.0567)	(.0541)	(.0663)	(.0631)
			Weibull		
B_0	−2.9531	−2.7994	−2.8200	−3.8733	−3.5229
	(.0173)	(.0168)	(.0160)	(.0180)	(.0174)
B_1	.0632	−.0559	−.0417	.5229	.3363
	(.0078)	(.0069)	(.0061)	(.0074)	(.0068)
			Gompertz		
B_0	−3.0776	−3.2618	—[a]	−3.2260	−2.9768
	(.0336)	(.0802)		(.0204)	(.0215)
B_1	.0768	.0439	—	.0448	.0155
	(.0021)	(.0028)		(.0014)	(.0011)

Note: Standard errors are given in parentheses. 28 weeks, 52 weeks, and None are censoring points.
[a]Converged at inadmissible parameter values ($B_1 < 0$).

and wound up with estimated cumulative distribution functions having a regular interior maximum. Obviously the calculation of tail-area probabilities or means is meaningless in such circumstances.) As the purpose of fitting these forms is extrapolation to unobserved durations and reconstruction of the underlying distribution, estimates which violate parameter restrictions are not reported. These also include all log-linear estimates, and some versions of the Gompertz form.

The results in Tables 10.5 and 10.6 suggest that models which allow nonconstant hazard rates are superior to the constant-hazard exponential for both men and women. The Weibull form appears to fit most versions of the data better than the exponential form, according to a likelihood ratio test, as do several forms of the Gompertz distribution with admissible parameter values. It should be noted, however, that the exit rate derived from CPS data increases with elapsed duration, and the CM exit rates usually decline over time. Since the Weibull and Gompertz model are not nested, we cannot choose between them on the basis of a likelihood ratio test.

More important than the fit of each model to the data used to estimate

Table 10.7. *Summary statistics from alternative hazard function models for adult men*

			Proportion of spells with duration less than		
Censoring point	Mean	Median	8 weeks	28 weeks	52 weeks

Exponential					
CM data					
28 weeks	9.03	6.26	.588	.955	.997
52 weeks	10.84	7.51	.522	.924	.992
None	14.82	10.27	.417	.849	.986
CPS-like data					
28 weeks	12.20	8.46	.481	.899	.986
52 weeks	12.89	8.93	.462	.886	.982
Weibull					
CM data					
28 weeks	12.97	7.98	.501	.875	.972
52 weeks	14.65	7.96	.501	.843	.951
None	14.56	7.96	.501	.845	.952
CPS-like data					
28 weeks	12.09	9.72	.419	.927	.997
52 weeks	12.92	9.49	.438	.893	.987
Gompertz					
CM data					
28 weeks	10.23	8.42	.480	.968	.999
CPS-like data					
28 weeks	12.09	9.26	.446	.920	.998
Actual	14.20	8.00	.510	.845	.907

it is the ability of each parametric model to predict the actual (unobserved) distribution of unemployment spells. In the case of uncensored CM data, these considerations coincide, since the entire distribution is used in estimation. We can compare this "best possible" fit of simple parametric forms to those achieved when data are simply censored and, in turn, to those that result when CPS-like monitoring and reporting procedures are used.

We focus on three aspects of the distribution of unemployment spells: the duration of a typical spell as measured by the mean and median, the frequency of very short spells, and the frequency of very long spells. Predicted values of these magnitudes from all acceptable parametric models are presented in Tables 10.7 and 10.8, together with the true values from

Table 10.8. *Summary statistics from alternative hazard function models for adult women*

Censoring point	Mean	Median	Proportion of spells with duration less than		
			8 weeks	28 weeks	52 weeks
Exponential					
CM data					
28 weeks	12.30	8.53	.478	.897	.985
52 weeks	14.71	10.19	.420	.851	.971
None	18.57	12.87	.350	.779	.939
CPS-like data					
28 weeks	15.79	10.94	.398	.830	.963
52 weeks	15.89	11.02	.396	.828	.962
Weibull					
CM data					
28 weeks	16.63	12.07	.361	.817	.962
52 weeks	18.73	12.38	.368	.776	.932
None	18.50	12.38	.366	.780	.936
CPS-like data					
28 weeks	15.11	13.18	.277	.887	.996
52 weeks	15.92	13.18	.299	.850	.987
Gompertz					
CM data					
28 weeks	10.76	10.00	.399	.989	1.000
52 weeks	14.87	13.31	.307	.879	.999
CPS-like data					
28 weeks	14.42	12.89	.318	.892	.999
52 weeks	15.92	12.34	.352	.832	.983
Actual	18.40	12.70	.353	.819	.913

the CM sample. (Closed-form solutions exist for the exponential and Weibull mean value functions, and these were used in Tables 10.7 and 10.8. The Gompertz mean values were obtained via numerical integration. Median values were obtained from the fitted survivor functions.)

Means and medians

When uncensored data are used, the estimated mean and median unemployment durations are very close to their true values for both men and women, regardless of the parametric model used. (The only exception is that the exponential model overestimates the median for men only by about two weeks.) If the CM data are censored, however, the choice of a model becomes very important. CM52 performs nearly as well as CMall with the Weibull form but usually results in a significant underestimate of both mean and median with either of the other forms. CM28 does even worse, but the undershooting is kept to a minimum by the Weibull distribution.

With CPS data, the degree of censoring has almost no effect on the predicted means and medians. In sharp contrast to the CM data, use of the Weibull or Gompertz form does not generally improve the predictions. When compared to Weibull estimates using CM data with similar censoring, CPS28 and CPS52 lead to more serious underestimates of mean durations and slightly worse estimates of medians.

Frequency of short spells

One well-known feature of the CPS sampling method is that short spells of unemployment are undercounted. For example, ignoring the overall sampling rate, as interviews are conducted at 4-week intervals, a spell with a complete duration of 4 weeks or more is certain to be caught, a 2-week spell has a .5 probability of being detected, and so forth. Since shorter spells of unemployment are less likely to be included in the CPS sample, the distribution of completed spell lengths may be biased.

How important are these missing spells? Tables 10.7 and 10.8 show that in this sample, 51% of men's unemployment spells are less than 8 weeks long, as are 35% of women's. Using the Weibull distribution results in good estimates with CM data, regardless of censoring. With the same distribution, CPS-like data do appear to lead to length bias, as the proportion of short spells is significantly underestimated for both men and women. This impression does not persist, however, if we turn to the exponential distribution, where for women the bias is in the opposite direction. Although CPS sampling results in censoring at the lower and upper tails of the distribution, the resulting bias in the estimated distribution depends solely on how well the assumed parametric model fits in the lower tail.

Frequency of long spells

Table 10.7 and 10.8 contain the actual and predicted proportions of unemployment spells that end in less than 28 or 52 weeks for men and women, respectively. Even with uncensored data, the models we use proved too simple to fit these tail probabilities consistently. For men prediction is good up to 28 weeks, but the number of extremely long spells is underestimated. For women prediction is reasonably good for 52 weeks but underestimates the proportion of spells less than 28 weeks. The shape of the actual distributions in the upper tails clearly does not conform well to these standard distributions. Note that this leads to some rather important considerations: under ideal data conditions, the best estimate suggests that 5% of men's unemployment spells are longer than 52 weeks, yet the true proportion is over 9%.

As might be expected, censored versions of the data do even worse. None of the models pick up the fat upper tail of the actual distribution for men; the proportion of long spells is consistently underpredicted. For women there is a clear trade-off between predicting the proportion of spells less than 28 weeks and predicting the proportion less than 52 weeks. The Weibull model fits well at 28 weeks with CM28 and 52 weeks with CM52.

Predictions using CPS data are remarkably insensitive to changes in functional form or censoring and are remarkably poor. For men long spells are underpredicted by a very large amount (8 points for over 52 weeks). For women the exponential model predicts well at 28 weeks, but all models do very badly at 52 weeks.

General goodness-of-fit

Table 10.9 presents a chi-squared test for the fit of each model for the first 17 4-week intervals and the maximum distance between the predicted and actual distribution functions. [The chi-squared statistic is formed as $\chi^2 = N\Sigma_{t=1}^{17}[\hat{F}(t) - F(t)]^2/\hat{F}(t)$, where N is the number of spells of unemployment in the sample, $\hat{F}$ is the predicted distribution, and F is the empirical distribution. The summation runs over the 17 duration intervals reported.] The results have already been suggested by the preceding discussion. The best fit is achieved by the Weibull model applied to CM data. CM52 is nearly as good as CMall; CM28 is only a little worse. CPS data do best with the exponential model but are always clearly inferior to the best of the CM models. Censoring has no effect on the fit of the CPS-exponential model.

Several conclusions are suggested by the preceding results:

1. A simple and commonly used functional form – the Weibull – fits the actual distributions of unemployment durations well. This is true for both men and women, with the only major problem

Table 10.9. *Goodness-of-fit measures over first 68 weeks of duration distribution*

Censoring point	Adult men		Adult women	
	x^2	$\max\|\hat{F} - F\|$	x^2	$\max\|\hat{F} - F\|$
Exponential				
CM data				
28 weeks	52.4	.11	62.4	.14
52 weeks	26.4	.08	20.6	.08
None	31.3	.10	4.3	.05
CPS-like data				
28 weeks	19.0	.08	10.0	.05
52 weeks	19.0	.08	9.3	.05
Weibull				
CM data				
28 weeks	11.1	.07	4.6	.05
52 weeks	7.4	.04	4.3	.05
None	7.5	.05	3.7	.05
CPS-like data				
28 weeks	51.1	.09	57.8	.10
52 weeks	28.9	.08	28.5	.07
Gompertz				
CM data				
28 weeks	45.2	.12	88.7	.19
52 weeks	—	—	31.1	.10
CPS-like data				
28 weeks	34.3	.09	31.1	.11
52 weeks	—	—	10.2	.07

being an inability to fit the upper tail of the male distribution in this sample.

2. With CM data, censoring at 52 weeks does not lead to a marked deterioration of the fit, and censoring at 28 weeks leads to only moderate problems when the Weibull form is used.

3. CPS-like data censored at 52 weeks fit the actual distributions badly, and the use of functional forms more general than the exponential one generally makes the fit even worse. Censoring at 28 rather than 52 weeks makes almost no difference.

The implications for our current knowledge of the unemployment-duration distribution, which is derived from the CPS, are almost entirely negative.

Although the results reported here are specific to our data set, it seems likely that predictions from parametric models applied to CPS data are no better than those from our very similar CPS28 data. Even more disturbing, these predictions can probably not be improved by using more general parametric forms or by extending the censoring limit to make additional data available. With existing sampling techniques, we cannot do much better than leave the censoring at 26 weeks and estimate an exponential hazard model. The major problem appears to be the imprecision with which unemployment durations are measured by the CPS; in turn, this is the result of once-a-month sampling plus the aggregation of initial durations into 4-week intervals. Measurement error obscures the hazard rate patterns in CPS data that are so evident in the CM data.

How serious is the poor fit that results? The underprediction of very long spells and the bias in predicted mean duration might be reduced in magnitude by a more representative data set with fewer long spells. The apparent unreliability of estimates derived from CPS data is likely to be a more persistent problem. On the basis of how well they fit available CPS data, we would prefer parametric forms other than the exponential. We have shown, using the true duration distribution, that such criteria may be very misleading; the "preferred" estimates may fit the actual distribution very badly.

10.5   Conclusions

The findings reported in this study are specific to the data set used, and other data sets could, in principle, produce different results. Yet to our knowledge, the DIME data provide the only means of assessing the value of using data derived from point-in-time sampling, such as that reported in the CPS, to estimate durations of comleted spells of unemployment. Our results indicate that the bias in mean durations is about 2–3 weeks and the frequency of long spells is underpredicted. More important, we find that the currently popular method of estimating hazard functions on censored and aggregated data to provide estimates of the complete distribution and of functions of the complete distribution are quite unreliable. This arises in part because durations are censored and some parameterizations yield defective distribution functions but primarily because CPS sampling and reporting techniques introduce measurement error into observed unemployment durations. Functional forms that fit the true distribution well produce misleading estimates when applied to CPS data. Consequently, we conclude that there is little to be coaxed out of CPS unemployment data other than what is present in nonparametric estimates of the distribution function available from the censored data.

Acknowledgments

We have benefited from comments by Dale Mortensen, Lars Muus, Richard Startz, Neils Westergard-Nielsen, and Chris Winship. The usual disclaimers apply. This research has been supported by grants from the National Science Foundation and the National Commission on Employment Policy. Research assistance by Beth Asch and Douglas MacIntosh is gratefully acknowledged.

References

Abowd, John, and Zellner, Arnold (1982), "Estimation of Gross Labor Force Flows From the Current Population Survey," H. G. B. Alexander Mimeo Series, Chicago: University of Chicago.

Akerlof, George A., and Main, Brian G. M. (1980), "Unemployment Spells and Unemployment Experience," *American Economic Review*, 70, 885–893.

Bjorklund, A. (1981), "On the Duration of Unemployment in Sweden, 1965–76," *Scandinavian Journal of Economics*, 83, 167–183.

Bowers, J. K., and Harkess, D. (1979), "Duration of Unemployment by Age and Sex," *Economica*, 46, 239–260.

Burdett, Kenneth E., Kiefer, Nicholas M., Mortensen, Dale T., and Neumann, George R. (1984), "Earnings, Unemployment, and the Allocation of Time Over Time," *Review of Economic Studies*, 51, 559–578. Chapter 5 in this volume.

Clark, Kim B., and Summers, Laurence H., (1979), "Labor Market Dynamics and Unemployment: A Reconsideration," *Brookings Papers on Economic Activity* (1), 13–60.

Cripps, T. F., and Tarling, R. J. (1974), "An Analysis of the Duration of Male Unemployment in Great Britain," *Economic Journal*, 84, 289–316.

Frank, Robert H. (1978), "How Long Is a Spell of Unemployment?" *Econometrica*, 46, 285–301.

Green, Gloria P., Devens, Richard M., and Whitmore, Bob (1978), "Employment and Unemployment – Trends During 1977," *Monthly Labor Review*, 101, 12–23.

Hall, Robert E. (1972), "Turnover in the Labor Force," *Brookings Papers on Economic Activity* (3), 709–756.

Kaitz, Hyman (1970), "Analyzing the Length of Spells of Unemployment," *Monthly Labor Review*, 93, 11–20.

Kalbfleisch, John D., and Prentice, Ross L. (1980), *The Statistical Analysis of Failure Time Data*, New York: John Wiley.

Keeley, Michael C., Robins, Philip K., Spiegelman, Robert G., and West, Richard W. (1978), "The Estimation of Labor Supply Models Using Experimental Data," *American Economic Review*, 68, 873–887.

Kiefer, Nicholas M., and Neumann, George R. (1982), "Wages and the Structure of Unemployment Rates," in *Workers, Jobs and Inflation*, ed. M. N. Baily, Washington, DC: Brookings Institution, pp. 325–351. Chapter 9 in this volume.

Luckett, James P. (1978), "The Estimation of Completed Spell Durations from Published Data Under Non-Steady State Conditions," paper presented at the Winter Econometric Society meeting. Chicago, August 30.

Lundberg, Shelly, J. (1980), "Unemployment and Household Labor Supply," unpublished Ph.D. dissertation, Northwestern University, Dept. of Economics.

Marston, Stephen T. (1976), "Employment Instability and High Unemployment Rates," *Brookings Papers on Economic Activity* (1), 169–203.

Salant, Steve W. (1977), "Search Theory and Duration Data: A Theory of Sorts," *Quarterly Journal of Economics*, 91, 39–57.

Silcock, H. (1954), "The Phenomenon of Labor Turnover," *Journal of the Royal Statistical Society*, Ser. A, 107, 429–440.

Smith, Nina (1982), "Varighed of Ledighedsperioder og Indstromning tie Arbejdsloshed: En Analyse Pa Danske Data 1965–1978" [Duration of Unemployment and the Flow into Unemployment: An Analysis of Danish Data 1965–1978], Working Paper 82-5, Aarhus University, Dept. of Economics, Denmark.

Tuma, Nancy B., and Robins, Phillip K. (1980), "A Dynamic Model of Employment Behavior: An Application to the Seattle and Denver Income Maintenance Experiments," *Econometrica*, 48, 1031–1052.

Woltman, Henry (1980), "Possible Effects of Response Variance on the Estimate of Gross Changes From Month-to-Month in the CPS," in *Using the Current Population Survey as a Longitudinal Data Base*, Technical Report 608, Washington, DC: U.S. Department of Labor, Bureau of Labor Statistics, pp. 11–13.

PART IV

Mobility and contracting

CHAPTER 11

Employment risk and labor market diversification

In this chapter, we examine labor market structure as an explanation of the persistent geographic differences in unemployment rates in the United States. Specifically, we focus on the insurance role that diversified labor markets can play. It is sometimes argued that employment variability has increased in the 1970s and 1980s and that this has led to higher aggregate unemployment and greater dispersion in local unemployment rates.[1] A related view of the effect of labor demand variability on unemployment recognizes that the equilibrium level of unemployment in a labor market is partially determined by uncertainty about current and future states of labor demand. For example, in competitive models with costly search among spatially distinct "islands," an increase in the variability of labor demand will increase the amount of search unemployment and increase mobility (Lucas and Prescott 1974). Neither view provides an explanation of the two central empirical facts about geographic unemployment rates: (1) Unemployment rate differences persist over time, although the actual levels vary, and (2) migration does not appear to be affected by differences in labor market unemployment rates. The goal of this chapter is to provide a consistent explanation of both empirical findings.

The plan of the chapter is as follows. In Section 11.1 we present a simple one-sector contracting model that illustrates the essential aspects of labor force allocation under uncertainty. A one-sector description of market equilibrium is inadequate if local markets consist of firms (or industries) with imperfectly correlated demands. Section 11.2 extends the model to the multiple-sector case and provides an explanation of how within-market job mobility affects equilibrium unemployment rates. The final section summarizes these results.

This chapter was written by George R. Neumann and Robert H. Topel.

[1] See, e.g., Lilien (1982 a,b). This explanation of changes in unemployment is called the sectoral shift hypothesis.

11.1   Demand uncertainty and intermarket differences in equilibrium unemployment

Uncertainty about the level or sectoral distribution of demand can affect individual decisions and unemployment in a number of ways. To illustrate the effects of demand uncertainty, we consider a model with identical workers on the supply side. Each worker possesses a concave utility function $u(c + k)$, where c is consumption and k the fixed value of nonmarket time. Firms seek to maximize profit, and each faces stochastic product demand characterized by the distribution function $G(\theta)$. Technology is such that the workers' labor supply is indivisible: Either the worker is employed and consumes no leisure, or he or she is unemployed and receives the full value of k.

In this market, an optimal policy sets the wage independent of demand for employed workers and will provide some compensation to unemployed workers. Since mobility between sectors is costly, firms compete for workers ex ante by offering "contracts" consisting of a wage W while workers are employed and payment B while they are unemployed. The assumptions made about preferences ensure that, in equilibrium, $W - B = k$, so workers are indifferent between employment and unemployment.[2] The typical firm then faces the allocation problem of choosing N_i workers to whom contracts will be offered and how to deploy those workers in each demand state θ. With only one sector in a market, efficient employment decisions are the solution to

$$\max_{L_i(\theta), N_i} E\pi_i(W, B, G) = \int_0^{\bar{\theta}} (\theta_i F(L_i) - WL_i - B(N_i - L_i))DG(\theta) \tag{1}$$

$$\text{subject to} \quad L_i(\theta) \leq N_i \ \forall \ \theta. \tag{2}$$

The first-order conditions characterizing the solution are

$$\theta F'(L(\theta_i)) - (W - B) - \lambda(\theta) = \theta, \tag{3a}$$

$$B - \int_0^{\bar{\theta}} \lambda(\theta) \, dG(\theta) = 0, \tag{3b}$$

$$(N_i - L_i(\theta)) \geq 0; \quad \lambda(\theta)(N_i - L_i(\theta)) = 0 \ \forall \ \theta. \tag{3c}$$

---

[2] The utility function we have chosen to illustrate this equilibrium is fortuitous in that it has no income effects on the demand for leisure; hence, consumption and leisure are completely ensured. This implies that observed wage rates are uncorrelated with unemployment rates across markets, which is broadly consistent with empirical evidence (see Hall 1979).

Here $\lambda(\theta) \geq 0$ is the shadow value of having an additional worker in demand state θ, associated with constraint (2). When demand is "low," that is, $\theta < \theta^* = k/F'(N)$, not all workers are employed, so $\lambda(\theta) = 0$. If $\theta \geq \theta^*$, $\lambda(\theta) = \theta F'(N) - k \geq 0$, and $\lambda'(\theta) = f'(N) \geq 0$. Hence, $\lambda(\theta)$ is convex in θ. The optimal N is determined by the expectation of $\lambda(\theta)$, as in (3b).

If we consider mean-preserving spreads of the distribution G as the measure of risk in the sense of Rothschild and Stiglitz (1970), the convexity of $\lambda(\theta)$ and (3) imply that $dN_i^*/d\sigma \geq 0$, where σ is the measure of spread. Intuitively, an increase in risk increases the likelihood that low states of demand will occur, where the contribution of an extra worker to profit is zero, but also increases the likelihood of high states of demand where $\lambda(\theta) > 0$. The increased probability of these high states of demand makes it efficient to carry a larger inventory of workers to meet contingent production in high demand. Here, this inventory is achieved through higher average unemployment.

If markets differ only in the distribution of demand, the allocation of workers across labor markets can be shown directly. We substitute $\lambda(\theta)$ from (3a) into (3b) and use the definition of θ^* to arrive at

$$B - \int(\theta F_i'(N_i^*) - k)\, dG(\theta)_i \equiv 0, \tag{4}$$

which implies that $dN_i^*/dw < 0$. Now, if there are $\bar{N}$ workers in total, the allocation of workers across markets is straightforward. Other things equal, markets with greater demand uncertainty would have higher ex ante demand for labor, and relatively more workers would be employed in those markets. Similarly, increases in risk will increase demand in a particular market, and also the aggregate demand $\Sigma N_i(W, G_i)$. Ex ante competition for workers will drive up the market clearing wage W (and hence B), which will be paid to all participants. Thus, the equilibrium labor force is larger in riskier markets, which is analogous to results in standard "peak load" problems of productive capacity under variable demand,[3] though there are no equalizing wage differences for unemployment among markets.

The increase in the optimal size of the work force brought about by increased risk has implications about the expected level of unemployment in each labor market and in the aggregate. Specifically, the set of states in which unemployment occurs is increasing in σ since $\theta^* = k/F'(N(\sigma))$ and $\partial\theta^*/\partial\sigma > 0$. Whether the expected unemployment rate increases in

[3] Topel (1982) provides a more general analysis.

σ depends, as is commonly the case, on third-derivative properties of the production function. The unemployment rate is $U(N, \theta) = 1 - L(\theta)/N$, whch is nonzero only for $\theta < \theta^*$ and declining in θ. Thus, a sufficient (though not necessary) condition for a mean-preserving spread in $G(\theta)$ to increase expected unemployment is that $u(N, \theta)$ be globally convex, which requires $\partial^2 L(\theta)/\partial \theta^2 \leq 0$. For this to hold, it is sufficient that $F_i''' \leq 0$. With these conditions, if $G(\theta;\sigma)$ is a mean-preserving spread of $G(\theta;0)$ we have

$$
\begin{aligned}
E(U \mid G(\sigma)) &= \int \left(1 - \frac{L_i(\theta)}{N_i(\sigma)}\right) dG(\theta; \sigma) \\
&\geq \int \left(\frac{1 - L_i(\theta)}{N_i(0)}\right) dG(\theta; \sigma) \\
&\geq \int \left(1 - \frac{L_i(\theta)}{N_i(0)}\right) dG(\theta; 0) = E(U \mid G(0)).
\end{aligned} \tag{5}
$$

The first inequality follows from $N(\sigma) \geq N(0)$, and the second from the convexity of U in θ. Under the stated conditions, an increase in employment risk increases the unemployment rate in a particular market, and also in the aggregate since total unemployment is a labor-force-weighted (i.e., $N_i/\overline{N}$) average of local unemployment rates, and the weight on the riskier market is increasing in σ_i.

11.2   Equilibrium unemployment with multiple-sector markets

This one-sector description of market equilibrium is inadequate if local markets consist of multiple sectors with imperfectly correlated demand disturbances. Then, labor mobility within a market may serve to diversify employment risk and reduce the optimal demand for unemployment as a labor inventory. To illustrate, consider a two-sector market characterized by production functions $F_i(L_i)$ and productivity shifters θ_i, $i = 1, 2$. Let the joint density of demand shifters by $g(\theta_1, \theta_2)$. With mobility among sectors the relevant constraint on sectoral employment is $L_1 + L_2 \leq N$, so efficient allocations satisfy

$$
\theta_i F_i'(L_i) - k = \lambda(\theta_1, \theta_2), \qquad i = 1, 2, \tag{6}
$$

$$
\iint \lambda(\theta_1, \theta_2) g(\theta_1, \theta_2) \, d\theta_1 \, d\theta_2 = B, \tag{7}
$$

where $\lambda(\theta_1, \theta_2)$ is the shadow price of N, which depends on *both* θ_i in

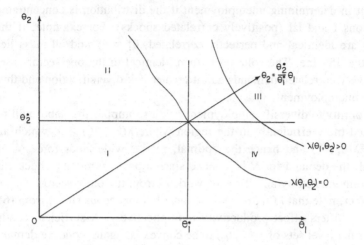

Figure 11.1. Unemployment and diversifiable demand risks.

the market. Thus, with mobility, marginal surplus $(\theta_i F_i - k)$ is equated across sectors for each demand pair (θ_1, θ_2), while the expectation of $\lambda(\theta_1, \theta_2)$ over all states of demand determines optimal labor force size N.

The role played by diversification is shown in Figure 11.1. In the figure, θ_1^* and θ_2^* are the critical levels of demand that just yield full employment in each sector in the *absence* of labor mobility, as above. Thus, full employment is associated with pairs (θ_1, θ_2) in the upper right quadrant, labeled III, while there is unemployment in both sectors in region I. Now consider the impact of mobility. Holding $N = N_1 + N_2$ fixed, for each $\theta_1 < \theta_1^*$ there is now a $\theta_2 > \theta_2^*$ that will just support market-wide full employment, and conversely. This defines the upper boundary of points where $\lambda(\theta_1, \theta_2) = 0$. Again, this boundary is convex if $\partial^2 L_i/\partial\theta_i^2 \leq 0$, since unemployment is constant (zero) along it.

The key point about intersectoral mobility is that it increases the set of market-wide full-employment demand pairs by the areas in regions II and IV that lie above the boundary $\lambda(\theta_1, \theta_2) = 0$. For other points in these regions total employment must rise since workers are reallocated to the sector where the constraint $L_i = N_i$ would otherwise be binding. Since total employment is unaffected in regions I and III, N being held fixed, the expected unemployment rate must fall so long as the density $g(\theta_1, \theta_2)$ allocates positive mass in regions II and IV. The magnitude of this effect clearly depends on the form of $g(\theta_1, \theta_2)$: Diversification is least relevant in determining unemployment if the distribution is concentrated in regions I and III (positively correlated shocks). For example, if the sectors are identical and perfectly correlated, $\theta_1^* = \theta_2^*$ and all mass lies along the 45° line. The solution is then identical to the one-sector case. Negatively correlated demands admit greater risk diversification and thus reduce unemployment.

The ability to diversify employment risk also implies that labor will be allocated more efficiently in the region where $\lambda(\theta_1, \theta_2) > 0$, which affects $E\lambda(\theta_1, \theta_2)$ and hence the optimal, market-wide labor force N. In general, the demand for N is reduced since a positive relative shock can be accommodated by an inflow of workers from the other sector. To see this effect, note that $\lambda(\theta_1, \theta_2) + k$ is linear homogeneous since, from (6), demand shifters affect productivity multiplicatively. A sufficient condition for the level sets of $\lambda(\theta_1, \theta_2)$ to be convex is, again, concave demand curves ($F_i''' \leq 0$), so $\lambda(\theta_1, \theta_2)$ is a convex cone. Now consider the ray $\theta_2 = (\theta_2^*/\theta_1^*)\theta_1$, shown in Figure 11.1. Along this ray $\lambda(\theta_1, \theta_2) = \lambda_1(\theta_1) = \lambda_2(\theta_2)$ since employment in each sector is fixed at its optimal level. Because without mobility $d\lambda_i/d\theta_i F'_i(N_i)$, $\lambda(\theta_1, \theta_2)$ lies everywhere below the plane $A(\theta_1, \theta_2) = \alpha\lambda_1(\theta_1) + (1 - \alpha)\lambda_2(\theta_2)$, where $a = \theta_2^* F_2''$ $(N_2)/(\theta_1^* F_1''(N_1) + \theta_2^* F_2''(N_2))$, and is tangent to $A(\theta_1, \theta_2)$ from below in the region where $\lambda(\theta_1, \theta_2) > 0$. Finally, since $\lambda(\theta_1, \theta_2) = 0$ for all points where one $\lambda_i(\theta_i) > 0$, we have that

$$\int\int [\lambda(\theta_1, \theta_2) - A(\theta_1, \theta_2)]g(\theta_1, \theta_2)\, d\theta_1\, d\theta_2 < 0. \tag{8}$$

The condition that $\lambda(\theta_1, \theta_2)$ be quasi-concave is stronger than necessary for this result. The upshot is that labor mobility and efficient allocation *reduce* the expected shadow price of N, which implies a reduction of the equilibrium labor force for any density $g(\theta_1, \theta_2)$. Graphically, the equilibrium boundary $\lambda(\theta_1, \theta_2) = 0$ shifts leftward in Figure 11.1 in order that the expectation of $\lambda(\theta_1, \theta_2)$ remain fixed. This negative effect on the efficient labor force reinforces the previous impact of diversification on unemployment, so the expected market unemployment rate must decline for any distribution of demands.

11.3   Summary

This characterization of the relation between unemployment and demand uncertainty is a steady-state description of the response to idiosyncratic differences in local demand structures. The model implies not only that average unemployment will be higher in riskier markets, subject to the stated conditions, but that increasing uncertainty will generally lead to both rising unemployment in a market and growth of the labor force. Thus, *equilibrium* unemployment differentials will not lead workers to migrate to low-unemployment areas, and an increase in unemployment caused by a change in the structure of demand may actually be associated with net in-migration of labor. These facts offer a sharp contrast to the incentives normally studied in the empirical literature on migration, and they help to explain why differences in local unemployment ratios have little impact on migration flows. For these reasons, it appears important to distinguish equilibrium, or permanent, unemployment levels from transitory levels when examining cross-section data on mobility or on wage changes.

Acknowledgments

This research was supported by NSF Grant SES-85-10295 and by a grant from the U.S. Department of Labor, Office of the Assistant Secretary for Policy. The opinions expressed here are those of the authors and not necessarily those of the NSF or the Department of Labor. We have benefited from discussions with Dale Mortensen, Kevin M. Murphy, and Lars Muus and from workshop participants at Aarhuus, Chicago, LSE, MIT, North Carolina State, Cal Tech, and UCLA. We remain responsible for any errors.

References

Greenwood, Michael, "Research on Internal Migration in the United States: A Survey," *Journal of Economic Literature*, 8 (June 1975), 397–443.
Hall, Robert E., "A Theory of the Natural Rate of Unemployment and the Duration of Unemployment," *Journal of Monetary Economics*, 5 (April 1979), 153–69.
Lilien, David, "Sectoral Shifts and Sectoral Unemployment," *Journal of Political Economy*, 90 (August 1982), 777–93.
"A Sectoral Model of the Business Cycle," paper presented at the Hoover Conference on Labor Economics, Hoover Institute on War, Peace, and Revolution, Stanford University, December 1982.
Lucas, Robert E., Jr., and Edward Prescott, "Equilibrium Search and Unemployment," *Journal of Economic Theory*, 7 (1974), 188–209.
Rothschild, Michael, and Joseph Stiglitz, "Increasing Risk 1: A Definition," *Journal of Economic Theory*, 2 (1970), 225–43.
Topel, Robert, "Local Labor Markets," *Journal of Political Economy*, 94(3), pt. 2. (June 1986).

CHAPTER 12

A proposition and an example in the theory of job search with hours constraints

Employment agreements often involve, implicitly or explicitly, far more than the posting and acceptance of a wage rate. This chapter considers the optimal behavior of a worker choosing among jobs characterized by wage–hour pairs. The usual analysis of worker behavior characterizes jobs by wages alone and typically assumes that the worker is free to adjust hours freely, given the wage. The assumption of continuously adjustable hours seems extreme, given the many jobs requiring shifts of fixed length. The model studied here is the other extreme. Jobs have associated wages and hours; workers can adjust hours only by changing jobs. Other characteristics of jobs are undeniably important as well – working conditions, fringe benefits, and pensions, to name a few. These could be incorporated into the structure used here. For the present I take the view that hours are probably the most important job characteristic after wages, so for simplicity I will concentrate on hours and wages. This chapter also concentrates attention on worker behavior; optimizing behavior by firms is suppressed, as is the discussion of equilibrium. On the other hand, the model is specifically empirically oriented – it delivers, with additional functional form assumptions, a likelihood function suitable for use with micro data on turnover. No error term need appear mysteriously in an "empirical section." The model is stochastic from the outset.

This chapter concentrates on two labor market states, employment and nonemployment, which for convenience will frequently be referred to as unemployment. Introduction of nonparticipation in the labor force as a separate state makes the model more suitable for empirical work but does not really change the results available. Workers receive, at random intervals, "shocks" or changes in offered terms of employment. These shocks arrive to both employed and unemployed workers. It seems reasonable to assume that the shocks arrive more frequently to unemployed (search-

This chapter was written by Nicholas M. Kiefer. It is reprinted from the *Journal of Labor Economics*, vol. 5, no. 2 (1987); © 1987 by the University of Chicago.

ing) workers, in the form of job offers, than to employed workers. On receiving an offer, the worker decides whether to become (or remain) employed on the offered terms or to remain (or become) unemployed, hoping that better terms will be offered in the near future. The offered terms consist of a wage–hour pair. These are assumed to be drawn from a distribution that is fixed over time. Draws are independent over time (of course, wages and hours can be correlated in offers). The model has the same structure as that studied by Burdett et al. (1984), except that there jobs were characterized by wages alone. A general survey of search models is given by Lippman and McCall (1976).

This chapter examines the effect of changing mean wages on turnover and "natural rates." When hours are fixed across jobs, a translation of the wage–offer distribution leads to an increase in the probability that a draw from the offer distribution will be acceptable and a corresponding increase in the employment rate. This result is established in a utility-maximizing framework. The notion here is that individuals may, as a result of previous investment decisions, restrict their search to specific occupations or industries in which hours variation across jobs is negligible. If so, then the effect of a wage translation is as expected on the basis of the static model.

When hours of work vary across jobs, however, no such results can be established. Translating the offer distribution along the wage axis necessarily leads to an increase in reservation utility; however, the new optimal strategy can yield a smaller employment probability and a lower employment rate. This is demonstrated by an example. The example is robust to minor changes in assumptions and specification and does not require "pathological" preferences. The broad implication is that "standard" results from the theory of job search, which have now become a part of our intuition, cannot be routinely expected to hold in contracting models and need to be checked.

It is important to note the purpose of the exercise of studying these translations. The purpose is to obtain predictions for relations between characteristics (here, mean wages) and outcomes (employment rates), looking across individuals with different characteristics in a cross section. The method used is to imagine that an individual is behaving optimally in one environment and then to change the environment, calculate the new optimal behavioral policy, and compare it with the first. The purpose, however, is to get implications for differences in observable outcomes for otherwise identical individuals in the two environments. We are not considering the dynamics of movement from one equilibrium to another. Indeed, it should be clear that the exercise here is, as usual in the labor supply literature, a partial equilibrium exercise. Full equilibrium models can be studied and are certainly of interest. Burdett and Mortensen (1980) study the equilibrium in a model in which jobs differ in both wages and layoff rates. For present purposes, however, the partial equilibrium framework is adequate.

12.1   The model with hours fixed across jobs

Consider a consumer-worker whose instantaneous utility flow is a function of instantaneous consumption and leisure. With the assumption that hours are not variable across jobs, leisure is fixed at the total time available for allocation if the consumer is not employed or fixed at that time less the fixed hours if employed. We really need to consider, therefore, only a fixed value of utility associated with unemployment (we are abstracting from variable unemployment insurance benefits) and a utility function for the employed worker that depends only on consumption. Since we will be concerned with the effects of wages, it is convenient to define utility as a function of the wage; this is done using the budget constraint and the assumption that income is exhausted, apart, perhaps, from some fixed amount of saving that does not depend on the particular realization of the wage rate (as long as the wage rate is such that the job in question is acceptable). This utility function will be assumed to have the conventional properties.

>   *Assumption 1.* The state-dependent utility flows are as follows:
>   (1) utility $= u(w)$, $u_w(w) > 0$, $u_{ww}(w) < 0$ (employed at wage w);
>   and (2) utility $= A$ (unemployed).

The next task at hand is to specify the mechanism by which unemployed workers obtain offers of employment and the mechanism by which employed workers become unemployed. Suppose that an unemployed worker is actively engaged in looking for employment opportunities and that his efforts result in a fixed arrival rate of offers μ_u. Thus, for short intervals of search time, the probability of obtaining an offer in a given interval is proportional to the length of the interval. The spirit of this assumption is to rule out variations in search intensity through the course of a spell of unemployment. Suppose the offers, when obtained, consist of a wage rate drawn from a distribution F; suppose further that these draws are independent. With F fixed, there is neither human capital deterioration nor learning through the course of a spell of unemployment.

If our interest were confined to the effects of shifts in the wage-offer distribution on the unemployment-to-employment transition, we could make the common simplifying assumption that jobs are held forever and proceed to analyze the acceptance strategies. However, specifying a complete model of transitions allows us to consider the effects of wage differences on long-run or steady-state employment and unemployment rates. I adopt an extremely simple specification, namely, that the employed worker obtains from time to time a change in his employment conditions characterized as a new draw from the distribution F. Thus from time to time the employed worker is presented with a draw from F, and at those times he must choose whether to remain employed under the new conditions or to enter the pool of unemployed so as to devote more time and attention to search. Suppose that the employed worker obtains new offers at rate μ_e. Clearly, $\mu_e < \mu_u$ if the model is to make economic sense. This specification is discussed at greater length in Burdett et al. (1984). In short, assume the following.

> *Assumption 2.* Unemployed workers receive offers at rate μ_u and employed workers at rate μ_e, with $\mu_e < \mu_u$. An offer is a draw from the wage distribution F, and the draws are independent.

With these assumptions, we are able to specify the state-dependent value functions for a worker in this labor market. These are

$$V_e(w) = (\rho + \mu_e)^{-1}[u(w) + \mu_e T],$$
$$V_u = (\rho + \mu_u)^{-1}(A + \mu_u T),$$
$$T = E \max\{V_e, V_u\},$$

where ρ is the discount rate. The value function associated with employment depends on the realized wage. The value function for unemployment does not. Both functions depend on the opportunities available as reflected in the offer distribution; this dependence is indicated in the expectation operator in the definition of T, the maximized value. At any given moment the worker in this market will choose the labor market state associated with the highest value. Since the values do not change over the course of a period between offers, choices need be made only when offers arrive. Arrival of an offer does not change the value of unemployment V_u, but it does change V_e. Since V_e is monotonically increasing in the offered wage (note that T does not depend on the offered wage) and V_u does not depend on the offered wage, the optimal policy is a reservation wage policy. There exists a wage w^* such that offers above w^* will be accepted and offers below w^* will be rejected. The reservation wage w^* is defined implicitly by setting $V_e = V_u$. Note that it is possible that w^* will be set so that no offers are acceptable or that all offers are acceptable.

With this structure in place, we are in a position to examine the model's implications for turnover. Define the employment-acceptance probability on a draw

$$\pi_e = \int_{\omega^*}^{\infty} dF.$$

Then the transition rate from unemployment to employment is

$$\lambda_{ue} = \mu_u \pi_e,$$

the product of the arrival rate of offers and the probability of the offer's being acceptable. Similarly,

$$\lambda_{eu} = \mu_e(1 - \pi_e).$$

These transition rates characterize the turnover process as a continuous-time Markov process. This structure is sensitive to changes in the assumptions about the offer arrival processes and the offer sequence. Given the transition rates, we can solve for the steady state by setting flows into employment equal to flows out and normalizing

$$\lambda_{ue} p_u = \lambda_{eu} p_e,$$
$$1 = p_e + p_u.$$

Solving yields

$$p_e = \lambda_{ue}(\lambda_{eu} + \lambda_{ue})^{-1},$$
$$p_u = 1 - p_e.$$

The steady-state distribution can be interpreted as the distribution of time spent in each state for an individual over time or as the employment and unemployment rates for a large group of identical individuals.

I now wish to examine the effects of a translation in the offer distribution. It seems clear that an upward translation of the offer distribution will lead to an increase in the reservation wage. Less clear is the answer to the question, What happens to the employment probability when the wage-offer distribution is shifted toward higher wages? It is this question that must be answered in order to determine the effects on labor transitions and employment rates. In the income-maximizing case the answer is known: The increase in the offers leads to an optimal strategy with a higher employment probability (Kiefer and Neumann 1979; Burdett et al. 1984; Burdett and Ondrich 1985). The utility-maximizing case does not follow directly from this result since a translation of the wage-offer distribution is not a translation of the utility-offer distribution. Nevertheless, it is possible to establish the following.

Proposition 1. Let $\overline{w}$ be the location of the wage-offer distribution. Then an increase in $\overline{w}$ implies an increase in the employment probability on a draw.

Proof. Decompose the offered wage as $w = \overline{w} + \varepsilon$, and let F be the distribution function for ε. The value functions can be written out

$$V_e(\varepsilon, \overline{w}) = (\rho + \mu_e)^{-1}[u(\overline{w} + \varepsilon) + \mu_e T(\overline{w})],$$
$$V_u(\overline{w}) = (\rho + \mu_u)^{-1}[A + \mu_u T(\overline{w})],$$
$$T(\overline{w}) = E \max\{V_e, V_u\}.$$

The expectation is taken with respect to F, the distribution of ε. The reservation deviation from $\overline{w}$, $\varepsilon(\overline{w})$, is defined by $V_e[\varepsilon(\overline{w}), \overline{w}] = V_u(\overline{w})$. If $\varepsilon(\overline{w})$ is decreasing in $\overline{w}$, then the employment probability is increasing in $\overline{w}$. The implicit-function theorem gives an expression for $\varepsilon'(\overline{w})$:

$$\varepsilon'(\overline{w}) = -(\partial V_e/\partial \overline{w} - \partial V_u/\partial \overline{w})/(\partial V_e/\partial \varepsilon - \partial V_u/\partial \varepsilon).$$

The denominator of this expression is the $(\rho + \mu_e)$-discounted value of the value of the marginal utility of w, evaluated at the reservation wage. As this term is unambiguously positive, the sign of $\varepsilon'(\overline{w})$ is the same as the sign of $\partial V_u/\partial \overline{w} - \partial V_e/\partial \overline{w}$. Now differentiate $T(\overline{w})$ to obtain

$$T'(\overline{w}) = \partial \left[\int_{\varepsilon(\overline{w})}^{\infty} V_e(s, \overline{w})\, dF(s) + \int_{-\infty}^{\varepsilon(\overline{w})} V_u(\overline{w})\, dF(s) \right] \Big/ \partial \overline{w}$$

$$= \int_{\varepsilon(\overline{w})}^{\infty} [\partial V_e(s, \overline{w})/\partial \overline{w}]\, dF(s) + \int_{-\infty}^{\varepsilon(\overline{w})} [\partial V_u(\overline{w})/\partial \overline{w}]\, dF(s)$$

$$= PE(\partial V_e/\partial \overline{w}|V_e > V_u) + (1 - P)(\partial V_u/\partial \overline{w}),$$

using the fact that $V_e[\varepsilon(\overline{w}), \overline{w}] = V_u(\overline{w})$ and defining

$$P = \int_{\varepsilon(\overline{w})}^{\infty} dF.$$

We have thus obtained $T'(\overline{w})$ as a weighted average of $\partial V_u/\partial\overline{w}$ and the expected value of $\partial V_e/\partial\overline{w}$, with the expectation conditioned on $V_e(\varepsilon, \overline{w}) > V_u(\overline{w})$. Now

$$\partial V_u/\partial\overline{w} = (\rho + \mu_u)^{-1}\mu_u T'(\overline{w}) < T'(\overline{w});$$

consequently,

$$E(\partial V_e/\partial\overline{w}|V_e > V_u) > T'(\overline{w}).$$

Writing out the expectation, note that

$$E(\partial V_e/\partial\overline{w}|V_e > V_u) = P^{-1}\int_{\varepsilon(\overline{w})}^{\infty} [\partial V_e(s, \overline{w})/\partial\overline{w}]\, dF(s)$$

$$< P^{-1}\int_{\varepsilon(\overline{w})}^{\infty} \{\partial V_e[\varepsilon(\overline{w}), \overline{w}]/\partial\overline{w}\}\, dF(s)$$

$$= \partial V_e[\varepsilon(\overline{w}), \overline{w}]/\partial\overline{w},$$

where the inequality follows since $\partial V_e(\varepsilon, \overline{w})/\partial\overline{w}$ depends on ε only through the term $u_w(\overline{w} + \varepsilon)$, which is a decreasing function of ε. Hence

$$\partial V_e[\varepsilon(\overline{w}), \overline{w}]/\partial\overline{w} > \partial V_u(\overline{w})/\partial\overline{w},$$

which implies

$$\varepsilon'(\overline{w}) < 0.$$

The proposition implies that the transition rate from employment to unemployment is decreased, that the transition rate from unemployment to employment is increased, and that the steady-state employment rate is increased.

12.2   The model with wage-and-hours variation in offers

In this section I consider a model in which the worker receives from time to time an offer consisting of a wage and hour pair. The worker must decide, on receipt of an offer, whether to accept employment on the offered terms or to become (or remain) unemployed and search. The model is essentially the same as that in the previous section except that we can no longer suppress the dependence of utility on hours worked, and of course the offer distribution is now a bivariate distribution. Write utility as a function of the wage rate and of hours worked. This is an unusual notion of a utility function; it is neither the direct nor the indirect utility function. If the utility function defined over consumption and leisure has the usual properties (increasing and concave), and if in addition the cross derivative is positive, then it can be shown that the utility function defined over wages and hours satisfies the conditions given in assumption 2a.

Assumption 2A. The state-dependent utility flows are as follows: (1) utility $= u(w, h)$, where $u_w > 0$, $u_h >(<) 0$, as $h <(>) h(w)$, $u_{ww} < 0$, $u_{hh} < 0$, where $h(w)$ is the ordinary labor supply function (employed at wage w and hours h); and (2) utility $= A$ (unemployed).

The results of this section are weak relative to that given in the case of hours fixed across offers, in the sense that I provide here an example illustrating that a proposition corresponding to Proposition 1 cannot be established when hours vary across offers. In constructing the example, I might as well choose as simple a case as possible, providing that the simplicity introduced does not make the model "special." Consequently, I abstract completely from flows out of employment and establish that the effect of a translation of the joint wage–hour distribution along the wage axis can be to increase or decrease the employment probability on a draw from the distribution. Thus assume the following.

Assumption 2B. Unemployed workers receive offers at rate μ_u; employed workers do not receive offers (i.e., $\mu_e = 0$). An offer is a draw from the joint distribution of wages and hours, and the draws are independent.

Note that the draws are independent from draw to draw for an individual; wages and hours will no doubt be dependent in the offer distribution. As will be clear from the construction below, introducing transitions from employment to unemployment will complicate the calculations but will not introduce any new issues.

The result of this section is given as follows.

Proposition 2. Increasing the mean wage of the offer distribution can increase or decrease the probability that employment will be the acceptable state given a draw from the offer distribution.

Proof. By example. Begin by setting A, the utility flow while unemployed, equal to zero. This is clearly a harmless normalization. With the simplifications we have made, the value functions are given by

$$V_e(w, h) = \rho^{-1}u(w, h),$$
$$V_u = \mu_u(\mu_u + \rho)^{-1}T$$
$$T = E \max\{V_e, V_u\}.$$

It is clear at this point that increasing the mean of the offer distribution can increase the employment probability; indeed this is the "expected effect" on the basis of intuition. To establish this, suppose the distribution of w and h is such that utility is negative for all realizations of (w, h). Then the optimal strategy is to reject all offers, achieving a T of zero. If the distribution becomes positive for some possible offers, the optimal policy will be to accept some possible offers, so the employment probability on a draw rises.

The other case, employment probability on a draw falling with an increase in wages, is less intuitively clear. Consider the two-point distribution

$$(w, h) = (11.11, .1),$$

with probability .1, and

$$(w, h) = (4.0, .5),$$

with probability .9, and the utility function

$$u(w, h) = [wh(1 - h)]^{.9},$$

which assigns utility one to the two points above. Since A is zero in this example, the optimal strategy is clearly to accept any offer; the employment probability on a given draw is one.

Now consider a translation of this distribution along the wage axis. Suppose the translated distribution is

$$(w, h) = (13.11, .1),$$

with probability .1, and

$$(w, h) = (6.0, .5),$$

with probability .9. The corresponding utilities are $u(13.11, .1) = 1.1605$ and $u(6, .5) = 1.4404$. Take $\mu_u/(\mu_u + \rho) = .9$, so offers arrive rapidly relative to the discount rate. With this information the values can be calculated. The optimal strategy is to accept $(6, .5)$ and to reject the other offer if it occurs. This strategy gives a value of $\rho T = 1.4246$ and has a corresponding employment probability on a given draw of .9, down from one (the next best strategy is to accept either offer; this leads to $\rho T = 1.4124$).

The utility function in this example is Cobb–Douglas in consumption and leisure. This is hardly a pathological specification. Further, the conclusion is robust to small changes in the specification of the probability distribution. To develop some intuition, note that hours = .5 is on the ordinary labor supply curve for any positive value of the wage. A wage increase at this value of hours is worth more in utility terms than an equal wage increase elsewhere (starting from indifference). The indifference curves in (w, h) space, where $w > 0$ and $0 < h < 1$, are symmetric around the line $h = .5$ and are closer together along that line than along any other. It is clear from a graphic consideration of this situation that many other examples could be constructed without difficulty.

This proposition implies that the transition rate into employment and the equilibrium employment rate can rise or fall as the general level of wages rises.

12.3 Conclusions

The first result of this chapter is that a worker searching for a job optimally is, loosely speaking, more likely to find an acceptable job offer when the distribution of offers he faces is translated toward higher offers. This intuitively appealing (obvious?) result extends existing results that deal with the income-maximizing worker. The extension is nontrivial in that a translation of a wage distribution does not typically induce a translation of the corresponding utility distribution.

The second result is that a similar theorem does not hold when the worker is searching over jobs characterized by an hours requirement as well as a wage. This was illustrated by a nonpathological example in Section 12.2. The general lesson seems to be that, when dealing with multifactor contracts, an unambiguously favorable shift in the offer distribution can lead to the employment probability associated with following the optimal strategy going down. The intuition here is that, when the joint distribution of wages and hours is translated upward along the wage axis, workers can afford to be more choosy about hours in deciding their acceptance strategy. In general, when prospects for one attribute of a contract improve, it is possible to be more particular about the other attributes. In this sense, the result is working like an income effect.

246   Mobility and contracting

Acknowledgments

I am grateful to Ken Burdett and Dale Mortensen for helpful discussions of this material and to the National Science Foundation for research support.

References

Burdett, K.; Kiefer, N. M.; Mortensen, D. T.; and Neumann, G. R. "Wages, Employment, and the Allocation of Time over Time." *Review of Economic Studies* 51 (1984): 559–78. Chapter 5 in this volume.
Burdett, K., and Mortensen, D. T. "Search, Layoffs, and Labor Market Equilibrium." *Journal of Political Economy* 88 (1980): 652–72.
Burdett, K., and Ondrich, J. "How Changes in Labor Demand Affect Unemployed Workers." *Journal of Labor Economics* 3 (1985): 1–10.
Kiefer, N. M., and Neumann, G. R. "Estimation of Wage Offer Distributions and Reservation Wages." In *Studies in the Economics of Search*, edited by J. J. McCall and S. A. Lippman. Amsterdam: North-Holland, 1979. Chapter 2 in this volume.
Lippman, S., and McCall, J. "The Economics of Job Search: A Survey, Pt. 1." *Economic Inquiry* 14 (June 1976): 155–89.

CHAPTER 13

Interfirm mobility and earnings

Cross-section studies invariably show a positive and usually concave relation between earnings and labor market experience. The pervasiveness and stability of this pattern has generated a substantial amount of theoretical investigation. One economic explanation of the pattern is that it is a reflection of investment in job-specific capital. The theoretical literature on mobility focuses on three specific versions of job-specific investment: job search, job matching, and on-the-job training. According to the first version, an individual worker's wage is stationary on a given job but differs across jobs. Information about the location and nature of jobs is imperfect and takes time to acquire. Hence, a worker earning a higher wage relative to alternatives is less likely to quit. In the second version, a worker's productivity is initially uncertain, but the degree of uncertainty diminishes with experience on the job as a consequence of repeated observations. "Good" matches, those on which the worker experiences wage growth, endure. In the third and best known version of the job-specific capital hypothesis, a worker acquires job-specific skills through learning and training on the job. Consequently, the worker's wage increases with job tenure relative to offers on alternative jobs, which implies that the propensity to separate diminishes. An important question for empirical research on mobility is, Which of these versions of the job-specific capital explanation fits the facts? Do these versions have different observable implications for the separation propensity or for the probability distribution of the wage earned on the next job, or are they observationally equivalent even in panel data?

The purpose of this chapter is to examine the implications of the alternative forms of job-specific investment and to provide empirical evidence on the returns to job mobility. The first section discusses the implications of each of the three forms of job investment and considers the differences that could be empirically tested. A complete treatment of the

This chapter was written by Dale T. Mortensen and George R. Neumann.

various models requires that one estimate the structural model described in Mortensen (1984), but that would require knowledge of the time sequence of individuals' reservation wages while employed. Alternatively, one can proceed by examining the conditional separation functions and the conditional wage function on the next job. The second section provides the raw "facts" about job mobility based on panel data from the Denver (DIME) and Seattle (SIME) Income Maintenance Experiments. The advantage of using these data sets is that they contain detailed information on the timing of job changes for 48 months. In the third section we examine some of the implications of the different models for mobility and wage changes in a regression context. The final section sets forth our conclusions.

13.1   Job mobility and earnings

The empirical facts of interest are the behavior of wages over time for an individual and the probability of separation from a particular job. For job separation – mobility – to make sense, there must be some uncertainty about jobs. Otherwise individuals would start and remain in the job paying the highest lifetime wage.[1] In comparisons among alternative explanations of the wage profile, this uncertainty will be either about conditions on the current job or about alternative jobs. In making such comparisons we will treat the case of a wealth-maximizing worker with an infinite horizon facing a discount rate of r.[2]

Jobs as pure search goods

In Burdett's (1978) model individuals face a common distribution of job opportunities, $F(w)$. On any particular job an individual's wage is constant and equal to his or her productivity. While employed, an individual can search for an alternative job, and the intensity of search will affect the arrival rate of offers, $\gamma(s)$. If an alternative arrives that pays a higher wage, the worker quits his or her current job to accept the higher offer. The instantaneous probability of a worker quitting is the product of the

---

[1] There is an obvious exception in that jobs could be a hierarchy in requiring a certain amount of time spent in level j before a higher-paying job $j + 1$ could be held. Why these jobs would be in different firms is not obvious.

[2] A complete characterization of the different models of job-specific investment is contained in Mortensen (1984). The discussion in the text is based on that treatment.

arrival rate of offers and the probability that an offer exceeds the individual's reservation wage, $-q(w) = \gamma(s)[1 - F(w)]$. By assumption there is no on-the-job wage growth, yet cross-section and panel data will show a positive relation between wages and time in the labor market ("experience") and between wages and duration on a particular job (tenure). Moreover, since search intensity depends on the expected wage gain, γ is declining in w and the quit probability will be negatively related to tenure and experience.[3] Thus, Burdett's model produces the two characteristics found in empirical studies: Wages are positively correlated with experience and tenure, whereas quit probabilities decline with both.

These patterns predicted in this pure search model are pure statistical artifacts induced by the selectivity process that is at work. More experienced workers receive higher wages not because they are more productive but because they have had more time to find better jobs. Similarly, workers with greater tenure on a particular job receive higher wages not because tenure increases wages in any sense but because higher wages make it less likely that a superior alternative will be found.[4] Indeed, the conditional quit rate $q(w)$ is independent of tenure and experience.

Job as pure experience goods

Jovanovic's (1979a, 1979b) models of learning about the characteristics of a particular job provide an alternative explanation of wage growth and separation probabilities. All jobs initially look alike to workers, and all workers (of similar observable characteristics) look alike to firms. "True" productivity, which is stationary on any particular job, is the outcome of a stochastic matching process, the observations on which are noisy. Over time the quality of a match is revealed as successive information on productivity becomes available. Individuals who quit a job start the process anew. Wages are equal to the expected value of the worker's productivity, which depends on the sample evidence of the productivity realizations. The reservation wage – the wage that makes an individual indif-

---

[3] We will frequently need to distinguish between the unconditional probability of a quit, the average over all individuals, and the quit probability conditional upon the wage being earned, $q(w)$, the average over all individuals with wage $= w$. The term "conditional quit rate" will be used for the latter, it being implicit that the conditioning refers only to the wage.

[4] In Burdett's model the probability of receiving an acceptable offer declines because the probability that an offer is acceptable is declining in the current wage and because the search intensity, hence the arrival rate of offers, is also declining in w.

ferent between continuing on the job and quitting to start the process anew
– depends on both the wage currently earned and tenure on the job. Also,
if A is the wage paid on a newly commenced job and $\mu(w, n)$ is the
reservation wage of an individual earning w with tenure n, then

$$A \leq \mu(w, n) \leq w. \tag{1}$$

If information about productivity on the job arrives at a rate α, the conditional quit rate is

$$q(w, n) = \alpha F(\mu(w, n), n), \tag{2}$$

where $F(', n)$ is the distribution of estimated productivity after n observations. In Jovanovic's setup $F(', n)$ is stochastically dominated by
$F(', n + 1)$, that is,

$$\int_0^z F(w, n)\, dw \geq \int_0^z F(w, n + 1)\, dw, \qquad \text{for all } z \in W. \tag{3}$$

This follows because the variance (more generally, scale) of the distribution of true productivity is declining in n; that is, the current estimate
is becoming more precise. However, since workers can always obtain A
with certainty, workers prefer jobs in which productivity is more uncertain. In other words, since downside risk is held constant, workers prefer
greater upside risk. (This is the option pricing result in the labor market.)
This implies that reservation wages fall as tenure increases.

   This model predicts that wages will be positively correlated with tenure
because only "good" matches last. As in the pure search model, the unconditional quit rate exhibits negative duration dependence due to the
selection process. However, here the unconditional quit rate exhibits positive duration dependence because of the increasing precision of the estimate of true productivity. Also, because the reservation wage is declining in tenure for any given level of wages, the possibility is admitted that
workers might voluntarily take wage cuts to accept a new job. An additional distinguishing feature of this model is the prediction that wages
on a particular job can be described as a martingale with diminishing
variance. This will be true for any individual, but the selection process
implies that it will not hold across individuals – that is, only good matches
endure.

Jobs as pure investment goods

In the simplest and most well known model of job-specific investment
(Mincer 1974), wages and productivity are deterministic functions of the

amount of on-the-job training or learning by doing. Empirical evidence and economic theory suggest that the increments to the wage should be positive and convex in tenure. Thus, the wage process on a particular job will have

$$w_n = w_{n-1} + x_n, \qquad n = 1, \ldots; \qquad w_0 = A; \qquad \text{with} \quad x_n \geq x_{n+1}. \tag{4}$$

If wage growth is deterministic, no mobility occurs: Workers go to the best alternative and leave only when the job disappears. In this case quit rates are constant (trivially) and independent of both wages and tenure.

Alternatively, if the increments to the wage process are random with expectation equal to x_n in each period, mobility can occur. In this case, the reservation wage depends positively on the wage currently earned and negatively on tenure on the current job. The negative relation between the reservation wage and tenure is derived solely from the shape of the wage increments profile [equation (4)]: Whatever things are today, future growth is expected to be less. Consequently, this model of job-specific investment has the same empirical implications about mobility and wages as does the matching model of Jovanovic. Wages increase and unconditional quit rates decline with tenure, while conditional quit rates decrease with higher wages and increase with higher tenures. In contrast to the matching model, however, on-the-job wage growth is predicted here to be a submartingale with constant variance over time.

Empirical implications

Pure forms of these alternative interpretations of the job-specific capital model of mobility can be investigated simply by observing the wage growth in job-to-job transitions. The pure on-the-job search version is rejected if a wage decline is observed.[5] Similarly, the specific training version would be rejected by observation of wage increases with the movement to a new job. The pure form of the job-matching version can account for both wage increases and wage declines in the movement across jobs.[6] In this case, the pure hypothesis can be rejected only by the absence of positive duration dependence in the probability of taking a wage cut.

Of course, rejection of the pure form of any of the alternative versions of the job-specific capital model is a straw man. It is generally to be

---

[5] A decline in wages for workers who "lose" rather than "leave" their jobs would, of course, be expected. Identification of such individuals is subject to considerable uncertainty.

[6] In order to generate wage increases there must be some initial distribution of productivities across jobs, as in Jovanovic (1984).

expected that each version contributes something to mobility; the relevant question is how much of the observed growth in wages over a worker's lifetime can be attributed to each source. To answer this question completely it would be necessary to estimate a general structural model that included each of the three explanations of wage change as alternatives. In principle, a general model of the individual's employment history can be modeled as a continuous-time Markov process, provided that one defines the state space appropriately. A state here is a specification of whether a worker is employed and the wage–tenure pair (w, n), given employment. Given data on the sequence of the job wages and an indicator of when a worker changes jobs, one can estimate the structure, provided that the wage distributions, both on the job $F_n(x, w)$ and across jobs $F_0(x, m)$, is known up to a parameter vector.

Although it is possible in principle to estimate such structural models, in practice there are several obstacles. Most important is the problem of selection: Individuals remain on a job only if the wage exceeds their reservation wage and no better outside alternative has arrived. Both the job-matching and job-training explanations imply that the reservation wage, conditional upon the wage received, will exhibit negative duration dependence that is linked in a crucial way with the form of the on-the-job wage process F_n. Although some progress has been made in solving for reservation wage functions from particular wage distributions (see Mortensen 1984 and Whittle 1983), the current state of knowledge about general solutions and computational methods in this area makes this approach an unattractive one. Data issues also cause two problems in implementing a structural model. The first is the problem of identifying those individuals who jobs "disappeared" but who did not pass through unemployment. This is a pure data problem that in the future could be solved by asking the appropriate questions of job changers. The second problem is more substantial. An essential element of matching and training models is that wage adjustments occur in response to the arrival of some "news" about productivity. In a world of inflation, however, some wage changes will be observed even when there has been no change in the perception of productivity. Since, as an empirical matter, firms do not appear to adjust wages continuously to inflation, there is a problem in distinguishing inflation adjustments from real wage changes.

Using a more reduced-form approach one can still derive some insights from data on mobility. Wage rates on a new job, for example, are drawings from the cross-job distribution of productivities, with the distribution depending upon the worker's characteristics and his reservation wage. This reservation wage will depend on, among other things, the wage rate earned on the previous job and on the length of time on the previous job. Separation rates will, for the same reasons, depend on the same factors. One prediction of matching and training models that can be tested is whether job tenure has any effect on subsequent wages. Although problems of unobserved heterogeneity make it difficult to draw precise inferences about tenure effects, it is of some interest to see what the raw data indicate. In what follows we examine the outcomes of the job-change process in this reduced-form manner. The description of the process so obtained will be of use, it is hoped, in the construction of more detailed structural models.

13.2 Empirical evidence on job mobility

Although much progress has been made in developing alternative theoretical models of the job mobility process, comparatively little empirical work has been done, the major exceptions being the work of Mincer and Jovanovic (1981) and Bartel and Borjas (1981). The essential difficulty that arises in studying job mobility is the need for panel data, which until recently were unavailable. Accordingly, the "raw facts" that are the basis for discriminating among theories are scarce. In this section we present a listing of these facts based on data collected from the Seattle (SIME) and Denver (DIME) Income Maintenance Experiments. Because the time pattern of job transitions is important in classifying job changes, we discuss the data in some detail.

Data

The data that we use in this chapter come from the control observations from the SIME and DIME experiments. These data have been extensively discussed elsewhere;[7] here we will describe the features of the data that are important for mobility studies. The control portion of the sample is used in order to eliminate the effects of the income maintenance aspect of the experiments. The restriction of the observations to the control portion of the experiments is relevant for two reasons. First, the control subjects received only token payments for reporting their labor market status,

---

[7] See Keeley et al. (1978), Kiefer and Neumann (1982), Lundberg (1980), and Tuma and Robbins (1980) for descriptions of the SIME–DIME data. The data come from the Public Use Files constructed by Mathematica Policy Research.

and thus the pronounced experimental effects are not present to confound the empirical issues. Second, inclusion in the experiments was conditional upon income levels at the start of the program. Ex post it appears that the income cutoffs were less strictly applied for controls, implying that the control portion is more representative of the population.[8]

The feature of the data that we exploit in this chapter is the presence of detailed information on the wage rate that an individual receives on the job with the longest hours each month, the employment status of an individual, which is recorded in continuous fashion, and whether an individual has switched employers in a given month. Specifically, a variable – SWITFLAG – exists for each of the 48 months covered in the SIME and DIME experiments. This variable takes on the value 0 if the person is not employed, 1 if the employer this month is the same as the employer last month, 2 if the individual has returned to a previous employer (e.g., after a temporary layoff), and 3 if the individual has begun a job with a new employer.[9] Thus, in the typical case, a worker who suffers unemployment due to layoff and returns to the same employer will be represented in the data as having a sequence of 1's for SWIT-FLAG, followed by some 0's and by a 2. Likewise, a job change will be signaled by a sequence of 1's, perhaps some 0's (if any unemployment or nonparticipation occurred), followed by a 3.

An important issue in the study of mobility is whether the job change occurred with or without a spell of unemployment or labor force with-

[8] Eligibility for the experiments was restricted on income, age, and family status. Excluded were families with heads over 58 years old or under 18 at the start of the program or families with permanently disabled heads; families of four with a preexperiment income of $9,000 for one-earner families (or $11,000 for two-earner families); and individuals who did not belong to a family. These eligibility rules do not appear to have been evenly applied to control and experimental subjects. For example, Ashenfelter (1980) finds that 22.6% of the controls had incomes of greater than $11,204 in the first year of the experiment, while 34% would have been expected to have incomes as high if there were no truncation on income at all.

[9] The actual meaning of the SWITFLAG variable is somewhat more complicated than indicated in the text. In each month the SIME and DIME data sets record information on the job with the longest number of hours worked and the job, if any, with the second longest number of hours worked. The value that the SWITFLAG variable takes depend on whether the job with the longest hours this month is the same as the job with the longest hours worked last month. Spurious job changes could be inferred due to a worker having a full-time and part-time job each month and temporarily, say due to a vacation or a layoff, working fewer hours at the full-time job than at the part-time job. This can be easily corrected because information about the individual's occupation and industry is available for all jobs. As a practical matter, this type of event was uncommon.

drawal. For such spells that last more than a month, the SWITFLAG variable alone would be sufficient to distinguish the presence or absence of nonemployment. In the case of shorter spells, resort must be made to the more detailed indicators of the fraction of the month that the individual was employed. In essence, the SIME and DIME data provide information on the labor force status at the beginning and end of each month as well as the fraction of the month the individual is not employed, with the reason for nonemployment being sufficiently detailed that distinctions of unemployment and nonparticipation can be made using Current Population Survey definitions.[10]

The wage variable used is the pretax, hourly wage rate exclusive of overtime payments. In contrast to other data sets this variable is not obtained by dividing weekly (or annual) earnings by the number of hours actually worked. For individuals paid on an hourly basis it is the response to a direct question about hourly wages; for those paid on a weekly, monthly, or annual basis it is obtained by dividing the periodic payment by the normal periodic hours worked; for example, for workers paid on a monthly basis it is monthly earnings (exclusive of overtime) divided by normal monthly hours. The measure that we use of wage change from one job to another is the nominal wage rate in the first month on the new job relative to the nominal wage rate on the last month on the previous job. A moment's reflection will suggest that this measure may have several infirmities in an environment of inflation. An individual who leaves a job in 1970 and returns to the same or a similar job in 1974 paying the same real wage as in 1970 would show a nominal wage *increase* of about 20 percent. This would appear to indicate that long spells between jobs lead to higher wages. For most of the comparisons that we will examine this is not a problem and can be controlled in part via regression covariates. Given that wage adjustment methods in the United States appear to be discrete, it is not obvious that one can get a more meaningful measure by deflating by some monthly index of purchasing power such as the consumers price index. We address the issue directly in the following section by examining the relative wage gains of movers versus stayers;

[10] See Chapter 10, this volume, for more details on the exact comparability between CPS and SIME–DIME definitions of unemployment and nonparticipation. For the purposes of this study the important issue is that it is possible to identify those individuals who are not at work during a particular period but who have new jobs to go to within 30 days and who are thus not classified as unemployed by the Current Population Survey (CPS). We follow this classification.

Table 13.1. *Fraction of workers changing employers, by age and sex*

Age	Denver	Seattle
Adult males		
20–29	.27	.31
30–39	.19	.24
40+	.24	.28
Adult females		
20–29	.21	.29
30–39	.16	.20
40+	.09	.10

in comparisons of all job movers, however, some care is needed in interpreting the wage-change magnitudes for job transitions that involve nonemployment, particularly for women.

The facts

An essential part of any mobility theory is the relation of job mobility and labor market experience. Mobility frequency is measured here as the ratio of all individuals who changed employers (regardless of how many times during the year) during the year divided by the number of individuals employed during the year. The numbers recorded in Table 13.1 are the four-year averages of the annual mobility frequency. For adult females the negative relation between turnover and age is readily apparent. For adult males, the mobility pattern has a U shape with regard to age. Despite the rather different labor market circumstances in Denver and Seattle, the mobility patterns do not differ much between the two areas.

   Movement between jobs either may be a direct move with no intervening unemployment, or it may involve periods of both unemployment and/or nonparticipation. Table 13.2 provides a breakdown by age of the fraction of job changes that occur without an intervening spell of nonemployment.[11] Age effects are noticeable for both males and females in Den-

[11] We use the term "nonemployment" as a shorthand expression covering both unemployment and nonparticipation. Technically, using CPS definitions of labor market status, an individual who has a job to report to within 30 days is counted as employed. Thus, a job transition in these data could involve a period in which no work was performed.

Table 13.2. *Percentage of job changes without unemployment or nonparticipation, by age and sex*

Age	Denver (%)	Seattle (%)
Adult males		
20–29	56.76	43.68
30–39	61.86	48.28
40+	61.76	36.72
Adult females		
20–29	38.80	34.34
30–39	49.40	54.35
40+	54.91	48.10

ver and in Seattle, suggesting that older workers who change jobs are more likely to do so with a specific alternative in mind than are younger workers. A major exception to this pattern is the case of workers over 40 in the Seattle area. Both males and females in this age group have a lower probability of changing jobs without nonemployment than do individuals in the 30–39 age group, and for males, the likelihood is even less than that of the 20–29 age group. This suggests that the incidence of job loss brought about by unusually severe economic conditions, such as prevailed in Seattle, where the unemployment rate rose from 4.0% to 12.5% in 18 months, has a proportionately greater effect on older workers.

The differences by sex in the manner by which a job change occurred also show the effects of the different economic conditions in the two areas. Given that females are more likely to be out of the labor force than males, some spells of nonparticipation will be recorded in these data as a job change with an intervening spell of nonemployment. Thus, particularly for women in the prime years of childrearing, one would expect that the fraction of job changes without nonemployment would be lower than that for similarly aged males. For the same reasons one would expect this difference to decline with age. For Denver females this is precisely the pattern observed, but in Seattle the pattern is perverse: Older females actually have higher probabilities of making a job transition without nonemployment than do males. The differences are almost entirely due, however, to the reduced rates for older males. It is of some interest that the overall fraction of workers changing jobs without an intervening spell of nonemployment – 53.3 percent in Denver and 43.2 percent in Seattle –

Table 13.3. *Average percent wage change for job movers, by age, sex, and transition type*

	Denver (%)		Seattle (%)	
Age	Transitions without nonemployment	Transitions with nonemployment	Transitions without nonemployment	Transitions with nonemployment
Adult males				
20–29	10.98	11.46	12.81	14.26
30–39	12.40	9.27	9.87	7.67
40+	12.43	13.21	6.92	1.66
Adult females				
20–29	15.13	8.91	21.23	11.85
30–39	5.83	8.04	11.17	2.79
40+	9.16	4.76	11.01	3.41

conforms to the patterns reported by Mattila (1974).[12] In particular, in stationary economic conditions a substantial fraction – roughly 59 percent for males and 45 percent for females – change jobs without unemployment.

Taken by itself, the form by which a transition from one job to another is made has little meaning, in part because most spells of unemployment are so short. To the extent that the occurrence of unemployment or nonparticipation implies that workers lost jobs rather than left them, there is a potential difference brought about by the differences between the reservation wage on a job and that value while an individual is unemployed. That there is substantive meaning to the form of job change is indicated by the patterns of wage change indicated in Tables 13.3 and 13.4. In these tables the average percent wage change is obtained from the wage rate in the last month on the job being left and the wage rate in the first month on the new job. Any growth that would occur due to better matching, more opportunities for investment, or the presence of institutionally set programs such as probationary periods with lower earnings is not in-

[12] Mattilla's evidence is based primarily on the Bureau of Labor Statistics (BLS) studies "Job Mobility in 1961" and "Job Mobility of Workers in 1955" (BLS 1957, 1963). The 1961 data by sex on all job changers indicates that 56.6% of the males and 54.0% of the females who changed jobs in that year did so without unemployment. These estimates are remarkably close to those for the Denver area, which perhaps more resembles the economic conditions prevailing in 1961, but are significantly higher than the estimates for Seattle. Of course, this is what would be expected from what is known about the cyclical behavior of quit rates.

Table 13.4. *Percentage of job changers receiving a wage cut, by age, sex, and transition type*

	Denver (%)		Seattle (%)	
Age	Transitions without nonemployment	Transitions with nonemployment	Transitions without nonemployment	Transitions with nonemployment
Adult males				
20–29	35.24	41.25	29.82	35.37
30–39	27.40	34.44	30.61	36.19
40+	41.25	36.54	25.53	43.21
Adult females				
20–29	28.46	43.81	26.47	36.15
30–39	31.33	42.35	28.19	45.24
40+	29.73	31.15	23.68	34.15

cluded in these comparisons.[13] Several patterns stand out in these data. Generally, the average wage change upon a move is greatest for young workers, which is consistent with the view that the returns to matching are greatest in the earlier years. This is not a universal phenomenon, however, as the absence of any age pattern for adult males in Denver indicates. Except for younger males, a job change accompanied by a spell of nonemployment makes a significant difference, particularly for older workers, again with the exception of males in Denver. These effects of nonemployment are more pronounced in the volatile demand area of Seattle than in the steadier circumstances of Denver.

An alternative way of looking at the outcome of the job transition process that is particularly relevant to the on-the-job-search explanation of wage growth is given in Table 13.4. Indivduals are classified as having incurred a wage cut in the obvious manner: If the wage on the new job is less than the wage on the old job, a wage cut has occurred. From the results in Table 13.4 it is apparent that a substantial number of job changes results in an initial decline in wages. About 30–40 percent of the males who change jobs without an intervening spell of nonemployment incur a wage cut, with the fraction being somewhat higher in Denver. Job changes

[13] Comparisons of pre- and postmove wages are notoriously sensitive to measurement error. As a check on the results in the text we compared two-month moving averages of pre- and postmove wages, finding little difference from the results reported. Longer-period comparisons are treated in the following section of the text.

that include a spell of nonemployment lead on average to about 6 percent more individuals incurring a wage cut. Note that the age pattern in the fraction of workers taking a wage cut is less apparent than it was in the average wage change figures in Table 13.3

The preceding discussion suggests that the empricial job mobility process can be summarized as follows: Mobility declines with age, as is well known, but it still occurs among a nontrivial fraction of workers over 40. About one-half of all job changes (somewhat higher for females, less for males) result in a spell of unemployment or nonparticipation, and the outcome of such spells generally is a lower wage than if the transition had been made directly to another job. In particular, the probability of a wage cut increases if a spell of nonemployment occurs. Aggregate demand appears to have relatively little effect on the overall amount of job mobility, influencing instead the composition of the sample between those who transit directly to a new job and those who incur a spell of unemployment or labor force withdrawal. In percentage terms the greatest wage gains to mobility occur among younger and female workers. Even among workers who transit directly from job to job, a large fraction experience wage cuts, which suggests that even among this group a pure job search model cannot account for all the facts.

Although this characterization of empirical mobility patterns is somewhat crude, it does capture the main patterns of wages and turnover that appear in these data. In the following sections we investigate via regression means whether these patterns reflect observable heterogeneity or whether they persist after adjustment for individual characteristics.

13.3   Wage functions of job changers

The empirical facts discussed in the previous section indicate that there are significant differences in wages due to changing jobs and that these differences are related to the form in which the transition takes place. A question of empirical interest is whether these patterns merely reflect differences among individuals in such measurable characteristics as education and age, or whether they reflect real differences due to the type of job change being made. In this section we examine these patterns in more detail. In particular, we examine the relation of these wage changes to tenure on the job, and we compare the wages of movers and stayers.

Tables 13.5 through 13.8 contain alternative regression specifications relating the (logarithm) of the hourly wage earned on the new job to

Table 13.5. *Wage regression: Denver, adult males, all job changers*

	(1)	(2)	(3)	(4)	(5)	(6)
Constant	2.1710	2.2209	2.6904	2.4758	2.9244	2.9712
	(12.552)	(12.784)	(15.607)	(14.076)	(16.300)	(16.537)
White	0.0207	−0.0268	−0.0183	−0.0385	−0.0278	−0.0340
	(−0.813)	(−1.050)	(−0.767)	(−1.521)	(−1.150)	(−1.405)
Hispanic	0.0290	0.0292	0.0128	0.0110	0.0061	0.0058
	(1.067)	(1.078)	(0.504)	(0.412)	(0.240)	(0.231)
Age/100	0.1570	0.1336	0.1471	0.2085	0.1978	0.1569
	(0.976)	(0.831)	(0.980)	(1.329)	(1.204)	(1.053)
$(\text{Age})^2/1{,}000$	0.0121	0.0136	0.0224	0.0089	0.0182	0.0197
	(0.631)	(0.714)	(1.248)	(0.480)	(1.021)	(1.109)
Kids < 6 years	0.0177	0.0153	0.0126	0.0139	0.0113	0.0087
	(1.474)	(1.276)	(1.118)	(1.188)	(1.011)	(0.778)
(Net equity)/1,000	0.0026	0.0021	0.0036	0.0027	0.0035	0.0079
	(1.867)	(1.464)	(2.698)	(1.967)	(2.670)	(2.234)
Education	0.0048	0.0049	0.0096	0.0065	0.0073	0.0030
	(0.935)	(0.959)	(1.96)	(1.255)	(1.482)	(1.596)
(Spouse's monthly earnings)/100	−0.0020	−0.0017	−0.0026	−0.0025	−0.0031	−0.0028
	(−0.396)	(−0.345)	(−0.548)	(−0.505)	(−0.667)	(−0.606)
$\ln w_{-1}$	0.6089	0.6056	0.5118	0.5543	0.4836	0.4794
	(22.253)	(22.171)	(18.883)	(19.941)	(17.497)	(17.378)
Unemployed/ nonparticipant		−0.0500				−0.0510
		(−2.393)				(−2.590)
Industry controls	No	No	Yes	No	Yes	Yes
Occupation controls	No	No	No	Yes	Yes	Yes
R^2	.4103	.4145	.4928	.4525	.5112	.5154
SEE	.2836	.2828	.2643	.2747	.2608	.2599
F	62.233	56.911	45.558	38.74	33.010	32.228
N	814	814	814	814	814	814

Table 13.6. *Wage regression: Seattle, adult males, all job changers*

	(1)	(2)	(3)	(4)	(5)	(6)
Constant	2.0890	2.272	2.3159	2.4450	2.5831	2.7216
	(9.004)	(9.706)	(10.054)	(10.270)	(10.819)	(11.362)
White	0.0139	0.0152	0.0428	0.0140	0.0410	0.0438
	(0.455)	(0.506)	(1.437)	(0.467)	(1.390)	(1.501)
Age/100	0.2519	0.2386	0.2751	0.2739	0.2712	0.2646
	(1.313)	(1.261)	(1.505)	(1.474)	(1.521)	(1.502)
$(\text{Age})^2/1{,}000$	−0.0164	−0.0056	−0.0087	−0.0181	−0.0063	0.0003
	(−0.762)	(−0.261)	(−0.418)	(−0.863)	(−0.307)	(0.161)
Kids < 6 years	0.0301	0.0329	0.0239	0.0181	0.0132	0.0173
	(1.774)	(1.967)	(1.475)	(1.093)	(0.826)	(1.096)
(Net equity)/1,000	0.0004	0.00007	0.0008	0.0018	0.0023	0.0020
	(0.264)	(0.017)	(0.560)	(1.177)	(1.497)	(1.352)
Education	−0.0101	−0.0130	−0.0002	−0.0103	−0.0051	−0.0071
	(−1.747)	(−2.255)	(−0.039)	(−1.661)	(−0.834)	(−1.172)
(Spouse's monthly earnings)/100	−0.0023	−0.0012	−0.0017	0.0002	0.0001	0.0009
	(−0.364)	(−0.190)	(−0.284)	(0.026)	(0.023)	(0.145)
ln w_{-1}	0.6571	0.6394	0.5782	0.5921	0.5370	0.5231
	(16.899)	(16.551)	(14.706)	(15.124)	(13.620)	(13.351)
Unemployed/ nonparticipant		−0.0973				−0.0834
		(−3.675)				(−3.332)
Industry controls	No	No	Yes	No	Yes	Yes
Occupation controls	No	No	No	Yes	Yes	Yes
R^2	0.4497	0.4664	0.5152	0.5003	0.5525	0.5642
SEE	0.2686	0.2648	0.2545	0.2584	0.2468	0.2439
F	44.131	41.864	28.157	26.531	21.404	21.491
N	440	440	440	440	440	440

Table 13.7. *Wage regression: Denver, adult females, all job changers*

	(1)	(2)	(3)	(4)	(5)	(6)
Constant	2.7223	3.0077	2.9331	2.8587	2.9725	3.2080
	(12.892)	(13.855)	(13.614)	(13.273)	(13.698)	(14.493)
White	−0.0725	−0.0671	−0.0614	−0.0634	−0.0547	−0.0521
	(−3.008)	(−2.828)	(−2.507)	(−2.611)	(−2.233)	(−2.157)
Hispanic	−0.0308	−0.0184	−0.0346	−0.0226	−0.0177	−0.0064
	(−1.119)	(−0.675)	(−1.267)	(−0.817)	(−0.647)	(−0.236)
Age/100	0.1370	0.0266	0.1383	0.0926	0.0876	−0.0222
	(0.885)	(0.169)	(0.874)	(0.583)	(0.555)	(−0.141)
$(\text{Age})^2/1{,}000$	−0.0354	−0.0306	−0.0334	−0.0307	−0.0325	−0.0286
	(−1.860)	(−1.630)	(−1.761)	(−1.610)	(−1.720)	(−1.531)
Kids < 6 years	0.0036	0.0079	0.0039	0.0061	0.0025	0.0061
	(0.257)	(0.572)	(0.275)	(0.437)	(0.180)	(0.441)
(Net equity)/1,000	0.0007	0.0007	0.0007	0.0004	0.0004	0.0004
	(0.509)	(0.536)	(0.505)	(0.269)	(0.285)	(0.327)
Education	0.0143	0.0118	0.0136	0.0103	0.0106	0.0084
	(2.827)	(2.346)	(2.632)	(1.935)	(2.004)	(1.607)
(Spouse's monthly earnings)/100	0.0050	0.0056	0.0048	0.0055	.0053	0.0058
	(2.153)	(2.441)	(2.042)	(2.382)	(2.286)	(2.524)
ln w_{-1}	0.4799	0.4465	0.4582	0.4567	0.4371	0.4104
	(12.651)	(11.738)	(12.086)	(11.877)	(11.455)	(10.754)
Unemployed/nonparticipant		−0.0958				−0.0884
		(−4.516)				(−4.147)
Industry controls	No	No	Yes	No	Yes	Yes
Occupation controls	No	No	No	Yes	Yes	Yes
R^2	.2934	.3177	.3189	.3122	.3425	.3621
SEE	.2425	.2385	.2395	.2407	.2370	.2334
F	26.482	26.678	16.594	16.087	12.682	13.222
N	583	583	583	583	583	583

263

Table 13.8. *Wage regression: Seattle, adult females, all job changers*

	(1)	(2)	(3)	(4)	(5)	(6)
Constant	3.0186	3.1127	3.1775	2.3070	3.4842	3.5366
	(9.780)	(9.991)	(10.150)	(10.425)	(10.773)	(10.891)
White	0.0589	0.0587	0.0465	0.0523	0.0432	0.0401
	(1.797)	(1.799)	(1.399)	(1.608)	(1.306)	(1.214)
Age/100	-0.1302	-0.2128	-0.0026	-0.1059	-0.0496	-0.1182
	(-0.604)	(-0.971)	(-0.012)	(-0.490)	(-0.225)	(-0.526)
$(\text{Age})^2$/1,000	-0.0070	-0.0021	-0.0110	-0.0121	-0.0138	-0.0092
	(-0.249)	(-0.073)	(-0.394)	(-0.434)	(-0.497)	(-0.329)
Kids < 6 years	0.0119	0.0144	0.0041	0.0012	-0.0058	-0.0040
	(0.535)	(0.648)	(0.185)	(0.055)	(-0.258)	(-0.176)
(Net equity)/1,000	0.0045	0.0048	0.0053	0.0038	0.0048	0.0050
	(2.210)	(2.347)	(2.572)	(1.819)	(2.280)	(2.406)
Education	0.0103	0.0085	0.0121	0.0038	0.0067	0.0064
	(1.195)	(0.992)	(1.376)	(0.410)	(0.711)	(0.679)
(Spouse's monthly earnings)/100	0.0026	-0.0034	-0.0010	-0.0031	-0.0015	-0.0020
	(-0.579)	(-0.759)	(-0.248)	(-0.705)	(-0.336)	(-0.456)
$\ln w_{-1}$	0.4372	0.4337	0.4082	0.4020	0.3762	0.3746
	(8.469)	(8.430)	(7.928)	(7.734)	(7.201)	(7.184)
Unemployed/ nonparticipant		-0.0597				-0.0477
		(-1.839)				(-1.456)
Industry controls	No	No	Yes	No	Yes	Yes
Occupation controls	No	No	No	Yes	No	Yes
R^2	0.2542	0.2632	0.2975	0.3093	0.3417	0.3470
SEE	0.2632	0.2621	0.2588	0.2566	0.2538	0.2533
F	11.758	10.917	7.595	8.031	6.183	6.031
N	284	284	284	284	284	284

various demographic characteristics, including the wage earned on the past job.[14] The sample consists of all job changes that occurred during the four years of the experiments for which there were complete data on all variables.[15] Two features stand out prominently in these data. First, regardless of the presence of other variables in the regression, the presence of a spell of unemployment or nonparticipation results in a lower reemployment wage. On average Denver males who obtain a new job after being unemployed earn about 5 percent less than those who transit directly to new employment; female job changers in Denver who incur nonemployment earn 9 percent less. In Seattle the effect of a spell of nonemployment is somewhat greater for males than it was in Denver – 8 versus 5 percent – but for females it was less (5 vs. 9 percent), although the precision with which the effect in Seattle is measured is low. Compared to the raw facts given in Table 13.3, the regression adjustment for females implies very little difference. For males, the regression adjustment yields differences due to the type of job transition that are slightly higher than implied by the raw data, although not by much. Put differently, the difference in wages that is related to how the job transition was made appears to be largely independent of standard measures of personal and job-related characteristics.

The second feature of note is the relative absence of predictive value to the standard regressors once previous wages and the transition type are controlled for. In regressions not shown, the conventional patterns of wages being a concave function of age or experience and positively related to education show up quite strongly, even allowing for the type of job transition. When the previous wage is conditioned upon, as in Tables 13.5– 13.8, no persistent pattern emerges. Education, for example, is related

---

[14] The variables included were race/ethnic group indicators, age and age squared, number of children less than six years of age, net wealth (defined as assets less liabilities), years of education, spouse's monthly earnings, one-digit SIC industry indicators (10), occupation codes (10), and an indicator of whether unemployment or nonparticipation occurred in the job transition. The dependent variable is the logarithm of the hourly wage, measured in cents per hour, on the new job. The wage on the previous job is conformably defined. All independent variables refer to conditions (e.g., industry, occupation, number of children) prevailing when the individual began the job transition. The exception here is for education, which in the SIME–DIME data refers to education level at the beginning of the experiment. Thus, increases in educational attainment are not reflected in these data.

[15] There were 92 observations excluded because of missing data. The bulk of these, 67, were excluded because age and/or education were missing; the remainder were excluded because of missing wage data.

to wage change in three of the groups, but in only one group (Denver females) is the effect measured with much precision. Although this empirical finding is not new, it is difficult to reconcile in terms of existing models of turnover. To see this, consider the following example. Assume for simplicity that there is no matching or specific capital accumulation, workers receive alternative offers at some exogenous rate γ, and jobs disappear at an exogenous rate α. Unemployed, workers receive $\$b$ per period, and the common cross-job wage distribution is exponential with mean μ.

In this situation job changers consist of two types: those who transit directly to a new job, because an offer arrived that paid more than their current wage, and those who transit to a new job after some period of nonemployment. For both groups the conditonal wage functions can be written as

$$E(w_j) = \mu + w^r_{j-1}, \tag{5}$$

where w^r_{j-1} is the reservation wage. For employed individuals the reservation wage is the wage currently earned; for unemployed workers the reservation wage is a function of all the parameters in the model – μ, α, γ, and r, the discount rate – but it necessarily is less than the previous wage.[16] If the mean of the wage distribution is related to individual characteristics by the linear regression

$$\mu = X_i\beta + \varepsilon_i, \tag{6}$$

then we have a direct interpretation of the regressions presented in Tables 13.5–13.8. This development suggests that a source of misspecification is the inclusion of the previous wage as a proxy for the reservation wage for those individuals who lost their jobs. Moreover, treating the problem as an errors-in-variables issue, the error introduced $(w_{j-1} - w^r_{j-1})$ in general will be correlated with the remaining variables in the wage regression, which might account for the general insignificance of those regressors. One way to deal with this is to allow for different effects of past wages for those who transited to a new job with a spell of nonemployment.[17]

---

[16] By definition the reservation wage while an individual is unemployed is the lowest wage that the individual would work at. Hence, any observed wage must exceed the reservation wage.

[17] This adjustment cannot fully explain the data patterns because, as Table 13.4 indicates, a significant number of individuals transited directly to new jobs, yet incurred a decrease in earnings. Such a pattern is impossible under the pure search interpretation, which is the basis for the adjustment suggested in the text.

Table 13.9. *Alternative wage specifications for Denver male job changers*

	(1)	(2)	(3)
ln w_{-1}	.4971	.4966	.5112
(without unemployment)	(18.41)	(18.76)	(17.71)
ln w_{-1}	.4733	.4719	.4676
	(16.37)	(16.94)	(15.89)
SEE	.2605	.2590	.2484

Table 13.9 contains a set of alternative regressions performed on the Denver male sample of job changers to test these conjectures. For each specification we have reported only the relevant coefficients on previous wages and the summary statistics. Column (1) reports the results of allowing the regression coefficient on previous wages to differ between the two groups, forcing all other coefficients to be the same and excluding the indicator variable for transition type. Both coefficients are higher than the corresponding constrained value reported in Table 13.5, but the difference between them is not significant. Column (2) shows the results when the indicator variable for transition type is included. As in the results of Table 13.5, the effect on wages is significant, even after allowing for different lagged wage effects. Finally, column (3) reports the results obtained by allowing all coefficients and variances to differ by transition type; that is, separate regressions were fit for each group. The difference in the error sum of squares in this case is asymptotically distributed as chi-square with 23 degrees of freedom.

A potentially important element that is missing so far from the empirical analysis is the effect of job tenure on subsequent earnings. As discussed above (and more fully in Mortensen 1984) the distinguishing characteristic of specific capital and matching models is the prediction of negative duration dependence in the on-the-job reservation wage. In terms of the example given above, this implies that the reservation wage is not equal to the currently earned wage, but in fact is less. Unfortunately, detailed information about actual job duration is rare in social science data sets, including SIME–DIME. The central problem is that few data sets initialize the process by inquiring about the duration of the initial job.[18] With the SIME–DIME data it is possible to construct job tenure

---

[18] The Michigan PSID data do initialize the process, but the subsequent questions on length of time with the employer result in internally inconsistent data on job duration for a substantial portion of the sample.

for all jobs that start during the experimental periods, using the same information that allowed us to identify job switches. In using these data on tenure we are constrained, therefore, to look at the effects of tenure of less than four years. With few exceptions, we are also constrained to look at a selected sample of multiple-job changers within a four-year period in analyzing the effect of job tenure.[19] Since learning about the quality of a match is likely to be most important during the early part of the relationship, the limitations imposed by the data may not be so severe.

Tables 13.10–13.13 contain regression specifications similar to those presented earlier, with the addition of job tenure. Length of time on the previous job has a positive effect on wages in the next job for all four groups, but is small and not precisely estimated. At conventional significance levels it would be judged significant only for Denver males. More important, the positive sign (or zero) is counter to what would be expected from matching and human capital models. If reservation wages decline with job tenure, holding current earnings constant, then the conditional wage functions holding previous earnings should also be lower. Some fiddling with the specification along the lines of Table 13.9 failed to show any evidence of a negative effect.

As an alternative method of looking at the effect of job tenure we examined the probability of taking a wage cut when making a job change. This measure is less sensitive to any outliers in the wage data, and it may be less affected by unobserved individual heterogeneity. The results, contained in Tables 13.14–13.17, provide very limited support for the role of job tenure.[20] For males, longer job durations decrease the probability of taking a wage cut, a result consistent with the regressions in Tables 13.10 and 13.11, while for females some evidence of negative duration dependence in reservation wages is indicated by the positive effects of job length on the probability of taking a wage cut. In all cases, however, the effects we are talking about are small and uniformly statistically insignificant.

As far as these data are concerned, the effects of job tenure on subsequent earnings appear to be nil, given that previous earnings are con-

---

[19] The exceptions occur for young individuals who take their first career job after they finish school. Although the samples are restricted to adults over 21, and hence most high school leavers are excluded, we nonetheless pick up some individuals who were in school for a number of periods and then enter the labor force.

[20] As indicated in Section 13.1, mobility can be treated endogenously if one proceeds along the structural lines described there. As we noted, there are formidable computational problems involved in solving such a model, but in principle it can be done.

Table 13.10. *Wage regression: Denver, adult males, multiple-job holders*

	(1)	(2)	(3)	(4)	(5)
Constant	2.3805	2.4365	3.0894	2.6962	3.2395
	(11.538)	(11.703)	(14.690)	(12.541)	(14.622)
White	−0.0199	−0.0241	−0.0298	−0.0272	−0.0225
	(−0.629)	(−0.755)	(−0.844)	(−0.846)	(−0.742)
Hispanic	0.0172	0.0171	0.0010	0.0098	0.0028
	(0.513)	(0.510)	(0.032)	(0.294)	(0.090)
Age/100	−0.0447	−0.0879	−0.1272	−0.0138	−0.0876
	(−0.223)	(−0.438)	(−0.681)	(−0.070)	(−0.465)
$(Age)^2/1,000$	0.0201	0.0211	0.0360	0.0128	0.0336
	(0.864)	(0.905)	(1.650)	(0.556)	(1.532)
Kids < 6 years	0.0195	0.0182	0.0081	0.0150	0.0081
	(1.333)	(1.243)	(0.590)	(1.035)	(0.591)
(Net equity)/1,000	0.0039	0.0037	0.0037	0.0034	0.0036
	(2.081)	(1.934)	(2.101)	(1.822)	(2.008)
Education	−0.0038	−0.0043	0.0019	−0.0019	0.0006
	(−0.586)	(−0.668)	(0.309)	(−0.287)	(0.088)
(Spouse's monthly	0.0015	0.0014	−0.0009	0.00003	−0.0019
earnings)/100	(0.240)	(0.225)	(−0.156)	(0.006)	(−0.333)
ln w_{-1}	0.5988	0.5924	0.4724	0.5412	0.4530
	(18.645)	(18.361)	(14.506)	(16.023)	(13.444)
Job length		0.0023	0.0040	0.0024	0.0036
		(1.272)	(2.364)	(1.332)	(2.134)
Unemployed/		−0.0273	−0.0378	−0.0248	−0.0321
nonparticipant		(−1.039)	(−1.543)	(−0.953)	(−1.307)
Industry controls	No	No	Yes	No	Yes
Occupation controls	No	No	No	Yes	Yes
R^2	.4265	.4305	.5183	.4596	.5292
SEE	.2826	.2822	.2615	.2770	.2606
F	43.715	36.221	29.397	23.234	21.275
N	538	538	538	538	538

trolled for. This finding is somewhat paradoxical because it conflicts with the pattern of wage cuts experienced by those who move directly to a new job. That is, the pattern of wage cuts suggests that training or matching is important in explaining job mobility and is inconsistent with a simple model of on-the-job search. The conditional wage functions, on the other hand, do not show any evidence of a declining reservation wage on the last job; indeed, they seem consistent with a simple on-the-job-search explanation. It may be that the type of learning that is important

Table 13.11. *Wage regression: Seattle, adult males, multiple-job holders*

	(1)	(2)	(3)	(4)	(5)
Constant	2.1520	2.3635	2.5594	2.7194	2.8620
	(7.473)	(8.117)	(8.945)	(8.839)	(9.477)
White	−0.0135	−0.0140	0.0092	−0.0067	0.0137
	(−0.325)	(−0.343)	(0.23ᴸ,	(−0.164)	(0.346)
Age/100	0.2364	0.2687	0.3014	0.2497	0.2929
	(0.886)	(1.024)	(1.207)	(0.966)	(1.194)
$(Age)^2/1,000$	−0.0090	0.0018	0.0182	0.0017	0.0224
	(−0.312)	(0.061)	(0.664)	(0.061)	(0.829)
Kids < 6 years	0.0470	0.0542	0.0449	0.0386	0.0319
	(2.067)	(2.421)	(2.104)	(1.703)	(1.482)
(Net equity)/1,000	0.0001	−0.0005	−0.0003	0.0015	0.0015
	(0.051)	(−0.253)	(−0.186)	(0.764)	(0.803)
Education	−0.0128	−0.0175	−0.0056	−0.0216	−0.0135
	(−1.751)	(−2.394)	(−0.764)	(−2.655)	(−1.698)
(Spouse's monthly earnings)/100	−0.0029	−0.0004	0.0007	0.0009	0.0017
	(−0.360)	(−0.044)	(0.097)	(0.120)	(0.228)
$\ln w_{-1}$	0.6561	0.6322	0.5544	0.5777	0.5110
	(13.789)	(13.385)	(11.591)	(11.894)	(10.597)
Job length		0.0033	0.0016	0.0030	0.0017
		(1.249)	(0.629)	(1.141)	(0.658)
Unemployed/ nonparticipant		−0.1087	−0.1183	−0.1000	−0.1110
		(−3.083)	(−3.51)	(−2.851)	(−3.326)
Industry controls	No	No	Yes	No	Yes
Occupation controls	No	No	No	Yes	Yes
R^2	.4772	.4997	.5648	.5352	.6011
SEE	0.2817	0.2766	0.2613	0.2705	0.2539
F	31.953	27.769	20.686	17.272	15.852
N	288	288	288	288	288

about jobs has a mean arrival time of longer than the maximum of four years that we are constrained to deal with in these data.

Mover–stayer comparisons

Comparisons of pre- and postmove wages are useful in providing insight into the mechanism of the job mobility process, but they do not tell us how individuals fared relative to those who did not move. Presumably, those who moved did so because their alternative was more favorable than

Table 13.12. *Wage regressions: Denver, adult females, multiple-job holders*

	(1)	(2)	(3)	(4)	(5)
Constant	2.9853	3.2594	3.3222	3.3387	3.3550
	(11.073)	(11.813)	(11.859)	(11.989)	(11.943)
White	−0.0971	−0.0902	−0.0900	−0.0792	−0.0778
	(−3.299)	(−3.100)	(−2.986)	(−2.661)	(−2.542)
Hispanic	−0.0726	−0.0569	−0.574	−0.0434	−0.0354
	(−2.098)	(−1.657)	(−1.666)	(−1.248)	(−1.016)
Age/100	0.0371	−0.0782	−0.0221	−0.1073	−0.0573
	(0.186)	(−0.392)	(−0.107)	(−0.531)	(−0.277)
$(Age)^2/1,000$	−0.0227	−0.0212	−0.0233	−0.0194	−0.0242
	(−0.990)	(−0.939)	(−1.015)	(−0.852)	(−1.055)
Kids < 6 years	0.0064	0.0096	0.0081	0.0119	0.0069
	(0.388)	(0.589)	(0.493)	(0.727)	(0.419)
(Net equity)/1,000	0.0016	0.0018	0.0018	0.0016	0.0016
	(1.051)	(1.179)	(1.195)	(1.031)	(1.068)
Education	0.0130	0.0091	0.0107	0.0068	0.0084
	(2.085)	(1.471)	(1.680)	(1.070)	(1.294)
(Spouse's monthly	0.0063	0.0071	0.0066	0.0073	0.0071
earnings)/100	(2.182)	(2.491)	(2.245)	(2.596)	(2.434)
$\ln w_{-1}$	0.4396	0.4102	0.3992	0.3935	0.3784
	(9.592)	(8.940)	(8.622)	(8.473)	(8.126)
Job length		0.0008	0.0008	0.0005	0.0006
		(0.478)	(0.460)	(0.284)	(0.344)
Unemployed/		−0.0925	−0.0873	−0.0878	−0.0874
nonparticipant		(−3.454)	(−3.201)	(−3.245)	(−3.208)
Industry controls	No	No	Yes	No	Yes
Occupation controls	No	No	No	Yes	Yes
R^2	.2849	.3098	.3223	.3285	.3490
SEE	.2411	.2375	.2375	.2364	.2351
F	16.734	15.342	9.751	10.031	7.762
N	387	387	387	387	387

the job at which they were employed. Similarly, those who did not change jobs had employment opportunities that were more favorable than their labor market alternatives. This is the classic problem of heterogeneity, which must be resolved if one seeks to answer the question "How much better off are movers than they would have been had they stayed on their previous job?" To answer this question one must have a theory of why people change jobs and a means of identifying the reasons for job change. For our purposes we treat mobility as predetermined and inquire whether

Table 13.13. *Wage regressions: Seattle, adult females, multiple-job holders*

	(1)	(2)	(3)	(4)	(5)
Constant	3.3418	3.4065	3.7306	3.6875	3.9368
	(7.200)	(7.231)	(7.946)	(7.572)	(8.001)
White	0.0732	0.0731	0.0340	0.0710	0.0418
	(1.425)	(1.425)	(0.673)	(1.370)	(0.800)
Age/100	−0.1001	−0.2441	−0.0916	−0.1734	−0.0330
	(−0.276)	(−0.653)	(0.244)	(−0.460)	(0.085)
$(Age)^2/1{,}000$	−0.0207	−0.0161	−0.0391	−0.0252	−0.0384
	(−0.444)	(−0.346)	(−0.869)	(−0.540)	(−0.830)
Kids < 6 years	−0.0085	−0.0066	−0.0138	−0.0290	−0.0305
	(−0.259)	(−0.198)	(−0.425)	(−0.847)	(−0.888)
(Net equity)/1,000	0.0062	0.0072	0.0087	0.0057	0.0079
	(1.985)	(2.273)	(2.735)	(1.718)	(2.363)
Education	0.0058	0.0023	0.0088	0.0003	0.0052
	(0.466)	(0.185)	(0.688)	(0.023)	(0.366)
(Spouse's monthly	−0.0021	−0.0035	−0.0038	−0.0045	−0.0044
earnings)/100	(−0.329)	(−0.533)	(−0.598)	(−0.684)	(−0.672)
$\ln w_{-1}$	0.3855	0.3876	0.3188	0.3518	0.3012
	(5.165)	(5.205)	(4.385)	(4.630)	(3.965)
Job length		0.0039	0.0032	0.0051	0.0042
		(1.240)	(1.009)	(1.630)	(1.269)
Unemployed/		−0.0509	−0.0545	−0.0323	−0.0419
nonparticipant		(−0.998)	(−1.101)	(−0.621)	(−0.807)
Industry controls	No	No	Yes	No	Yes
Occupation					
controls	No	No	No	Yes	Yes
R^2	0.1998	0.2139	0.3200	0.2795	0.3462
SEE	0.3092	0.3084	0.2934	0.3020	0.2946
F	4.993	4.300	4.180	3.445	3.178
N	168	168	168	168	168

there are significant differences in wages between movers and stayers.

For these comparisons we used as the dependent variables the hourly wage earned in December of each year. If this was missing, say due to unemployment, we used the wage rate for November if it was available. If neither was available, the observation was treated as having missing data and was excluded. A person was classified as being a job changer if a job change occurred at any time during the year. The type of job transition that occurred for job changers is defined implicitly by the variable "months not employed," which measures the total number of months

Table 13.14. *Probability of taking a wage cut: Seattle, adult males*

	(1)	(2)	(3)	(4)	(5)
Constant	0.3413	0.2310	0.2454	−1.3618	−1.9223
	(1.602)	(1.055)	(1.108)	(−2.921)	(−3.866)
White	0.0970	0.1026	0.1008	0.0783	0.0581
	(1.431)	(1.520)	(1.490)	(1.179)	(0.872)
Age/100	−0.2298	−0.2339	−0.2319	−0.7243	−0.0065
	(−0.546)	(−0.559)	(−0.553)	(−1.690)	(−1.542)
$(Age)^2/1,000$	0.0276	0.0190	−0.0175	0.0250	−0.0105
	(0.582)	(0.402)	(0.368)	(0.536)	(−0.229)
Kids < 6 years	−0.0790	−0.0833	−0.0839	−0.1174	−0.0966
	(−2.172)	(−2.294)	(−2.306)	(−3.211)	(−2.565)
(Net equity)/1,000	0.0247	0.0032	0.0032	0.0025	0.0003
	(0.803)	(1.035)	(1.025)	(0.836)	(0.089)
Education	0.0047	0.0091	0.0094	0.0129	0.0007
	(0.387)	(0.749)	(1.025)	(1.1074)	(0.052)
(Spouse's monthly	−0.0129	−0.0157	−0.0158	−0.0156	−0.0171
earnings)/100	(−0.971)	(−1.179)	(−1.183)	(−1.197)	(−1.344)
ln w_{-1}				0.2970	0.4600
				(3.892)	(5.699)
Job length			−0.0020	−0.0022	−0.0012
			(−0.461)	(−0.514)	(−0.279)
Unemployed/		0.1163	0.1125	0.1394	0.1459
nonparticipant		(2.011)	(1.924)	(2.422)	(2.562)
Industry and					
occupation controls	No	No	No	No	Yes
R^2	0.0301	0.0429	0.0425	0.0895	0.2105
SEE	0.4798	0.4774	0.4781	0.4673	0.4464
F	1.342	1.691	1.523	2.950	3.039
N	310	310	310	310	310

during the year that an individual was not employed.[21] For each group the regressions are presented on an annual basis for each of the four years in the experiment. These results are given in Tables 13.18–13.21.

Several patterns are obvious in these wage regressions. The odd-numbered columns show the coefficient estimates obtained without conditioning on the previous wage – here, last year's wage – and as noted above,

[21] Multiple-job changers within a year could be identified, but as a practical matter there were few such individuals outside of construction. If an individual did change jobs more than once during the year, the "months not employed" variable will record the total number of months an individual was not employed from all of the job changes during the year.

Table 13.15. *Probability of taking a wage cut: Denver, adult males*

	(1)	(2)	(3)	(4)	(5)
Constant	0.0125	−0.0295	−0.0286	−1.3880	−2.1916
	(0.070)	(−0.164)	(−0.159)	(−4.107)	(−5.838)
White	0.0801	0.0884	0.0879	0.0756	0.0622
	(1.542)	(1.694)	(1.680)	(1.469)	(1.210)
Hispanic	−0.0006	−0.0002	−0.0005	−0.0088	−0.0005
	(−0.010)	(−0.003)	(−0.010)	(−0.160)	(0.010)
Age/100	0.4091	0.4354	0.4430	0.4116	0.3726
	(1.258)	(1.338)	(1.354)	(1.281)	(1.178)
$(Age)^2/1,000$	−0.0022	−0.0052	−0.0048	−0.0132	−0.0259
	(−0.057)	(−0.134)	(−0.124)	(−0.347)	(−0.687)
Kids < 6 years	−0.0054	−0.0034	−0.0032	−0.0190	−0.0135
	(−0.227)	(−0.143)	(−0.135)	(−0.800)	(−0.576)
(Net equity)/1,000	−0.0088	−0.0081	−0.0081	−0.0098	−0.0095
	(−2.812)	(−2.570)	(−2.568)	(−3.163)	(−3.101)
Education	0.0230	0.0232	0.0234	0.0223	0.0147
	(2.168)	(2.187)	(2.197)	(2.135)	(1.393)
(Spouse's monthly	−0.0049	−0.0050	−0.0050	−0.0020	−0.0017
earnings)/100	(−0.485)	(−0.501)	(−0.498)	(−0.204)	(0.175)
ln w_{-1}				0.2467	0.3924
				(4.718)	(6.876)
Job length			−0.0007	−0.0020	−0.0032
			(−0.241)	(−0.710)	(−1.123)
Unemployed/		0.0610	0.0584	0.0658	0.0775
nonparticipant		(1.475)	(1.366)	(1.567)	(1.876)
Industry and occupation controls	No	No	No	No	Yes
R^2	.0310	.0347	.0348	.0714	.1525
SEE	.4816	.4811	.4815	.4727	.4582
F	2.264	2.259	2.035	3.943	3.651
N	575	575	575	575	575

one sees the familiar pattern of age and education in explaining wages. When the previous wage is included, individual characteristics are not important in explaining current wages.

The effect of having changed jobs appears to vary both across years and between the Denver and Seattle samples. From the results that do not condition on previous earnings, a worker who changes jobs without any unemployment on average has wages that are about 5 percent less than a stayer for Denver males and females, about 8 percent less for Seattle females, and essentially the same for Seattle males. When the

Table 13.16. *Probability of taking a wage cut: Denver, adult females*

	(1)	(2)	(3)	(4)	(5)
Constant	0.5200	0.2606	0.2316	−2.7194	−2.7768
	(2.537)	(1.232)	(1.084)	(−5.329)	(−5.311)
White	0.1131	0.0996	0.0981	0.0984	0.0861
	(2.000)	(1.789)	(1.762)	(1.845)	(1.545)
Hispanic	0.0719	0.0338	0.0354	0.0585	0.0403
	(1.089)	(0.515)	(0.539)	(0.929)	(0.633)
Age/100	−0.3034	−0.0749	−0.0744	0.1392	−0.0122
	(−0.794)	(−0.197)	(−0.196)	(0.381)	(−0.033)
$(Age)^2/1{,}000$	−0.0370	−0.0417	−0.0404	−0.0249	−0.0158
	(−0.853)	(−0.977)	(−0.948)	(−0.608)	(−0.381)
Kids < 6 years	−0.0246	−0.0318	−0.0303	−0.0251	−0.0208
	(−0.757)	(−0.994)	(−0.946)	(−0.819)	(−0.672)
(Net equity)/1,000	−0.0003	−0.0008	−0.0008	−0.0021	−0.0008
	(−0.096)	(−0.254)	(−0.277)	(−0.737)	(−0.294)
Education	0.0064	0.0150	0.0149	0.0082	0.0082
	(0.529)	(1.247)	(1.234)	(0.704)	(0.676)
(Spouse's monthly earnings)/100	−0.0134	−0.0152	−0.0152	−0.0141	−0.01031
	(−2.367)	(−2.728)	(−2.733)	(−2.652)	(−2.398)
ln w_{-1}				.5367	.5552
				(6.313)	(6.406)
Job length			0.0032	0.0020	0.0016
			(0.964)	(0.641)	(0.509)
Unemployed/ nonparticipant		0.2016	0.2127	0.2548	0.2426
		(4.020)	(4.133)	(5.123)	(4.779)
Industry and occupation controls	No	No	No	No	Yes
R^2	.0285	.0637	.0657	.1453	.1884
SEE	.4959	.4874	.4874	.4667	.4625
F	1.581	3.250	3.017	6.614	3.843
N	439	439	439	439	439

previous wage is included, movers have wages about 3 percent greater than stayers for Denver males and females and Seattle females, and essentially the same for Seattle males. This pattern implies that it is the relatively lower paid workers who change jobs, and when they do so, there is a greater increase in their wages than in those of similar workers who did not move. The exception to this pattern is adult males in Seattle, which perhaps can be explained by the unusual conditions brought about by the slump at Boeing and the related local recession that occured during this period. In any event, although the patterns seem, on the whole, to

Table 13.17. *Probability of taking a wage cut: Seattle, adult females*

	(1)	(2)	(3)	(4)	(5)
Constant	0.7426	0.6166	0.6162	−1.5149	−1.9725
	(2.405)	(1.915)	(1.909)	(−2.246)	(−2.688)
White	0.0831	0.0851	0.0859	0.0706	0.0770
	(1.064)	(1.092)	(1.098)	(0.931)	(0.958)
Age/100	−0.9257	−0.7803	−0.7908	−0.6554	−1.0511
	(−1.747)	(−1.446)	(−1.454)	(−1.241)	(−1.850)
(Age)^2/1,000	0.0449	0.0385	0.0385	0.0545	0.0598
	(0.666)	(0.571)	(0.569)	(0.830)	(0.882)
Kids < 6 years	−0.0118	−0.0179	−0.0184	−0.0009	−0.0103
	(−0.244)	(−0.369)	(−0.378)	(−0.002)	(−0.204)
(Net equity)/1,000	−0.0028	−0.0032	−0.0032	−0.0056	−0.0054
	(−0.650)	(−0.743)	(−0.722)	(−1.309)	(−1.149)
Education	−0.0093	−0.0066	−0.0070	−0.0097	−0.0212
	(−0.504)	(−0.359)	(−0.377)	(−0.539)	(−0.573)
(Spouse's monthly	−0.0070	−0.0056	−0.0057	−0.0041	−0.0028
earnings)/100	(−0.738)	(−0.588)	(−0.593)	(−0.441)	(0.029)
ln w_{-1}				0.3830	0.4824
				(3.565)	(4.231)
Job length			0.0009	0.0008	−0.0002
			(0.189)	(0.171)	(−0.048)
Unemployed/		0.1006	0.1027	0.1150	0.1134
nonparticipant		(1.350)	(1.360)	(1.571)	(1.477)
Industry and occupation controls	No	No	No	No	Yes
R^2	0.0338	0.0435	0.0437	0.1071	0.1810
SEE	0.4909	0.4898	0.4911	0.4759	0.4747
F	0.910	1.028	0.913	2.146	1.520
N	189	189	189	189	189

be consistent with a standard job-matching model, the precision of the estimates is low. The pattern that does stand out, and is measured with precision, is the effect of nonemployment on subsequent earnings. In Tables 13.18–13.21 the coefficient estimates for nonemployment are almost always negative and generally are two to three times their associated standard error in size. There is also a remarkable consistency in the estimates, with the central tendency being −2% for each of the groups. Since an average job transition that does not go directly to a new job has a spell of nonemployment of 2.7 months, this implies a wage loss of 5 to 6 percent.

The consistency of this finding across the two different areas and in

Table 13.18. *Annual wage regressions: Denver adult males, 1971–4*

	1971		1972		1973		1974	
	(1)	(2)	(3)	(4)	(5)	(6)	(7)	(8)
Constant	4.9126	1.2183	4.9865	1.3710	5.4897	1.5410	5.6919	0.9386
	(22.50)	(6.15)	(22.26)	(6.50)	(21.19)	(6.95)	(17.19)	(3.21)
White	0.0276	0.0278	0.0667	0.0218	0.0224	-0.0228	0.0268	0.0103
	(0.87)	(1.36)	(2.13)	(1.03)	(0.64)	(1.06)	(0.67)	(0.41)
Hispanic	-0.0064	0.0255	0.0302	0.0473	0.0063	0.0020	0.0149	0.0347
	(0.18)	(1.12)	(0.87)	(1.99)	(0.16)	(0.08)	(0.33)	(1.22)
Age	0.0403	-0.0041	0.0398	0.0119	0.0212	-0.0100	0.0215	0.0062
	(3.66)	(0.57)	(3.60)	(1.56)	(1.70)	(1.28)	(1.39)	(0.62)
Age^2	-0.0005	0.0001	-0.0005	-0.0001	-0.0003	0.0001	-0.0002	-0.0001
	(3.51)	(0.55)	(3.49)	(1.42)	(1.86)	(0.78)	(1.67)	(0.72)
Education	0.0330	0.0061	0.0470	0.0275	0.0393	-0.0226	0.0545	0.0236
	(2.02)	(0.56)	(3.00)	(2.54)	(2.12)	(1.94)	(2.34)	(1.60)
Kids ≤ 6 years	0.0098	0.0056	0.0071	-0.0003	0.0078	0.0030	-0.0015	-0.0022
	(1.56)	(1.38)	(1.21)	(0.06)	(1.22)	(0.76)	(0.21)	(0.48)
Net worth ('000's)	0.0037	0.0005	0.0055	0.0013	0.0058	0.0006	0.0077	0.0028
	(2.37)	(0.45)	(3.46)	(1.81)	(3.21)	(0.55)	(3.28)	(1.87)
Spouse's earnings	-0.0214	-0.0086	-0.0133	-0.0025	-0.0013	-0.0026	-0.0014	0.0039
	(2.66)	(1.65)	(1.95)	(0.53)	(0.20)	(0.65)	(0.22)	(0.95)
Job changer	-0.0768	0.0088	-0.0261	0.0463	-0.0514	0.0386	-0.0462	0.0126
	(2.26)	(0.39)	(0.84)	(2.10)	(1.45)	(1.73)	(1.04)	(0.42)
Months not employed	-0.0251	-0.0195	-0.0252	-0.0362	-0.0162	-0.0124	-0.0600	-0.0227
	(3.36)	(2.33)	(3.15)	(3.30)	(1.42)	(1.56)	(4.31)	(1.70)
ln w_{-1}	—	.7975	—	0.7340	—	0.7989	—	0.8366
		(26.21)		(25.54)		(26.40)		(22.76)
R^2	0.1426	0.6505	0.1188	0.6162	0.0700	0.6453	0.1548	0.67428
F	8.401	76.803	6.927	66.414	3.396	69.778	7.108	59.234
N	516	467	525	467	464	434	399	374

Note: Dependent variable is ln(hourly wage). Absolute value of asymptotic "*t*"-statistics in parentheses.

Table 13.19. *Annual wage regressions: Seattle adult males, 1970–3*

	1970		1971		1972		1973	
	(1)	(2)	(3)	(4)	(5)	(6)	(7)	(8)
Constant	5.1099	1.3903	5.3912	1.8705	5.1776	0.8576	5.5824	1.9128
	(21.07)	(6.88)	(21.29)	(6.28)	(16.68)	(2.38)	(17.72)	(6.14)
White	0.0430	0.0170	0.0333	0.0471	0.0456	-0.0148	0.0010	-0.0133
	(1.38)	(0.95)	(1.04)	(2.03)	(1.23)	(0.55)	(0.03)	(0.53)
Age	0.0378	0.0014	0.0249	0.0097	0.0394	0.0240	0.0294	-0.0002
	(3.13)	(0.19)	(2.02)	(1.01)	(2.68)	(2.25)	(1.69)	(0.02)
Age^2	-0.0005	-0.0000	-0.0003	-0.0001	-0.0005	-0.0003	-0.0003	-0.0000
	(3.04)	(0.27)	(2.17)	(0.15)	(2.73)	(0.19)	(1.91)	(0.13)
Education	0.0014	0.0053	0.0073	0.0013	0.0014	-0.0042	0.0091	0.0029
	(0.24)	(1.55)	(1.22)	(0.29)	(0.20)	(0.82)	(1.37)	(0.63)
Kids ≤ 6 years	0.0382	0.0015	0.0253	0.0102	0.0211	0.0205	0.0259	0.0177
	(2.25)	(0.15)	(1.46)	(0.81)	(0.94)	(1.28)	(1.12)	(1.09)
Net worth ('000's)	0.0053	0.0003	0.0064	0.0013	0.0059	-0.0002	0.0046	0.0007
	(2.60)	(0.25)	(3.37)	(0.89)	(3.19)	(0.13)	(3.34)	(0.76)
Spouse's earnings	-0.0041	-0.0006	-0.0026	-0.0049	-0.0070	0.0054	-0.0032	-0.0018
	(0.56)	(0.15)	(0.37)	(0.97)	(0.99)	(1.04)	(0.51)	(0.41)
Job changer	0.0061	-0.0170	-0.0026	-0.0049	0.0070	0.0054	-0.0032	-0.0018
	(0.12)	(0.55)	(0.71)	(0.47)	(2.78)	(2.49)	(0.38)	(0.77)
Months not employed	-0.0171	-0.0222	-0.0137	-0.0200	-0.0446	-0.0264	0.0170	-0.0009
	(1.84)	(2.70)	(1.85)	(2.60)	(4.45)	(2.19)	(1.22)	(0.08)
ln w_{-1}	—	0.7564	—	0.6585	—	0.7947	—	0.7025
		(24.76)		(14.49)		(15.48)		(16.89)
R^2	0.1907	0.7263	0.1140	0.5332	0.1467	0.5410	0.0917	0.6069
F	4.163	74.039	4.389	28.675	5.233	28.875	2.761	33.814
N	314	290	317	262	284	256	256	230

Note: Dependent variable is ln(hourly wage). Absolute value of asymptotic "t"-statistics in parentheses.

278

Table 13.20. Annual wage regressions: Denver adult females, 1971–4

	1971		1972		1973		1974	
	(1)	(2)	(3)	(4)	(5)	(6)	(7)	(8)
Constant	4.6923	0.6950	5.1186	1.5511	5.2366	1.4273	4.9204	0.9752
	(20.53)	(3.30)	(21.45)	(5.90)	(19.94)	(5.67)	(15.62)	(3.28)
White	−0.0326	−0.0012	0.0081	0.0003	−0.0487	−0.0315	−0.0483	−0.0348
	(1.13)	(0.07)	(0.28)	(0.02)	(1.69)	(1.53)	(1.40)	(1.44)
Hispanic	−0.0171	−0.0175	0.0403	0.0168	−0.0469	−0.0012	−0.0291	0.0063
	(0.51)	(0.80)	(1.21)	(0.65)	(1.37)	(0.05)	(0.72)	(0.22)
Age	0.0232	0.0032	0.0085	−0.0067	0.0017	−0.0154	0.0241	0.0095
	(2.05)	(0.44)	(0.75)	(0.73)	(0.14)	(1.64)	(1.64)	(0.89)
Age^2	−0.0003	−0.0001	−0.0002	0.0001	−0.0000	0.0002	−0.0003	−0.0001
	(2.12)	(0.58)	(1.12)	(0.53)	(0.25)	(1.46)	(1.87)	(0.91)
Education	0.0343	−0.0008	0.0325	0.0081	0.0378	0.0146	0.0375	0.0130
	(5.20)	(0.18)	(4.83)	(1.60)	(5.58)	(2.89)	(4.61)	(2.13)
Kids ≤ 6 years	0.0091	0.0195	0.0126	0.0245	0.0263	0.0123	0.0115	0.0047
	(0.48)	(1.47)	(0.66)	(1.58)	(1.28)	(0.74)	(0.46)	(0.26)
Net worth ('000's)	0.0021	−0.0003	0.0031	0.0003	0.0021	0.0010	0.0005	−0.0006
	(1.40)	(0.27)	(1.98)	(0.22)	(1.25)	(0.81)	(0.24)	(0.42)
Spouse's earnings	−0.0109	−0.0005	−0.0102	−0.0031	−0.0029	−0.0014	−0.0043	−0.0006
	(2.42)	(0.16)	(2.94)	(1.13)	(0.90)	(0.56)	(1.41)	(0.27)
Job changer	−0.0232	0.0895	−0.0745	0.0289	−0.0783	0.0084	−0.0532	0.0154
	(0.55)	(3.10)	(2.40)	(1.18)	(2.40)	(0.34)	(1.30)	(0.51)
Months not employed	−0.0195	−0.0348	−0.0175	−0.0183	−0.0179	−0.0093	−0.0241	−0.0203
	(3.04)	(4.94)	(3.09)	(2.38)	(3.29)	(1.32)	(3.07)	(2.71)
ln w_{-1}	—	0.8758	—	0.7444	—	0.7902	—	0.7877
		(33.16)		(16.28)		(18.41)		(21.12)
R^2	0.1711	0.7146	0.1843	0.6105	0.1972	0.6492	0.1546	0.6230
F	8.566	76.942	9.781	48.864	10.805	58.049	7.318	50.934
N	426	350	448	355	451	357	411	351

Note: Dependent variable is ln(hourly wage). Absolute value of asymptotic "t"-statistics in parentheses.

Table 13.21. *Annual wage regressions: Seattle adult females, 1970–3*

	1970		1971		1972		1973	
	(1)	(2)	(3)	(4)	(5)	(6)	(7)	(8)
Constant	4.4422	0.5646	4.4021	1.8275	5.1323	1.0708	5.4410	1.4992
	(16.26)	(3.36)	(15.65)	(6.28)	(15.05)	(3.18)	(14.15)	(5.02)
White	0.0099	0.0158	0.0229	0.0460	0.0063	0.0145	0.0383	0.0530
	(0.30)	(1.12)	(0.70)	(1.87)	(0.18)	(0.57)	(1.02)	(2.27)
Age	0.0388	-0.0011	0.0425	0.0131	0.0056	0.0195	-0.0078	-0.0195
	(2.83)	(0.18)	(3.04)	(1.20)	(0.34)	(1.52)	(0.43)	(1.73)
Age^2	-0.0005	0.0000	-0.0006	-0.0002	-0.0001	-0.0002	0.0001	0.0002
	(2.73)	(0.02)	(3.16)	(1.49)	(0.42)	(1.39)	(0.25)	(1.60)
Education	0.0354	0.0059	0.0404	0.0167	0.0387	0.0208	0.0451	0.0139
	(4.27)	(1.59)	(4.98)	(2.59)	(4.30)	(3.06)	(4.74)	(2.22)
Kids ≤ 6 years	0.0257	0.0331	0.0369	0.0171	0.0064	0.0173	-0.0197	-0.0073
	(1.10)	(3.10)	(1.57)	(0.88)	(0.24)	(0.76)	(0.67)	(0.37)
Net worth	-0.0007	0.0009	0.0048	0.0023	0.0040	0.0005	0.0030	0.0003
('000's)	(0.30)	(0.93)	(2.10)	(1.32)	(1.93)	(0.29)	(1.60)	(0.24)
Spouse's earnings	-0.0033	-0.0030	-0.0100	-0.0044	-0.0050	0.0005	0.0030	0.0003
	(0.64)	(1.34)	(2.52)	(1.15)	(1.19)	(0.61)	(2.39)	(1.19)
Job changer	0.0183	0.1210	-0.1645	-0.0523	-0.1306	0.0392	-0.0489	0.0451
	(0.32)	(4.18)	(3.92)	(1.57)	(2.62)	(0.91)	(1.06)	(1.47)
Months	-0.0224	-0.0299	-0.0077	-0.0023	0.0001	-0.0195	-0.0198	-0.0145
not employed	(2.80)	(3.96)	(1.16)	(0.32)	(0.01)	(2.11)	(2.58)	(2.12)
ln w_{-1}	—	0.8957	—	0.6120	—	0.7025	—	0.7911
		(32.73)		(13.24)		(15.38)		(19.91)
R^2	0.1536	0.8606	0.2513	0.5958	0.1463	0.6428	0.2121	0.7252
F	5.383	127.786	10.035	28.744	5.274	25.450	7.864	54.113
N	277	218	279	206	287	208	273	216

Note: Dependent variable is ln(hourly wage). Absolute value of asymptotic "t"-statistics in parentheses.

both the mover–stayer and the all-job-changer comparisons suggests that the method by which a job change occurs is important, but not of overwhelming importance, for the distribution of earnings. Whether this difference can be attributed entirely to differences in reservation wages between employed and unemployed job changers is an interesting question that can be addressed only in a complete structural model.

13.4 Summary and conclusions

Job mobility is a pervasive feature of labor markets, for both women and men. Although turnover is highest in the early part of an individual's career and declines steadily with age, it is nonnegligible even for workers over 40. Although the most visible sort of turnover is that associated with the closing of a factory and the subsequent unemployment of some workers, the data studied here indicate that this is only a part of turnover. For males, about 60 percent of all job changes occur without an intervening spell of unemployment or labor force withdrawal; about 50 percent of the job changes made by females do not involve a spell of nonemployment. As one might expect, labor markets, such as Seattle, that experience sudden declines in demand have a smaller fraction of job changes without nonemployment.

While the average male or female job changer receives a higher wage on the new job, a surprisingly large fraction of job changers actually receive a wage cut: 37 percent of the male and 36 percent of the female job changers in Denver experienced a wage cut. One might have expected the frequency of wage cuts to be higher in Seattle, but this was not the case: 34 percent of the males and 32 percent of the females experienced wage cuts. It would seem natural to describe these wage cuts as being due to the loss of firm specific capital, but as noted above, job matching would produce the same pattern of results. Indeed, in these data a substantial fraction of individuals who moved directly to a new job experienced wage cuts: 32 percent of the males and 30 percent of the Denver females who transited without nonemployment incurred wage cuts, while for Seattle the percentages were 29 for males and 25 for females. The relative abundance of wage cuts for individuals who move directly to a new job is inconsistent with the simple view of on-the-job search models and suggests that job matching and/or specific human capital acquisition are important factors in the turnover process.

One empirical pattern stands out strongly in both the raw data and the more refined regression comparisons: Job transitions that involve a spell of unemployment or nonparticipation on average result in wage that are about 5–6 percent less than the wage of individuals who moved directly to a new job. The regressions of current wage on demographic characteristics as well as previous earnings and the type of job transition made (with or without nonemployment) indicated that very little of the variance in wages could be explained by personal characteristics such as age and education, given the level of previous earnings. In particular, length of time on the previous job appeared to have no effect on subsequent earnings that was not already included in the wage on the previous job. Although this result is subject to a number of qualifications concerning the limited range of values that the tenure measure could take on and the effects of unmeasured heterogeneity, taken on its face it suggests that the duration dependence implied by matching and specific capital models of mobility is quantitatively unimportant.

Acknowledgments

This research has been supported by a grant from the U.S. Department of Labor, Office of the Assistant Secretary for Policy Analysis and Research. The opinions expressed are the authors' and not necessarily those of the Department of Labor.

References

Ashenfelter, Orley, "Discrete Choice in Labor Supply: The Determinants of Participation in the Seattle and Denver Income Maintenance Experiments," Princeton University Industrial Relations Section Working Paper 136 (Princeton, NJ, May 1980).

Bartel, Ann, and George Borjas, "Wage Growth and Job Turnover: An Empirical Analysis," in Sherwin Rosen, ed., *Studies in Labor Markets* (University of Chicago Press, 1981), pp. 65–84.

Burdett, Kenneth, "A Theory of Employee Search and Quit Rates," *American Economic Review, 68* (March 1978), pp. 212–20.

Bureau of Labor Statistics, "Job Mobility in 1961," Special Labor Force Report No. 35 (1963).

Bureau of Labor Statistics, "Job Mobility of Workers in 1955," Current Population Reports, no. 70, (1957).

Jovanovic, Boyan, "Job Matching and the Theory of Turnover," *Journal of Political Economy, 87,* no. 5, pt. 1 (1979a), pp. 972–90.

"Firm-Specific Capital and Turnover," *Journal of Political Economy, 87,* no. 6 (1979b), pp. 1246–60.

"Matching, Turnover, and Unemployment," *Journal of Political Economy, 92,* no. 1 (1984), pp. 108–22.

Keeley, M., P. Robins, R. Spiegelman, and R. West, "The Estimation of Labor Supply Models Using Experimental Data," *American Economic Review, 68,* (December 1978), pp. 873–87.

Kiefer, Nicholas, and George Neumann, "Wages and the Structure of Unemployment Rates," in Martin Baily, ed., *Workers, Jobs, and Inflation* (Washington, DC: Brookings Institution, 1982), pp. 325–51.

Lundberg, Shelly, *Unemployment and Household Labor Supply,* unpublished dissertation (Northwestern University, August 1980).

Matilla, James, "Job Quitting and Frictional Unemployment," *American Economic Review, 64,* (1974), pp. 235–9.

Mincer, Jacob, *Schooling, Experience, and Earnings* (New York: Columbia University Press, 1974).

Mincer, Jacob, and Boyan Jovanovic, "Labor Mobility and Wages," in Sherwin Rosen, ed., *Studies in Labor Markets* (University of Chicago Press, 1981), pp. 21–63.

Mortensen, Dale, "Quit Probabilities and Job Tenure: On the Job Training or Matching?" (Northwestern University mimeo, August 1984).

Tuma, Nancy, and Phillip Robins, "A Dynamic Model of Employment Behavior: An Application to the Seattle and Denver Income Maintenance Experiments," *Econometrica, 48,* (May 1980), pp. 1031–52.

Whittle, Peter, *Optimization Over Time: Dynamic Programming and Stochastic Control,* Vols. 1 and 2 (New York: Wiley, 1983).

CHAPTER 14

Methods for analyzing employment contracts and other agreements

The neoclassical model of demand is the economist's basic tool for studying the relationship among prices, incomes, and quantities consumed. The theory is intuitively pleasing and delivers empirically meaningful restrictions which may form the basis for specification checking. There is an extensive literature on the estimation and interpretation of models of demand in this tradition; important treatments include Deaton and Muellbauer (1980), Phlips (1974) and Theil (1975). The neoclassical model predicts the behavior of the consumer who takes prices as parametric, and who adjusts quantities consumed continuously so that the marginal utilities per dollar spent are equal across commodities. An important class of purchases do not fit well into this framework, namely tied sales and negotiated agreements. An important case in point is the employment agreement.

This chapter considers methods of inferring utility (or demand) function parameters from data on negotiated agreements. These parameters are important for understanding consumer behavior, and practically for predicting responses to policy changes or changes in institutions, whether or not the neoclassical model is appropriate. As we shall see, the specification of the stochastic structure of the model is crucial to the problem of inference when agreements are involved. Additive "errors" cannot simply be tacked on to deterministic demand functions as is typically done when the neoclassical model is applied (but see Theil (1975) for a supporting theory). Section 14.1 reviews briefly the standard model, Section 14.2 introduces a simple model in which one price is "negotiated" and considers its implications, Section 14.3 considers approaches to the statistical analysis of the model, and Section 14.4 treats a very preliminary example based on the labor market data from the Denver Income Maintenance Experiment.

This chapter was written by Nicholas M. Kiefer. It is reprinted from *Business and Economic Statistics Section Proceedings of the American Statistical Association* (1984).

14.1   The neoclassical model of demand

Consider the utility-maximizing consumer who chooses quantities x_1 and x_2 of commodities 1 and 2 so as to maximize a utility function $u(x_1, x_2)$ subject to a budget constraint $p_1x_1 + p_2x_2 = m$. This consumer takes p_1 and p_2 as fixed and merely adjusts x_1 and x_2. Under well-known conditions utility is maximized at the point where $u_1/u_2 = p_1/p_2$ and the budget constraint and the indifference curve are tangent in x_1, x_2 space. When prices or incomes change, but the utility function does not, economists can exploit this tangency condition to make predictions about the resulting changes in quantities. For practical purposes, this means that differences in consumption between homogeneous individuals (that is, individuals assumed to have the same utility function) facing different prices (due perhaps to temporal or geographical dispersion) and with different incomes can be used to infer the interesting parameters of $u(x_1, x_2)$. These parameters must satisfy certain conditions; for example equal simultaneous changes in income and prices should not affect quantities consumed. A statistical test of these conditions can be interpreted as a test of the adequacy of the parametric specification of the model.

Empirical applications of the neoclassical model typically fit equations of the form

$$q_i = q(p, m_i, \beta) + \varepsilon_i,$$

where q_i is some transformation of a quantity, p is a vector of prices, m_i is income, β is a vector of unknown parameters, ε_i is "error," and i indexes individuals. It is difficult to arrive at a similar model when agreements are negotiated.

14.2   A model for negotiated sales

In order to simplify the analysis let us assume that the worker may buy and sell commodity 2 at price p_2 in any quantity. The problem, then, is to model the consumer's strategy in shopping or negotiating for his purchases of commodity 1. It seems reasonable to attach some cost to negotiation or haggling. We will suppose that the consumer enters the market for commodity 1 and receives offers consisting of x_1, p_1 pairs, that is, offers to sell x_1 units of commodity 1 at a price of p_1 per unit. As a method of imposing costs of shopping we will suppose that consumers who enter this market receive offers at random intervals. Since we are looking for simplicity, it is convenient to assume that offers to sell commodity 1 arrive according to a Poisson process with parameter η. The problem of the consumer is to select a shopping strategy which maximizes his expected utility. To this end note that we may write the utility function as a function of p_1 and x_1 rather than of x_1 and x_2 in view of the budget constraint $p_1x_1 + p_2x_2 = m$ and the maintained assumption that commodity 2 is traded at price p_2 in any quantity until the consumer's budget is exhausted. Call this utility function $u^*(p_1, x_1)$. We introduce a primitive dynamics into the model (otherwise shopping is not costly) by supposing that the rate of time preference is ρ and that u^* represents the instantaneous flow of utility from a purchase of commodity 1 on the terms x_1, p_1.

The consumer's problem is then to maximize his expected utility, where the expected utilities associated with accepting and rejecting an offered transaction at terms x_1, p_1 are V_A and V_R respectively, with

$$V_A = \rho^{-1}u^*(p_1, x_1),$$
$$V_R = (\rho + \eta)^{-1}(B + \eta E \max\{V_A, V_R\}),$$

where the expectation is taken with respect to the distribution of p_1, x_1 pairs and B is a "reference" utility flow in the absence of consumption of x_1.

Note that V_A is increasing in x_1 and decreasing in p_1, while V_R does not depend on the offered pair. Consequently, an optimal acceptance strategy exists; for given x_1 there is a value $p_1(x_1)$ such that if $p_1 < p_1(x_1)$ the offer is accepted; if not the consumer continues to search or to negotiate.

Since the familiar graphical analysis of this model occurs in x_1, x_2 space, it is useful to note that our discussion of x_1, p_1 pairs can be transformed into a discussion of x_1, x_2 pairs in view of the budget constraint and the assumption of budget exhaustion. Figure 14.1 illustrates the implications of the two models. In the standard neoclassical model the x_1, x_2 pairs all lie on tangencies between the budget constraints and the indifference curves; in our alternative model of tied sales or negotiated agreements the tangency condition simply cannot be expected to hold. The usual model predicts that, apart from "errors", x_1, x_2 pairs consumed will lie along the curve D as p_1 varies across consumers with the same income m. The addition of errors, typically attached to quantities or to some transformation of quantities, implies roughly that points observed will be clustered near the curve D. The model of negotiated sales merely implies that the bundle transacted will lie in the region A. Formally,

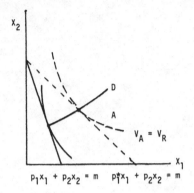

Figure 14.1. Acceptance sets; D = optimal (x_1, x_2) pair as p_1 varies in the standard model; A = acceptance set in the "agreement" model.

$A = \{x_1, x_2)|p_1 x_1 + p_2 x_2 = m; p_1 < p_1(x_1)\}$. Note that this model does not require the tacking on of errors in order to describe the observations. It is in this sense that the model is more complete than the usual.

14.3 Estimation

Is there any hope of identifying preference parameters from the data on negotiated sales? The answer is yes. We first consider the problem in the absence of any information whatever on the bargaining aspects of the problem. Then, we incorporate additional information in the form of assumptions about the functional form of the utility function and the distribution of p_1, x_1 pairs.

A nonparametric approach is feasible when individuals in the sample are homogeneous with respect to their incomes m and prices of other goods p_2 (as well as with respect to their utility functions). As a first approach we might simply connect the observed x_1, x_2 pairs after deleting observations x_1^*, x for which $x_1^* = x_1$ and $x_2^* > x_2$ or $x_2^* = x_2$ and $x_1^* > x_1$. Thus, we are attempting to trace out the boundary of the acceptance set A. This estimator is clearly consistent if either x_1 or x_2 is discrete. However, it is unlikely to be very useful in practice since little information about the shape of the indifference curve is incorporated and, as a result, the estimated indifference curve is unrealistically jagged (see Figure 14.2 below for an example). One obvious improvement on this estimator is obtained by requiring that the estimated indifference curve have negative slope throughout. This is a reasonable requirement as a positively sloped

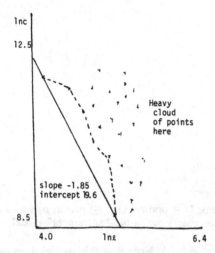

Figure 14.2. Plot of ln c and ln l. Slope, -1.85; intercept, 19.6.

indifference curve is economically unsound as long as consumers like commodities 1 and 2.

A further improvement can be made by imposing the requirement that the indifference curve be convex. The nonparametric estimator is then the southwest portion of the convex hull of the x_1, x_2 pairs. This estimator is easily seen to be consistent under quite general conditions on the process generating the x_1, p_1 (pairs). Figure 14.2 illustrates this estimator.

The next step is to assume a functional form for the indifference curve; this is most naturally accomplished by assuming a functional form for the utility function and deriving the implied indifference curve. The advantages of assuming a functional form are two: First, the shape of the indifference curve will be determined by a few parameters. Consequently the efficiency of estimation is likely to be greatly increased, provided the assumed form is appropriate. Second, the parameters typically have natural economic interpretations, simplifying considerably the subsequent use of the estimates for prediction or for comparison with other studies. Fitting a parametric model can, however, be problematic without an additional assumption. Intuitively, one would like to move the boundary of the acceptance set, whose shape is now given by the functional form assumption, as far to the northeast in the x_1, x_2 plane as possible without violating the natural condition that all transacted pairs lie in the acceptance set. In many institutions there may be several candidates for "farthest to the northeast," and a precise metric will have to be specified. To illustrate this possibility, suppose the functional form chosen implies that the indifference curve is a straight line. Then all lines containing line segments on the (southwest portion of the) convex hull of the x_1, x_2 pairs are candidate estimators of the boundary of the acceptance set. It is possible to choose one of the candidate lines arbitrarily, seeking comfort in the fact that as the sample size increases the relevant part of the convex hull of the data will consist of only one segment, and therefore any of the segments in a given sample yields a consistent estimator. This argument, while technically correct, is practically unappealing since in fact the candidate estimators could be quite different.

The next step is to specify the distribution of x_1, p_1 pairs from which the consumer samples. This distribution reflects characteristics of the bargaining process and institutions, as well as "supply" factors not modelled explicitly. It readily transformed into a distribution of x_1, x_2 pairs, which we will denote by $F(x_1, x_2)$, with associated density $f(x_1, x_2)$. The probability that any particular offer will be acceptable is the probability that the x_1, x_2 pair will lie in the acceptance region A,

$$P = \int_A f(x_1, x_2) \, dx_1 \, dx_2 \, ,$$

and the implied density function for the (x_1, x_2) pairs is

$$f(x_1, x_2)/P.$$

Consequently the log-likelihood function for a sample of N independent observations is

$$L = \sum_{i=1}^{N} \ln f(x_{1_i}, x_{2_i}) - N \ln P.$$

We now have a metric for choosing among alternative estimators of the acceptance set: We choose the estimator which minimizes $\ln P$.

14.4   Example: employment contracts

Consider a worker who is negotiating an employment contract. Suppose that the contract consists of a wage–hour pair, that is the worker and the firm agree to both a wage rate and the number of hours worked at that wage rate. In this model the transacted wage will not typically be interpretable as a measure of the marginal value of leisure. Workers, if asked,

Table 14.1. *Summary statistics (N = 444)*

Variable	Mean	Standard deviation	.25	Quantiles	.75
ln c	11.05	0.47	10.86	11.09	11.22
ln l	5.47	0.18	5.42	5.49	5.53

will often express a desire to work more or fewer hours than they do at the transacted wage. (Ham (1982) describes some data of this type.) Suppose workers sample from a distribution of wage–hour pairs. This distribution is easily transformed into a distribution of consumption and leisure pairs, corresponding to x_1 and x_2 of the previous sections, by assuming that hours not at work are spent at leisure (this is not really necessary) and that all earned income is consumed.

In order to fix ideas I have drawn a sample of 444 employed workers from the Denver Income Maintenance Experiment (DIME) data set. A detailed description of these data is available elsewhere (see SRI (1983)). The sample consists of white males ages 18 and over who were employed at the same job through a given month. Information on hours worked that month and on the wage rate is available. I have chosen to measure leisure as $l = 420 -$ hours worked, taking 420 hours per month, or roughly 100 hours per week, as total time available for allocation. Consumption c is defined for present purposes simply as wage income for the month; clearly c is a highly stylized notion of consumption. It is useful to measure both consumption and leisure in logarithms; this will be done throughout. The reason is that a natural starting point for parameterizing the utility function is the Cobb–Douglas form

$$U(c, l) = l^\alpha c^\beta,$$

for which the acceptance frontier is simply a line in the ln c, ln l plane with slope $-\alpha/\beta$. No generality is lost by measuring the variables in logs, but the data plots may be a little easier to interpret. Summary statistics for ln c and in ln l in our sample are given in Table 14.1.

A rough plot of the data in the ln c–ln l plane is given in Figure 14.2. The dashed line indicates the second nonparametric estimator discussed in Section 14.3. This line connects points on the southwest edge of the cluster of points subject to the constraint that the line have negative slope throughout. The solid line is the nonparametric estimator subject to convexity (but note that convexity when variables are measured in logs may not be so compelling) and also the parametric estimator under the assumption that the utility function is Cobb–Douglas. No difficulty in choosing the appropriate line segment arises in this data set; there is only one candidate. The slope of this estimator gives the identified preference parameter, namely $-\alpha/\beta$, with value -1.85. If the utility function is scaled so that $\beta = 1 - \alpha$ then the implied value of α is 0.65.

With an estimate of the acceptance frontier at hand it is straightforward to assume a functional form for f and to estimate its parameters by reference to the likelihood function. If we assume that the offer density $f(\ln c, \ln l)$ is normal with means μ_c and μ_l and variance parameters σ_c^2, σ_l^2, and σ_{cl}, then the density of observed pairs is given by

$$g(\ln c, \ln l) = f(\ln c, \ln l)/\Phi\left(\frac{\mu_c + (\alpha/\beta)\mu_l - k}{\sigma}\right), \qquad (\ln c, \ln l) \in A,$$

where $\sigma = (\sigma_c^2 + (\alpha/\beta)^2\sigma_l^2 + 2(\alpha/\beta)\sigma_{cl})^{1/2}$ and k is the intercept of the acceptance function. The maximum likelihood estimates of the parameters of f for this data set are essentially identical to the least-squares estimates given in Table 14.1. The only new parameter is σ_{cl}, which is estimated to be $-.047$. What is going on here is that the bulk of the observations lie so far from the frontier that the estimated probability of an observation at or below the frontier is nearly zero. The truncation is so far in the tail of the distribution that the truncated and untruncated distribution are essentially identical. This point clearly requires further exploration. The message is that acceptance policies on the part of workers are not providing most of the "action" in the data. Sharper modelling of the negotiation or arrival process (here exogenous and Poisson) may be profitable.

14.5   Conclusion

When sales are negotiated agreements, the tangency conditions familiar from microtheory need not hold (and generally will not hold) so the standard approach to analyzing demand functions will not lead to satisfactory estimates of preference parameters. This chapter illustrates the problem and proposes estimation methods for samples of homogeneous individuals. The major outstanding issues are (1) incorporation of heterogeneity in preferences, opportunities, and incomes and (2) provision of an economic model of the offer distribution.

Acknowledgments

I am grateful to a number of my colleagues for discussions of these issues. Special thanks to Professor Insan Tunali of Cornell for reviewing the manuscript. This research was supported by a grant from the National Science Foundation.

References

Deaton, A., and J. Muellbauer, (1980), *Economics and Consumer Behavior*, Cambridge University Press.
Ham, J., (1982), "Estimation of a Labor Supply Model with Censoring Due to Unemployment," *Review of Economic Studies* 49, 335–354.
Phlips, L., (1974), *Applied Consumption Analysis*, Amsterdam: North-Holland.
SRI International, (1983), *Final Report of the Seattle–Denver Income Maintenance Experiment*, U.S. Government Printing Office.
Theil, H., (1975, 1976), *Theory and Measurement of Consumer Demand*, Vols. I, II, Amsterdam: North-Holland.

Index